# A Daybook
# for June
# in Yellow Springs, Ohio

## A Memoir in Nature

and a Handbook for the Month,
Being a Personal Narrative and Synthesis of Common
Events in Nature between 1981 and 2022
in Southwestern Ohio, with Applications
for the Lower Midwest  and Middle Atlantic Region,
Containing Weather Guidelines
and a Variety of Natural Calendars,
Reflections by the Author
and Seasonal Quotations
from Ancient and Modern Writers

By

Bill Felker

*A Daybook for the Year in Yellow Springs, Ohio*
Volume 6: June

*Cover Image from a Watercolor by Libby Rudolf*

Copyright 2022 by Bill Felker

Published by The Green Thrush Press
P.O. Box 431, Yellow Springs, Ohio
Printed in the United States of America



ISBN-13: 978-1986757423

ISBN-10: 1986757420

For Maggie

Bill Felker

*No one suspects the days to be gods.*

Ralph Waldo Emerson

Bill Felker

# Introduction

*All my botanical walks, the varied impressions made by the places where I have seen memorable things, the ideas they have aroused in me, all this has left me with impressions which are revived by the sight of the plants I have collected.... The collection is like a diary of my expeditions, which makes me set out again with renewed joy, or like an optical device which places them once again before my eyes.... It is the chain of accessory ideas that makes me love botany. It brings together and recalls to my imagination all the images which most charm it: meadows, waters, woods, solitude and above all the peace and tranquility which one can find in these places  - all of it instantly conjures up before my memory.*

Jean-Jacques Rousseau
*Reveries of a Solitary Walker*  (tr. Peter France)

# Setting

The principal habitat described in this *Daybook* is that of Glen Helen, a preserve of woods and glades that lies on the eastern border of the village of Yellow Springs in southwestern Ohio. At its northern edge, the Glen joins with John Bryan State Park to form a corridor about ten miles long and half a mile wide along the Little Miami River. The north section of the Glen Helen /John Bryan complex is hilly and heavily wooded, and is the best location for spring wildflowers. The southern portion, South Glen, as it is usually called, is a combination of open fields, wetlands and wooded flatlands. Here I have found many flowers and grasses of summer and fall. Together, the two Glens and John Bryan Park provide a remarkable cross section of the fauna and flora of the eastern United States.

Other habitats in the daybook journal include my yard with its several small gardens; the village of Yellow Springs itself, a town of 4,000 at the far eastern border of the Dayton suburbs; the Caesar Creek Reservoir, twenty miles south of Yellow Springs and created by the Corps of Engineers in 1976. My trips away from that environment were mainly northeast to Chicago, Madison, Wisconsin and northern Minnesota, east to Washington and New

York, southeast to the Carolinas and Florida, southwest to Arkansas, Louisiana and Texas, and occasionally through the Southwest to California and the Northwest, two excursions to Belize in Central America, several to Italy and Spain.

## Weather

My daily, weekly and monthly weather summaries have been distilled from over thirty years of observations. They are descriptions of the local weather history I have kept in order to track the gradual change in temperatures, precipitation and cloud cover through the year. I have also used them in order to try to identify particular characteristics of each day. They are not meant to be predictions.

Although my interest in the Yellow Springs microclimate at first seemed too narrow to be of use to those who lived outside the area, I began to modify it to meet the needs of a number of regional and national farm publications for which I started writing in the 1980s. While the summaries are based on my records in southwestern Ohio, they can be and have been used, with interpretation and interpolation, throughout the Lower Midwest, the Middle Atlantic region and the East.

## Natural Calendar

In this section, I note the progress of foliage and floral changes, farm and garden practices, migration times for common birds and peak periods of insect activity. Some of these notes are second hand; I'm a sky watcher, but not an astronomer, and I rely on the government's astronomical data and a few other references for much of my information about the stars and the Sun. I am also a complete amateur at bird watching, and most of the migration dates used in the seasonal calendar come from published sources. And even though I keep close track of the farm year, the percentages listed for planting and harvesting are interpretations of averages supplied by the state's weekly crop reports.

At the beginning of each spring and summer month, I have included a floating calendar which lists approximate flowering times for many plants, shrubs and trees in an average Yellow Springs season. The floating chronology describes the relationship between events more than exact dates of these occurrences.

Although the flora of the eastern and central United States is hardly limited to the species mentioned here, the flowers listed are common enough to provide easily recognized landmarks for gauging the advance of the year. I found that a record of my drives south during April complemented the floating calendar and allowed me to see the approximate differences between Yellow Springs and other locations. I also learned that April in the Lower Midwest is more like March in the Southeast and more like May in the Upper Midwest. This *Daybook* and its Natural Calendar summaries, then, are records of moveable seasonal feasts that shift not only according to fixed geographical regions but also according to the weather in any particular year.

## Astronomical Data

Each month's notes include approximate dates for astronomical events, such as star positions, meteor showers, solstice, equinox, perihelion (the Sun's position closest to Earth), and aphelion (the Sun's position farthest from Earth).

I have included the sunrise and sunset for Yellow Springs as a general guide to the progression of the year in this location. Even though the day's length is almost never exactly the same from one town to the next, a minute gained or lost in Yellow Springs is often a minute lost or gained elsewhere, and the Yellow Springs numbers can be used as a simple way of watching the lengthening or shortening of the days, and, therefore, of watching the turn of the planet. For those who wish to keep track of the Sun in their own location, abundant sources are now available for this information in local and national media. Better yet, of course, a person might actually keep track of when the Sun rises and sets near his or her home!

## Average Temperatures

Local average temperatures are also part of each day's entry. Temperatures in Yellow Springs generally keep pace with temperatures in the Lower Midwest and Middle Atlantic region, and they can be helpful indicators of the steady progress of the year in those areas.

## Daybook Entries

The journal entries in the Daybook section provide the raw material from which I wrote the Natural Calendar digests. When I began to take notes about the world around me, I found that there were few descriptions of actual events in nature available for southwestern Ohio. There was no roadmap for the course of the year. My daily observations, as narrow and incomplete as they were, were especially significant to me since I had found no other narrative of the days, no other depiction of what was actually occurring around me. In time, the world came into focus with each particle I named. I saw concretely that time and space were the sum of their parts.

As my notes for each day accumulated, I could see the wide variation of events that occurred from year to year; at the same time, I saw a unity in this syncopation from which I could identify numerous sub-seasons and with which I could understand better the kind of habitat in which I was living and, consequently, myself. When I paged through the journal entries for each day, I was drawn back to the space in which they were made. I browsed and imagined, returned to the journey.

## Quotations

The passages from ancient and modern writers that accompany each day's notations are lessons from my readings, as well as from distant seminary and university training, here put to work in service of the reconstruction of my sense of time and space. They are a collection of reminders, hopes, and promises for me that I find implicit in the seasons. They have also become a kind of a cosmological scrapbook for me and the philosophical underpinning of this narrative.

## Companions

Many friends, acquaintances and family members have contributed their observations to the *Daybook*, and their participation has taught me that my private seasons are also community seasons, and that all of our experiences together help to lay the foundation for a rich, local consciousness of natural history.

### *The Month of June*
### *June Averages: 1981 through 2022*
### *Normal June Average Temperature: 70.5*

| Year | Average |
|------|---------|
| 1981 | 71.9 |
| 1982 | 66.7 |
| 1983 | 69.9 |
| 1984 | 72.4 |
| 1985 | 67.0 |
| 1986 | 71.3 |
| 1987 | 72.5 |
| 1988 | 71.4 |
| 1989 | 70.6 |
| 1990 | 70.2 |
| 1991 | 74.2 |
| 1992 | 68.1 |
| 1993 | 69.7 |
| 1994 | 74.3 |
| 1995 | 72.8 |
| 1996 | 71.2 |
| 1997 | 69.1 |
| 1998 | 70.5 |
| 1999 | 72.5 |
| 2000 | 70.7 |
| 2001 | 69.6 |
| 2002 | 72.5 |
| 2003 | 66.7 |
| 2004 | 69.3 |
| 2005 | 73.3 |
| 2006 | 68.5 |
| 2007 | 71.7 |
| 2008 | 71.6 |
| 2009 | 71.1 |
| 2010 | 73.3 |
| 2011 | 71.6 |
| 2012 | 72.3 |
| 2013 | 71.3 |
| 2014 | 73.6 |
| 2015 | 72.5 |
| 2016 | 73.0 |
| 2017 | 71.0 |
| 2018 | 73.3 |
| 2019 | 69.8 |
| 2020 | 73.1 |
| 2021 | 73.5 |
| 2022 | 73.1 |

## *June 1st*
## *The 152nd Day of the Year*

*The exuberance of June...It began at daybreak with the chirping and chattering of birds close at hand and in widening circles around us. And then, what greater wonder than the rising of the sun? Even the nights, as yet without insect choirs, were alive. Fireflies against the mass of trees were flashing galaxies, which repeatedly made and unmade abstract patterns of light, voiceless as the stars overhead....*

Harlan Hubbard

Sunrise/set: 5:09/7:57
Day's Length: 14 hours 48 minutes
Average High/Low: 78/57
Average Temperature: 67
Record High: 97 – 1895
Record Low: 42 – 1972

### *Weather*

Today brings a five-percent chance of highs in the 90s, forty percent of 80s, forty percent of 70s, fifteen percent of 60s. Rain occurs 35 percent of the time, and the sun shines eight years in a decade. A very slight chance (one to three percent) of light frost remains until the 14th of June.

### *The Weather of the Week Ahead*

The first week of June brings an end to the likelihood of highs in the 50s and 60s at average elevations along the 40th Parallel. Chances of that kind of cold were around 30 percent last week; this week chances of 60s fall to only 15 percent, and 50s are rare. Temperatures for the days of this week rise into the 70s on 35 percent of the afternoons, into the 80s on 40 percent, and into the 90s on ten percent. After June 6th, the likelihood of highs reaching into the 90s jumps to 20 percent, and reaches 35 percent by the middle of the month. About 15 percent of the nights bring temperatures in the 30s or 40s. Rainfall is usually lighter this week than last, and the sun shines more. Still, showers fall about 40 percent of the time each day, except for the 4th, which has just a 30 percent chance, and the 6th, one of the driest days of June in the Lower Midwest, which has just a 15 percent chance of precipitation.

### *The June Weather Outlook*

Normal temperatures rise at the rate of one degree every four days this month throughout most of the United States. In the Lower Midwest, average highs move from the upper 70s on the first of June to the middle 80s by the beginning of July. Lows climb from the mid 50s into the lower 60s. The average temperature for the entire month is usually in the low 70s, up about ten degrees from May. The coldest June recorded in Yellow Springs, Ohio, was 65.8 degrees in 1928. The warmest was 78.4 degrees in 1934.

A typical June temperature distribution looks like the following in much of the state: four days in the 90s, twelve days in the 80s, twelve days in the 70s, two days in the 60s, with a slight chance of one of those cooler days to be in the upper 50s.

The warmest June days, those that carry an 85 percent chance of afternoon highs above 80 degrees: June 13th, 14th, 15th, 21st, 26th. The 13th, 14th, and 15th are the June days most likely to produce highs in the 90s. The coldest days in the month, those with a 50 percent chance of a high below 80: June 2nd, 3rd, 4th, 5th, 10th, 30th. The driest June days, those with 20 percent chance of rain or less, are June 4th, 6th, 10th, 13th, 14th, 16th, 17th, 18th, 21st, 25th, 26th. The period between the 13th and the 26th is historically the best for fieldwork. The 25th and the 26th are almost always free from rain.

The sunniest June days, those which have a 90 percent chance of 12 out of 24 hours without clouds (a thunderstorm is possible, but all-day overcast conditions are rare): June 9th, 10th, 14th, 19th, 21st, 24th, 25th, 26th.

The wettest days this month, those with more than a 40 percent chance of rain: June 2nd, 3rd, 5th, 8th, 11th, 12th, 15th and 20th. The 15th and 20th are usually the rainiest days in June weather history. The first and the last weeks of the month generally provide the most precipitation. About eight thunderstorms occur in a Yellow Springs June.

### *Summercount*

Between the last week of May through the first week of September, approximately fourteen major cool fronts of summer cross the United States. As these high-pressure systems approach, atmospheric conditions become unsettled, and rain becomes more likely. After the passage of the fronts, weather is ordinarily suitable for outdoor work and recreation. Fronts will reach the Mississippi around the following dates; they will come through about two days earlier in the West, a day or two later in the East.

**June 2:** The June 2nd front can bring a light freeze along the Canadian border and at higher elevations, but the rest of the country is typically safe by this time in the year (except for a very slight danger of frost on the morning of the 5th). After this front weakens, chances of highs in the cool 60s along the 40th Parallel fall to only 15 percent, and 50s are rare.

**June 6:** The low-pressure system that accompanies the June 6th front initiates a four-day period during which there is an increased chance of tornadoes and flash floods. Even after this front passes to the east, storms often strike up to 40 percent of the years. Part of the reason for the rise in the risk for severe weather is the increase in the percentage of afternoons in the 80s and 90s almost everywhere in the continental United States. With the heat, however, comes more sunshine than during any other week so far in the year.

**June 10:** Good chances of a shower precede this weather system, and after its passage, chances are the best so far in the year for a major heat wave. In all but the northernmost states (and at the highest elevations), lows near freezing and highs only in the 50s or 60s now recede from the realm of serious possibility until late August. Although showers can be associated with warm temperatures, many of the days between this front and the next are dry. The sunniest June days usually occur between now and the 26th. Approximately 100 frost-free days now remain on most farms and gardens of the country.

**June 15:** Unsettled conditions often surround the arrival of this front (between the 13th and 16th) as Late Spring and Early Summer hold their final skirmishes along the nation's midsection. After summer is victorious, precipitation typically stays away for several days. Between the 15th and the 19th, average temperatures climb their final degrees, reaching their summer peak near solstice. The period between the 13th and the 26th is historically one of the best times of the month for fieldwork.

**June 23:** The June 23rd high-pressure system is typically cool and dry, and it is often followed by some of the sunniest and driest days of all the year. Cooler conditions in the 70s or even the 60s are most likely to occur on the 23rd and 24th, as the front arrives, but then the afternoons usually warm to the 80s or 90s. As the next June front approaches, the benign effects of the June 23rd system can be expected to give way to storms.

**June 29:** The final weather system of the month is often followed by the Corn Tassel Rains, a two-week period of intermittent precipitation that accompanies the Dog Days of Deep Summer. If the land has been dry throughout June, the Corn Tassel Rains bring the first real chance of midsummer moisture. In spite of the association of this rainy period with heat, however, the final two days of June are sometimes the coldest of the year's midsection, highs below 80 degrees occurring more than half the time above the Border States.

### *Key to the Nation's Weather*

The typical June temperature at average elevations along the 40th Parallel, the average of the high of 81 and the low of 63, is 72 degrees. Using the following chart based on weather statistics from around the country, one might calculate approximate temperatures in other locations close to the cities listed.

For example, subtract five degrees from the base of 72 you to estimate normal temperatures in Minneapolis. Or add five degrees to find out the average conditions in Atlanta during the month.

| | |
|---|---|
| Fairbanks | -14 |
| Cheyenne | -12 |
| Portland, | -9 |
| Minneapolis | -5 |
| Boston | -5 |
| Des Moines | -2 |
| **AVERAGE ALONG THE 40TH PARALLEL:** | **72** |
| Washington DC | +1 |
| Louisville | +2 |
| St. Louis | +3 |
| Little Rock | +5 |
| Atlanta | +5 |
| Miami | +8 |
| New Orleans | +9 |

### *A Floating Sequence*
### *For the Blooming of Shrubs, Trees, Wildflowers and Perennials*

The following list is based on my personal observations in southwestern Ohio over a period of 30 years. The dates are approximate, but I have tried to show a relatively true sequence of first blossoming times during an average summer. Although the dates on all flower calendars are somewhat arbitrary (and may vary by up to 60 days between the Canadian border and the South), a "floating calendar" can be used throughout the country by adjusting the sequence to fit the climate and the particular year.

Many of the events mentioned in this June daybook occur up to a month earlier in the South and up to a month later in the North. For example, if moth mulleins bloom in your yard or alley on May 15 instead of June 1 (see below), subsequent blooming dates will follow more or less in the order given, but on later dates. Since microclimates – as well as precipitation, temperature, soil quality and the day's length - determine blooming times, personal records can refine and reorder sequences to reflect local conditions.

| | |
|---|---|
| May 15: | Common Orange Day Lily *(Hemerocallis fulva)* |
| | Stella d'oro Lily *(Hemerocallis 'Stella de Oro')* |
| May 16: | Yucca *(Yucca filamentosa)* |
| | Blue Flax *(Linum lewisii)* |

|           |                                                      |
|-----------|------------------------------------------------------|
|           | Foxglove (*Digitalis purpurea*)                      |
|           | Blackberry (*Rubus villosus*)                        |
| May 17:   | Achillea (*Achillea millefolium*)                    |
|           | Swamp Iris (*Iris*)                                   |
|           | Wild Grape (*Vitis vinifera*)                        |
|           | Cow Vetch (*Vicia villosa*)                          |
|           | Peonies (*Paeonia*)                                  |
| May 18:   | Lamb's Ear (*Stachys byzantine*)                     |
|           | Kousa Dogwood (*Cornus kousa*)                       |
|           | Yellow Sweet Clover (*Melilotus officinalis*)        |
| May 19:   | Climbing Rose (*Rosa setigera*)                      |
|           | Tea Rose (*Rosoideae rosa*)                          |
|           | Fringe Tree (*Chionanthus*)                          |
| May 20:   | Blue-Eyed Grass (*Sisyrinchium angustifolium*)       |
|           | Corn Salad (*Valerianella locusta*)                  |
| May 21:   | *Catalpa (Catalpa speciosa)*                         |
|           | Pink Spirea (*Spiraea japonica*)                     |
|           | Wild Parsnip (*Pastinaca sativa*)                    |
| May 22:   | Privet (*Ligustrum*)                                 |
|           | River Willow (*Salix myrtilloides*)                  |
|           | Smooth Solomon's Seal (*Polygonatum biflorum*)       |
| May 23:   | Astilbe (*Astilbe arendsii*)                         |
|           | Panicled Dogwood (*Cornus racemosa*)                 |
|           | Poison Hemlock (*Coniu maculatum*)                   |
|           | Angelica (*Angelica*)                                |
|           | Birdsfoot Trefoil (*Lobus corniculatus*)             |
| May 24:   | Japanese Honeysuckle (*Lonicera japonica*)           |
|           | Motherwort (*Leonurus cardiac*)                      |
|           | Multiflora Rose (*Rosa multifora*)                   |
| May 25:   | Tree of Heaven (*Ailanthus altissima*)               |
|           | Yarrow (*Achillea millefolium*)                      |
|           | Curly Dock (*Rumex crispus*)                          |
| May 26:   | Poison Ivy (*Toxicosdendron radicans*)               |
|           | White Campion (*Silene latifolia*)                   |
|           | Common Cinquefoil (*Potentilla simplex*)             |
| May 27:   | Cottonwood (*Aigeiros*)                              |
|           | Honewort (*Cryptotaenia canadensis*)                 |
|           | Japanese Pond Iris (*Iris versicolor*)               |

May 28:     Elderberry  (*Sambucus*)
            Lesser Stitchwort  (*Stellaria graminea*)
May 29:     Lychnis  (*Lychnis coronaria*)
            Cow Parsnip (*Heracleum*)
May 30:     Canadian Thistle  (*Cirsium arvense*)
May 31:     Coreopsis  (*Coreopsis lanceolata*)
            Chicory  (*Cichorium intybus*)
            Daisy Fleabane  (*Erigeron annus*)
June 1:     Rugosa Rose  (*Rosa rugosa*)
            Floribunda Rose  (*Floribunda*)
            Delphinium  (*Delphinium*)
            Moth Mullein  (*Verbascum blattaria*)
June 2:     Feverfew  (*Tanacetum  parthenium*)
            Heliopsis  (*Heliopsis  helianthoides*)
            Quickweed  (*Galinsoga parviflora*)
June 3:     Swamp Valerian   (*Valeriana ulginosa*)
            Moneywort  (*Lysimachia nummularia*)
            Rape brassica (*Napus*)
June 4:     Campanula  (*Campanula rapunculus*)
            Wild Garlic   (*Allium ursinum*)
            Scarlet Pimpernel  (*Anagallis arvensis*)
            Nodding Thistle  (*Carduus nutans*)
            Common "Ditch" Lily"   (*Hemerocallis fulva*)
June 5:     Bindweed (*Convolvulus  arvensis*)
            Butterfly Weed (*Asclepias tuberosa*)
            Crown Vetch  (*Securigera varia*)
            Japanese Iris   (*Iris ensata*)
            Smartweed (*Polygonum hydropiper*)
June 6:     Pickerel Plant  (*Pontederia cordata*)
            Balloon Flower  (*Platycodon grandiflor*us)
            Deptford Pink (*Sianthus armeria*)
June 7:     Oakleaf Hydrangea  (*Hydrangea quercifolia*)
            Indian Hemp  (*Apocynum cannabinum*)
            Virginia Creeper  (*Parthenocissus quinquefolia*)
June 8:     Purple Coneflower  (*Echinacea purpurea*)
June 9:     Asiatic Lily  (*Lilium asiaticum*)
            Carnation  (*Dianthus caryophylus*)
            Blueweed  (*Echium vulgare L.*)
            Pokeweed  (*Phytolacca americana*)

| | |
|---|---|
| June 10: | Early Season Hostas |
| | Shasta Daisy  (*Leucanthemum maximum*) |
| | Queen Anne's Lace  (*Daucus carota*) |
| June 11: | Hollyhock  (*Alcea rosea*) |
| | Beardtongue  (*Penstemon barbatus*) |
| June 12: | Mallow  (*Malva sylvestris*) |
| | Avens  (*Geum urbanum*) |
| June 13: | Tall Meadow Rue  (*Thalictrum dasycarpum*) |
| | Great Mullein  (*Verbascum Thapsus*) |
| June 14: | Leatherflower  (*Clematis pitcher*) |
| | Common Sow Thistle  (*Onchus oleraceus*) |
| | Common Milkweed  (*Asclepias syriaca*) |
| June 15: | Large-Leafed Hostas |
| | Wild Petunia  (*Ruellia humilis*) |
| June 16: | White Sweet Clover (*Melilotus albus*) |
| | Lizard's Tail  (*Saururus cernuus L.*) |
| June 17: | Asiatic Dayflower (*Commelina communis*) |
| | Trumpet Creeper  (*Campsis radicans*) |
| June 18: | Narrow-Leaved  Cattail  (*Typha latifolia*) |
| June 19: | Russian Sage (*Perovskia atriplicif*olia) |
| | Black-Eyed Susan  (*Rudbeckia hirta)* |
| June 20: | Pale Touch-Me-Not (*Impatiens pallida*) |
| June 21: | Gooseneck  (*Lysimachia clethroides*) |
| | Woodland Sunflower  (*Helianthus divaricatus*) |
| June 22: | Enchanter's Nightshade  (*Circaea lutetiana*) |
| | Figwort  (*Scrophularia*) |
| June 23: | Catnip  (*Nepeta*) |
| | Ramps  (*Astilbe arendsii*) |
| | Yellow Sow Thistle (*Sonchus asper)* |
| | Compass Plant  (*Silphium laciniatum*) |
| June 24: | Thimbleplant (*Rubus parviflorus*) |
| | Wood Mint  (*Blephilia ciliate*) |
| June 25: | Bergamot  (*Monarda didyma*) |
| | Tall Nettle  (*Urtica dioica*) |
| | Horse Nettle  (*Solanum carolinense*) |
| June 26: | Creeping Bell Flower (*Campanula rapunculoides)* |
| | Heal All   (*Prunella*) |
| June 27: | Limelight hydrangea (Hydrangea paniculata) |

|  |  |
|---|---|
|  | Lopseed (*Parma leptostachya*) |
|  | Evening Primrose (*Oenothera biennis*) |
| June 28: | Rose of Sharon (*Hibiscus syriacus*) |
|  | Leafcup (*Polymnia laevigata bea*dle) |
| June 29: | Fringed Loosestrife (*Lysimachia ciliate*) |
|  | Wild Lettuce (*Lactuca virosa*) |
| June 30: | Teasel (*Dipsacus*) |
| July 1: | Bouncing Bets (*Saponaria officinalis*) |
|  | Wood Nettle (*Laportea canadensis*) |
|  | Thin-Leaved Coneflower (*Rudbeckia triloba*) |
| July 2: | Mid-Season Garden Phlox (*Phlox paniculata*) |
|  | Tall Bell Flower (*Campanula americana*) |
| July 3: | Oriental Lilies |
|  | Ginseng (*Panax*) |
| July 4: | Liatris (*Liatris spicata*) |
|  | Grey-Headed Coneflower (*Ratibida pinnata*) |
| July 5: | Obedient Plant (*Physostegia virginiana*) |
| July 6: | White Vervain (*Verbena urticifolia*) |
| July 7: | Oxeye (*Chrysanthemum leucanthemum*) |
|  | Horseweed (*Conyza canadensis*) |
| July 9: | Germander (*Teucrium canadense*) |
|  | Small-Flowered Agrimony (*Agrimonia parviflora*) |
| July 10: | Showy Coneflower (*Rudbeckia alpicola*) |
| July 11: | Skullcap (*Scutellaria lateriflora*) |
| July 12: | Fogfruit (*Phyla nodiflora*) |
|  | Great Indian Plantain (*Arnoglossum reniforme*) |
| July 14: | Wingstem (*Verbesina alternifolia*) |
|  | Blue Vervain (*Verbena hastate*) |
| July 16: | Butterfly Bush (*Buddleja davidii*) |

### *Estimated June Pollen Count*

On a scale of 0 - 700 grains per cubic meter:
Pollen from flowering trees is quite low except in northernmost states. Most of the pollen in the air this month comes from grasses.

|  |  |
|---|---|
| June 1: 80 | June 5: 60 |
| June 10 40 | June 15: 35 |
| June 25: 30 | June 30: 25 |

### *Estimated June Mold Count*
On a scale of 0 -7,000 grains per cubic meter:

| | |
|---|---|
| June 1: 2600 | June 5: 3000 |
| June 10: 2500 | June 15: 2600 |
| June 20: 3200 | June 25: 3700 |

June 30: 3000

### *June Phenology*

When the first monarch butterfly arrives from the Gulf, then young coyotes come after chickens and new lambs.

When May apples have fruit the size of a cherry and honeysuckle flowers have all come down, cucumber beetles reach the economic threshold on the farm.

When fireflies light up the night, chinch bugs hatch in the lawn, and powdery mildew becomes a problem in the garden phlox.

When yucca plants send up their stalks, young grackles have left their nests, and nettles have grown up to your chest. Then, Japanese beetles start to attack roses and ferns. Azalea bark scale eggs hatch, too.

When pie cherries ripen, painted turtles and box turtles lay their eggs, and giant (but harmless) stag beetles prowl the grass.

When the oakleaf hydrangea produces its first blooms, then fall webworms and mimosa webworm eggs are hatching.

When the first chiggers bite, all the soybeans are in the ground (except in the wettest years).

When daylilies bloom by the roadsides, watch for winter wheat to turn a soft, pale green.

When catalpa trees come into bloom, then look for the first raspberries to redden.

When bud clusters form on the milkweeds and hosta, then oaks, Osage orange and black walnut trees have set their fruit, and cherry pickers pick cherries across the nation's heartland.

When black-eyed Susans flower across the northern states, then the wheat harvest is over in the Gulf region.

When long seedpods have formed on the locust trees, then annual cicadas start to chant.

When you see the first black walnuts on the ground, then you know that this year's ducklings and goslings are nearly full grown.

When great mullein blooms in the fields, then mock orange petals have all fallen and water willows are blossoming beside the streams.

When elderberry bushes come into full flower and cottonwood cotton floats in the wind, then the first chiggers bite in the woods and garden.

When acorns form, then almost all the winter wheat is headed.

When all of the soybeans are planted and the black raspberries are ripening in the lower Midwest, then walleye fishing is at its best in Lake Erie.

When the tall spikes of the yucca are in bloom, then Japanese beetles invade the flowers.

When damselflies out along the waterways, pie cherries will be ripe for pie, and the second cut of alfalfa will be underway.

When milkweed and pokeweed flower, then the first winter wheat is ripe.

When quail whistle and mate in the woods, tent caterpillars emerge in the trees, and the first Canadian thistles go to seed.

When lizard's tail is in flower along the rivers and lakes, and when black raspberry season ends along the roadsides, then corn borers haunt the corn.

When enchanter's nightshade blooms in the woods, then the first soybeans are blossoming, too.

When black-eyed Susans bloom along the freeways, then turtles hatch near the rivers and lakes.

When blackberries are setting fruit, then the earliest field corn starts to tassel and the canola harvest is underway.

When green berries form on the poison ivy, then the days will soon be shortening.

When the first annual cicadas sing, then May apples are ready for May-apple jam.

When the first katydid appears at porch lights, then the

first cut of alfalfa is complete and the wheat is ready to cut.

When touch-me-nots bloom in the woods, then the best bullhead and crappie fishing ends for the year.

When potato leafhoppers raid the alfalfa, blight appears on the tomatoes.

When blueberries ripen, then cottony maple scale eggs hatch on the silver maples.

When long seedpods have formed on the locust trees, then chinch bugs start leaving brown patches in the lawn.

When the first apple and cherry tree leaves become yellow and drift to the ground, alewives head back to sea from their estuaries along the Atlantic.

When road kills increase in Dog Day heat, thunderstorms announce Deep Summer.

When teasel flowers along the roadsides and wood nettle blooms in the woods, then bagworms attack arborvitae, euonymus, juniper, linden, maple, and fir. Root diseases stalk the soybeans, and the wheat still standing in the fields may suffer from rust, powdery mildew, head scab, and glume blotch.

When elderberry flowers turn to fruit, then giant green June beetles appear in the garden and poisonous white snakeroot is budding in the woods. That's the time to dig garlic before the heads break apart, time also to put in autumn turnips.

When timothy is bearded with seeds, then the first rough-winged swallows migrate south.

When the rose of Sharon flowers, the summer apple harvest will soon be starting.

When the roadside grasses turn like the winter wheat, local sweet corn appears in the market.

When the first fourth of the oats crop is ripe, then spring's goslings and ducklings are almost all grown up.

### *Natural Calendar*

The first week of Early Summer lies between the growing Deep Summer heat of the states below the Ohio River and the cool of Late Spring to the north.

All along much of the 40th Parallel, foliage of the high canopy is almost complete. The winter wheat is just starting to turn. Banks of yellow Stella d'oro lilies open. Staghorns redden on the sumac, and cottonwoods spill their cotton. Poison hemlock and elderberries and daisies are in flower. Strawberries ripen. Honeysuckle blossoms have all come down, and garlic mustard is almost bare.

South of Cincinnati, the hemlocks are seeding, and Canadian thistles are in full bloom. A few miles north of Lexington, white sweet clover replaces the hemlock along the freeway, and cattails emerge, golden with pollen. Trumpet creeper is bright orange and Queen Anne's lace is silver three hours south of Yellow Springs at Berea, Kentucky.

Roadside tiger daylilies (ditch lilies) and milkweed pace the bee balm throughout Knoxville, Tennessee. Below Spartanburg, South Carolina, July's wild lettuce and horseweed follow the fencerows. Around Charleston, corn is already tasseling, some ears formed. Farmers have cut their wheat. Catalpa beans are over a foot long, August size for Yellow Springs.

But north to Michigan and Wisconsin, locust trees are still heavy with new flower clusters, their rich scent on the wind. Purple sweet rockets are lush all the way into northern Minnesota where the wheat is only six inches tall, the first corn just sprouted and sugar beets and peony buds are the size of new radishes. Lilacs and iris are still fragrant near the Canadian border, strawberries only past flowering.

### *Daybook*

*Look*
*how the shade pours*
*from the big branches - the ground,*
*the good ground, pubic*
*and sweet. The trees - who*
*are they? Their stillness, that*
*long silence, the never*
*running away.*

Tim Seibles

1982: The middle of strawberry season in the yard.

1984: Chicory still not blooming.

1986: Strawberries peaking in the garden. At Jacoby Swamp, 8:00 a.m., geese with goslings maybe a third grown, a flock of finches, biting flies, box turtle on the path, crickets strong. Huge prairie false indigo, *Baptisia leucantha*, late bloom in the high prairie up from the road (seen late May at South Glen in 1993). Cobwebs across the path. Fire pinks still in bloom. Gold-collared black flies mating, swarming. Wild roses and corn salad still in full bloom, heavily fragrant. First dragonfly. Several baby toads noticed. Violet swamp iris late full bloom. First large-petaled wild rose seen. Geese fly over the house at 8:40 p.m.

1987: No chiggers yet. Small toads seen at the lakeshore.

1988: The pieces of summer fitting together like a puzzle solving itself: goslings growing up along Yellow Springs Creek, box turtles out laying eggs in the warm river banks, cobwebs closing the paths. First sundrops blooming, sweet rockets most all to seed, last remnants of May. Catalpas in early bloom, many still budding. Yucca flower stalks two feet high, like huge, thick asparagus or bamboo. Tall meadow rue budding at South Glen, one covered with golden aphids. Multiflora roses all open. Spring field crickets chirping at night. Cardinals have been feeding their fledglings for about a week now.

1989: First ditch daylilies seen today

1990: Nodding thistle opening.

1991: Intense heat continues, accelerating Early Summer. John Poortinga brought a bowl of red mulberries to Jean, then two ripe cherries. Ranunculus and pyrethrums gone at the south wall. Dock, tree of heaven and astilbe full bloom, pokeweed heading and nearly open, primrose full, mallow budding, zinnias budding, two four o'clocks have trumpet buds. More tiger lilies are budding, lychnis blooming big and full. Vegetable garden totally out of hand, broccoli bolting, peas filling up, lettuce and radishes gone to seed. First raspberry reddening along the garden wall. Yucca open in town. At the bridge, blue cohosh has its first blue berry, and bottle grass has emerged.

1993: Locusts in front of Wesley Hall in Wilberforce dropping green florescence.

1994: First firefly seen tonight, despite the dry, cool May.

1997: First pink peony opened in the rain. Mock orange full, flags nearing full. Locusts and Osage still pretty bare. Many honeysuckle flowers falling. This may be the latest the canopy has closed since 1978.

1998: Jacoby, north to High Prairie: Hobblebush centers are budding. Wingstem, leafcup, touch-me-nots are up to my waist. Honewort and clustered snakeroot dominate the undergrowth. Gold-collared black flies are out, and buckeyes, skippers, damsel flies, small tan moths, spitbugs, many ichneumons – one red with black wings. Springs and brooks as full as I've ever seen them. Tulip tree petals gold and peach color, like seashells in the swamp water below the brooks. Maple seeds along the path, fallen in tandem. One-inch May apple fruit, shining under its foliage. Blue jays and crows screech. Very last rockets and multiflora roses. Bright red wild strawberries. Purple waterleaf long gone, white still in flower.

Thousands of blackberries fully fruited inside of High Prairie. Last ragwort petals along the river. Wild cherry fruit well set. Cattails almost up to last year's brown remnants, some with pollen. Dreadlocks of purple vetch at Middle Prairie, veins of golden moneywort in the mowed paths. First white yarrow. Old white violets still common. Wild garlic flowers, striped like spring beauties. Blue-eyed grass, fire pink. Some teasel headed along the highway. At home, the pyrethrums are gone. First water willow blooms in the pond. First great mullein flower opens. Fireflies in the yard after dark.

2000: I accidentally stepped on a camel cricket in the kitchen at 12:30 this morning; I saw another in the greenhouse at 6:00 a.m. My notes from May 31st last year record the first camel at 4:30

a.m. To northern Ohio: peonies full bloom there, sweet rockets, and columbine.

2001: Wood thrush call identified. First Stella d'oro daylily fully open. First pink achillea opens in the south garden.

2002: First violet scabiosa seen open. Peak now of daisies, late sweet rockets, spiderworts, poppies, sweet Williams, Japanese honeysuckles and privets. Peonies, rhododendrons, mock orange and locusts all ended together at the end of May.

2003: At the Santee-Cooper reservoir in South Carolina, wheat is dark brown, and corn is almost ready to tassel.

2007: No cedar waxwings seen in the white mulberry tree yesterday or today.

2009: First fireflies seen in the park.

2010: First Japanese iris open in the pond over night. Moth mullein blooming, bright fields of parsnips and hemlock on the way to Xenia. Catalpa flowers covering the trees and the ground. Pokeweed eight feet tall and budded in the alley. Wild lettuce eight feet, too. Buds seen on the Davis Street yucca. Two Queen Anne's lace plants have opened in the north garden. And Rick wrote the following about the number of fecal sacks from grackles last week: "Wouldn't you know that right about the time I was about to give up, the problem solved itself. The babies, wherever they were, all must have fledged at once because the onslaught abruptly stopped."

2011: Italy: Olive trees now in full bloom throughout the Umbrian countryside. At Gary's, the roses were not so lush as they were ten days ago. The money plant was all to seed. Large-flowered campanula was in full bloom, lavender in early bloom, and pink valerian, which I had seen throughout Rome, continued to flower.

2012: The first heliopsis flower and the first purple coneflower were fully open this morning in the rain. The first raspberry in the garden is ready to pick. Serviceberries are red. But after a mild night, this day never made it out of the 60s, and the wind is blowing steadily from the northwest. Birds fed hard all day, the first nuthatch fledgling seen. Last night's rain, probably close to two inches, has given all the sprouts and transplants the moisture they need to develop well throughout the next several weeks. Orange Asiatic lilies have peaked by now. A family of five starling fledglings playing in the pond, bathing on the lily pads. First Endless Summer hydrangea blossoms. First chigger bite on my ankle. Cattail stalks have emerged in the roadsides, soon to flower.

2014: To Madison, Wisconsin: Lush and green in the sun all the way north. Roadsides full of yellow sweet clover, red clover, crown vetch, purple vetch, small daisies, parsnips, honeysuckles, multiflora roses, hemlock. The first chicory of the year seen west of Indianapolis. Nodding thistles coming in. A few moth mulleins in flower. No cattails showing among their tall ditch leaves. Some cornfields had sprouts three to six inches high near Yellow Springs, but sprouting was spotty and inconsistent throughout the trip. Approaching the Wisconsin line, I saw bright yellow spurge all along the roads, blossoming all the way to Madison. The canopy seemed thinner toward northern Illinois, but Madison seemed just a little behind southern Ohio. One daffodil and one tulip were still open. Tat's prairie false indigo, her geums, columbines, wild geraniums, garlic mustard, sweet rockets were in full bloom. Her peonies in the sun were just ready to open. In the city, many locusts and catalpas were full of flowers.

2016: At the quarry, Jill and I found banks of yellow sweet clover and clusters of daisies, a patch of crown vetch, brome grass with golden pollen, green frogs croaking, tadpoles still hiding in the shallows of the pools, red-winged blackbirds in the cattails (which had produced long, thin flower buds) and killdeers swooping and crying back and forth. As we left, a small "V" of maybe two-dozen Canadian geese flew over, calling, flying to the northwest. From Goshen, Indiana, Judy reported many sweet rockets, lupines and Solomon's plume in flower along her bike path. By the quarry parking lot, I took a few clumps of daisies for the garden. In the yard last night, I saw my first fireflies (the 26th for Rick and Matt).

2017: The first Stella d'oro lily opened in the yard over night. A drift of large white-flowered anemone found along the path at Buck Creek Park, only honewort blooming in the deep woods. Cabbage white butterflies more common in the yard today. John's peony buds less than an inch across in southern Minnesota.

2018: First gold-collared blackflies seen in the garden today. Two cabbage whites and one azure seen (and a report of numerous swallowtails seen so far this year). The first chigger bite on my leg. Six Stella d'oro blossoms in the yard.

In the North Glen, leafcup huge and lush, touch-me-not foliage soft and floppy, skunk cabbage leaves spreading so wide, just a touch of decay, in the deep woods May apple foliage all rusted and raggedy, hobble bush just starting to bloom, clustered snakeroot with pollen, delicate and blooming honewort throughout the walk, late waterleaf remaining, occasional deep red fire pinks shining in the dense wet undergrowth, two poke milkweed plants with drooping umbels ready to open, the stone paths and stairs sleek and slippery from the nightly storms.

And in reference to Rick's note from this date in 2010, I wrote the following for my column in the *Yellow Springs News*:

### Onslaught of the Pooping Grackles

I have a small koi pond with a waterfall in my yard. The fish are beautiful in their reds and golds and silvers and have become my pets. I clean out the pond filter every few weeks to keep algae under control. On May 29, I did the cleaning but was surprised the find that the waterfall was producing white foam as though someone had come by during the night and threw in some dish soap. And the fish were racing around the pond. Something was not right.

In a few days, the water cleared up, but I didn't figure out what happened until I chanced upon my daybook entry of May 24, 2010. Rick had written to tell me that the grackles around his home were placing the fecal sacks of the newly hatched fledglings into his birdbath and pond.

"What started out last year as an occasional fecal sack in our birdbath (which can no longer be called such) has mushroomed into an onslaught, with there often being more than fifty popcorn-sized sacks by day's end. Moreover, these grackles have lined the rocks around our pond with white sacks, and sometimes don't even bother to land, bombarding the pond on their way over. One result, we surmise, is that our pond is getting too much nitrogen, why water from the waterfalls is frothing white. Something we haven't seen before."

By June 1, the crisis had passed: "Wouldn't you know," wrote Rick, "that right about the time I was about to give up, the problem solved itself. The babies, wherever they were, all must have fledged at once because the onslaught abruptly stopped."

In my case this year, the waterfall stopped foaming after two days. Then came a four-day, Pentecost-like burst of grackles and their young feeding and begging and clucking and scrawing and whining and grackling and speaking in tongues that lasted from morning until night. Then all was quiet and the pond stayed clear and the fish calmed down and were happy.

The grackles perform the celebratory ritual of bringing out their fledglings all together in a feeding frenzy in my yard every year. Up until this May they spared my pond. Maybe they finally left Rick alone.

2019: No grackle residue in the pond this year, so far. In the late afternoon, a walk at the quarry with Jill and Ranger: After all the rain, it seemed that the trees were so much bigger than they had been. But I hadn't been here for a while. Blooming: wild daisies, yellow sweet clover, small purple verbena, a yellow sedum on wet rocky patches, red clover, common fleabane, crown vetch, a milk thistle still green, and many budding panicled dogwoods. One small pool still had tadpoles. One huge red-black dragonfly. A handful of azure butterflies and two red admirals fluttered in the shade of the dense honeysuckle groves, and we surprised one black rat snake, maybe a yard long, crossing the road. Tat reports from Madison, Wisconsin, that her red peony opened today on schedule.

2020: Moya's mock orange is shedding as summer heat settles in. Honeybees, some laden with pollen, work the full-blooming spiderwort. A bee fly seen. Continuous robin peeping throughout the day, guiding fledglings.

2022: In the early sunlight, fold-wing skippers speed back and forth above the circle garden alliums. The first bright yellow sundrop primrose opened in the night, and Jill's red mulberry tree started to shed fat berries. A young rabbit, maybe the size of a small kitten, ran across her yard into the lilies that had been eaten off by deer. After dark, I saw my first firefly, a day later than Mat, Rick and Chris, and I heard the soft, slurred call of tree cricket in the honeysuckles.

*High noon*
*clovers and vetches,*
*bindweeds and sweet peas,*
*trumpet vines, chicory,*
*mullein and thistles,*
*honewort and fire pink,*
*parsnips and mint .*

Hepatica Sun

## *June 2nd*
## *The 153rd Day of the Year*

*When June is here – what art have we to sing*
*The whiteness of the lilies midst the green*
*On noon-tranced lawns? Or flash of roses seen*
*Like redbirds' wings? Or earliest ripening*
*Prince-Harvest apples, where the cloyed bees cling*
*Round winey juices oozing down between*
*The peckings of the robin, while we lean*
*In under-grasses, lost in marveling?*

James Whitcomb Riley

Sunrise/set: 5:08/7:58
Day's Length: 14 hours 50 minutes
Average High/Low: 78/57
Average Temperature: 68
Record High: 98 – 1895
Record Low: 41 – 1910

### *Weather*

Most June 2nds are pleasant and warm with highs in the 70s or 80s (35 percent chance of each), with the remaining 30 percent evenly divided between 90s and 60s. Completely cloudy conditions occur four days out of ten. Rain falls half the time on this date, but this is the last day until June 20th that chances of precipitation are so high.

### *Natural Calendar*

Not long after peonies and the exotic flowers of the yellow poplar end their seasons, just past the end of poppies, the last leaves of the canopy cover the land. When the high foliage is complete, then the wild multiflora roses and the domestic tea roses are in full bloom, the last Osage and black walnut flowers fall, clustered snakeroot loses its pollen in the shade, and parsnips, goat's beard and sweet clovers take over the roadsides. Rare swamp valerian blossoms by the water, and common timothy pushes up from its sheaths in alleyways.

Delicate Miami mist, pink yarrow, yellow moneywort, silver lamb's ear and the rough Canadian thistle bloom. Wild onions and domestic garlic get their seed bulbs. Poison ivy and tiger lilies and catalpas are budding. Daisies, golden Alexander, groundsel, sweet rocket and common fleabane still hold in the pastures, but garlic mustard and ragwort are gone. The bright violet heads of chives decay. Petals of mock orange, honeysuckle, scarlet pyrethrum, blue lupine and Dutch iris have dropped to the garden floor.

The columbines come apart as astilbe reddens. Nettles and grasses tangle with catchweed. July's wild petunia foliage is a foot tall. Giant yucca plants send up their firm stalks not only in Kentucky but also deep in the Caribbean.

### The Stars

At ten o'clock at night, Virgo lies due south, and bright Arcturus, the largest star in the central sky, is almost overhead. The Milky Way fills the eastern half of the sky, running from the north and "Z" shaped Cassiopeia, through Cygnus the Swan, then through Aquila and finally to Scutum and Sagittarius deep in the southeast.

### Daybook

1981: First strawberries from the garden for breakfast.

1982: First peonies decaying.

1983: Yarrow budding in far South Glen, sweet Cicely, garlic mustard, winter cress, spring cress declining, sweet rocket strong, a few wild geraniums left, touch-me-nots and nettles three feet tall, angelica six feet and blooming, tall meadow rue four feet, poison hemlock still not open, parsnips beginning, wild petunia foliage becoming prominent, about a foot high. First baby blackbird in the yard.

1984: First young blackbird in the yard today. Catalpas budding, Siberian iris bloom, first yellow sweet clover, buckeyes with smooth fruits.

1986: First Canadian thistle and blueweed found blooming along the railroad tracks. End of the peonies today

1989: First strawberries for breakfast.

1992: All iris, small and large, in late bloom. Mock orange holding, second tier of daisies opening, red pyrethrum older but still beautiful, rockets going to seed, some ranunculus gone, bright orange geum holding. Peak of strawberries. Multiflora roses seen from the road.

1993: All locust flower clusters are brown now. Sycamore leaves seem full size. Wild cherry gone on Dayton Street, most iris done. Long fence rows of white blackberry flowers along Grinnell. Feverfew open along High Street.

1994: The first Asiatic lily opened along the north border today, flowering pale orange from a short stalk. Sweet Williams are at their height now, only four or five iris left, peonies full bloom. In the south garden, the sweet rockets are almost finished. This week, the flicker in the back woods has been calling all day, loud, steady, raucous sounds.

1996: Privets budding. Late peonies, late iris, late blue flags, late honeysuckle, full mock orange. Late full daisies. Poppies gone. Pyrethrums waning, sweet rockets waning. Snow-on-the-mountain full along Dayton Street. Locust flowers falling to the sidewalk, their rich season finally disintegrating. I saw yellow sweet clover for the first time two days ago. Black medic full bloom, red and white clover too.

2000: On Kelly's Island in Lake Erie, red sunrise exactly at 6:00, eight to ten minutes ahead of Yellow Springs. The fish bit in the barometric trough before the storm, then disappeared as the high pressure moved through. The wind blew chilly and hard all night, high waves lifting the boat off the sand beach and tumbling it south along the shore.

2001: Walk through the Glen in the rain: petals of the yellow poplar common on the path, the woods deep green for summer.

2002: Yellow swallowtail sighted today. White moths at the front porch light.

2003: Returning from Santee-Cooper in South Carolina, I came across a swarm of red periodic cicadas at the first rest stop across the Virginia – North Carolina line. Through the mountains, locusts, wild cherry, and blackberries were in bloom, weeks behind Yellow Springs. When I arrived home, the first yellow sundrop was coming out, the last blue flag shriveling.

2004: To South Carolina: Full summer in southwestern Ohio, canopy complete. Banks of yellow Stella d'oro lilies in Cincinnati. Staghorns reddening. Sweet clover and crown vetch throughout. Poison hemlock in bloom, and golden staghorns, daisies. Catalpas still flowering in Kentucky. Seeding time for locusts and ashes. Elderberries in flower.

South of Cincinnati, hemlocks were seeding and Japanese honeysuckles were in full bloom Parsnips tall and gold. Teasel and milkweed two to three feet. Full Canadian thistles. A few miles north of Lexington, white sweet clover coming in, cattails thin, emerging, full of pollen. Chicory opening by 7:15. Trumpet creeper in Lexington. Nodding thistles full throughout. New tawny hay bales rolled in the field. Queen Anne's lace open three hours south of Yellow Springs at Berea. Roadside tiger daylilies at Knoxville, some nodding thistles holding there, many going to seed. Mimosa trees and milkweed blooming. Teasel headed. Kousa dogwood in the mountains of North Carolina. Fields of purple and orange poppies high in the mountains. Below Spartanburg, wild lettuce, horseweed. Near Columbia, myrtles. At Santee Cooper, water willow in bloom – at the same time as in Yellow Springs. Corn tasseling here, some ears formed. Some wheat dark, most fields cut. Water lilies open – American lotus early bloom. Catalpa beans nine-inches long.

2007: Primrose sundrops completely full and bright. Transplanted Stella d'oros have first blossoms. Pale violet pond iris have ended, Japanese pond iris in early full bloom. Rockets closing very quickly, mostly gone. Daylilies and Asiatics budding throughout. Two purple coneflowers have unraveled; the Heliopsis is starting to unravel. In the water garden, the first water willow bloomed today. Lizard's "tails" have developed over the past three or four days.

2008: Madison, Wisconsin to Yellow Springs: Parsnips, hemlock, yellow sweet clover, foxtail grass dominate the roadsides. Red-winged blackbirds nesting throughout the 500-mile drive. Wheat turning pale green-gold near Indianapolis.

2009: Hundreds of tiny spiders, pale gold on the top of the garbage can, hatched from about 11:30; then in about 30 minutes, they were gone, having climbed out and floated away on their own silk, vanished into the woods. Later, grackles chased a hawk that seemed to be carrying one of their young.

2010: Cathy wrote from Vermont today: "Just as a point of interest, the Friends of the Horticulture Farm at the University of Vermont sent a notice last week that they had had to cancel the annual Lilac Walk because all the lilacs were gone. I presume they mean the blooming is past. I can't remember this ever happening before."

2011: Spoleto to Castelluccio, Italy: Linden trees exuding sap on the car. We drove northeast through fields of poppies, late elderberries. At Castelluccio, the "great flowering" had not begun there – was predicted for two weeks from now, but numerous lintel plots were bright yellow with blossoms, and on brief walks into the hills I found red clover, white campion, a strange new plantain that had a long, pink inflorescence, a buttercup similar to the variety that blooms at home, burdock tall and budding, a plant that looked like a lone grape hyacinth – possibly an *Orchis moio*, a bright purple vetch – maybe *Veccia cracca*, white *Caryophillaceae* and so many more small yellow, white and violet flowers all across the vast expanse of this immense valley. Crickets were very loud at one stopping place, absent in another.

2012: First four raspberries from the garden. First three yucca blossoms in the north garden. Hollyhocks budded in the park gardens. One last weigela flower on our north garden bush. This morning, the cabbage whites number about a dozen, all feeding and playing together in the bellflowers and the catmint. Yellow daylilies, yellow rebloomers, and one orange daylily joining the gold Stella d'oros, encroachment of color. Red admiral butterfly drinking at the hummingbird feeder, then a hummingbird comes and joins her. At twelve o'clock noon exactly, a loud flock of crows descends on the north end of the village, crescendo of sound like a truck coming down the street from Dayton. The red "Indomitable Spirit" hydrangea continues in full bloom, opened maybe two weeks ago?

2013: Flew into Sicily this afternoon with Neysa and Ivano, the land so dry and brown compared to Umbria and Tuscany. Instead of small hills with villages and castles and small landholdings of grain and olives: vast rolling valleys and huge crags and cliffs near the clear, clear sea. The towns, so far, do not have the color of Italian towns, most of the buildings unpainted, gray or drab earth tones. There are few trees, but the sidewalks are often lined with large pots containing assorted tropical plants. Many cacti here, the largest ones, the *Opoatia ficus indice L* in bloom. Fennel found, and a kind of blackberry with pink flowers. Many orange, pink, red flowering shrubs (oleanders) near towns and farms. In some areas, tall grass like Johnson grass, which is really "canya" that feels and looks like bamboo when it is cleaned off. (A man was stripping off the thin bark and preparing it for use at one of the places we visited.) A Sicilian cress with pale pink petals growing in San Vito do Capo on the coast. Many bright orange poppies and drifts of yellow ginestra like in central Italy and hedges of blooming jasmine. Watched the Corpus Christi procession through the streets of S. Vito do Cabo.

2015: Madison, Wisconsin to Yellow Springs: Roadsides lush with fresh hemlock, parsnips, daisies, foxtail grass and yellow sweet clover. The first nodding thistle seen in Fairborn, and catalpa flowers close to home. Returning to the village, I am struck by the clear difference between the season I left five days ago (the last days of Late Spring) and the season in Madison (the full middle of

Late Spring).  Here at home: the first ditch lily in bloom, several Stella d'oros, two of the low, orange Asiatic lilies; the first open blossom on the hobblebush hydrangea; full late pond iris (only one in bloom the morning I left); the first water lily – large, yellow; lizard's tail with its first tails the first yellow tea rose from Jeanie's ancient bush; the first quickweed flowers; full bloom of spiderwort, penstemon, waterleaf, celandine, bright primrose, lamium, catmint, snow-on-the-mountain; peonies, rockets, perennial salvia, tall ragwort, Japanese wisteria, garlic mustard almost gone; geranium gone with the rhododendron and sweet Cicely; resurrection lily foliage flopped over like that of daffodils or hyacinths; buds showing a little gold on the heliopsis, And all of that contrasting with the full seasons of iris and peonies and lilacs and mock orange and drifts of sweet rockets I left in Madison.

2016: Peonies in the yard drooping, privet flowers falling from one hedge, one of Moya's white yarrows blooming,

2017: Grackle fledgling chasing its parent, begging at the back porch. Milkweed has started to bud in the yard, the buds more prominent in the downtown gardens. The first deep purple Japanese water iris bloomed today – in spite of having been saved from the koi and transplanted to the south garden. White-flowered maple waterleaf is in full flower.

2018: This morning, Jill and I stood picking ripe red mulberries from the low tree by her back porch. In her back yard, daisy fleabane has opened wide, all the rockets gone. At home, five Stella d'oros in flower, and the very first Japanese water iris. Peonies completely gone. I found one smartweed flower when I was clearing out the circle garden for zinnias. Grackle fledglings scrawing in the honeysuckles. I saw a large red finch and mate feeding in the lawn a little before afternoon. This evening after sunset, Jill saw the first firefly along the path at the Glass Farm preserve, and then we saw more in the adjacent vegetable gardens.

2019: I woke up to Grackle Pentecost once again, the excited clucking and scrawing of adults and fledglings in the back bushes and trees. The mulberries were reddening, the high locusts and the

Osage were done blooming, the canopy full. No Pentecostal wind, but a nice breeze, sun and warm. The primroses had opened overnight, along with one cream-violet day lily, the first lily of any kind in the yard this summer. Late in the afternoon, Ranger and I went into South Glen at the entrance past the Covered Bridge. I hadn't been there for over a year, and everything was overgrown, the vegetation growth reminding me of being in the jungle of Belize, all green with very little variety. Here, wood nettle was the dominant wildflower foliage, along with touch-me-nots, wingstem and honewort (the latter about the only plant in bloom). I saw several black damselflies along the water, but no butterflies. The entire area on the west side of the river had been allowed to grow uncut for years, and now what used to be the butterfly preserve and what I called High Prairie are swallowed up by honeysuckles, black walnut and box elder trees. The quarry habitat where I visited last week was more varied than this unkempt forest.

2020: More black walnut catkins on the ground. Cottonwood cotton in the wind. Peonies still at their peak. First fireflies seen at the Mills Lawn Park near the Catholic church.

2021: Winter wheat gray-green along the way to Fairborn.

2022: First daddy longlegs seen this year, hunting on a cup plant leaf.

> *Wide are the meadows of night,*
> *And daisies are shining there,*
> *Tossing their lovely dews,*
> *Lustrous and fair;*
> *And through these sweet fields go,*
> *Wand'rers 'mid the stars---*
> *Venus, Mercury, Uranus, Neptune, Saturn, Jupiter, Mars.*
> *'Tired in their silver, they move,*
> *And circling, whisper and say,*
> *Fair are the blossoming meads of delight*
> *Through which we stray.*

Walter de la Mare

### June 3rd
### The 154th Day of the Year

*I will measure one by one*
*through this sweetest afternoon,*
*strawberries, mulberries,*
*ducklings and dragonflies,*
*crickets and fireflies*
*under the waxing moon,*
*sundrops, angelica, yucca buds,*
*meadow rue, thistles and raspberries*
*lilies, astilbe,*
*telling the time in June.*

Hepatica Sun

Sunrise/set: 5:08/7:59
Day's Length: 14 hours 51 minutes
Average High/Low: 78/57
Average Temperature: 68
Record High: 99 – 1895
Record Low: 40 – 1929

### Weather

Today's high temperature distribution: 80s occur on 45 percent of all the days, 70s on 35 percent, 60s on 20 percent, 90s almost never. Thunderstorms develop half the years, but the sun returns 90 percent of the time.

### Natural Calendar

June ushers in the four-month-long season in which the entire canopy of leaves is complete in almost the entire United States. Under the green crown of summer, Multiflora Rose Season, Lamb's Ear Season, Heliopsis Season, Floribunda Rose Season, Oakleaf Hydrangea Season and Tea Rose Season are open in the garden. Moth Mullein Season, Sweet Clover Season, Canadian Thistle Season, Crown Vetch Season and Meadow Goat's beard Season mark the roadsides. Late Clustered Snakeroot Season shelters daddy longlegs in the shade. Scarlet Pimpernel Season complements the lawn. Along the rivers, it is the middle of Turtle Egg Laying Season.

Catalpa Season and Privet Season and Pink Spirea Season parallel Firefly Season and Cucumber Beetle Season, Daylily Season and Coreopsis Season, Purple Coneflower Season and Hollyhock Season, Chicory Season and Trumpet Creeper Season, Nodding Thistle Season and Great Mullein Season, Asiatic Lily Season and Sweet Ripe Black Raspberry Picking Season. Delicate Honewort Season declines through the forest as Pie Cherry Season fills the pies.

### *Daybook*

1983: Snowball viburnum almost gone, rockets still hold, and watercress. Lily-of-the-valley gone, milkweed three feet tall, two young blackbirds, just out of the nest, sitting on the lawn.

1984: Honeysuckles and bridal wreath spirea mostly completed in the yard, snowballs fading.

1985: Privet still full bloom, pink spirea has been open a few days. May apples fat at South Glen, honewort full, garlic mustard all bowing down, only an occasional rocket and white violet, green berries on the cohosh. Out in the field, cow parsnips full, full timothy, first tall meadow rue and dogbane flowering.

1986: Cardinals singing at 4:33 a.m. Black raspberries turning red, cherries ripening.

1987: Mulberries coming in, first ones completely ripe around the end of May. Blueweed suddenly open, first black raspberries darkening, cherries turning. Summer is advancing more quickly now with heavy rains, humidity, and temperatures in the 80s. Robin seen sitting on her eggs in the ginkgo outside my window.

1990: Osage flowers fall, catalpa buds are forming, peonies and iris still full in patches, privet time.

1991: Fishing at Caesar Creek, sun, warm, quiet: Around 10:00 a.m., three catfish in a row, a bullhead, two carp, then nothing for a while. Along the shores, carp splashing, sucking at the reeds and leaves, sometimes a low slurping, other times almost like the chucking of a squirrel. Bullfrogs croak from time to time, other frogs or toads high chanting, steady through the morning. Webworms in the water willows, cottonwood still drifting, one question mark butterfly, a tiger swallowtail, and a small blue. Cicadas swarming (Brood XIV) in a nearby ash tree, periodic cicadas: red heads, orange legs, light orange wing ribs. Pale blue-bodied dragonflies with black wings, orange dragonflies. Brown spotted butterfly, a buckeye, sat on my right hand, unafraid and sipping salt from my skin. I wanted it to change hands. I put out my left index finger. It tasted it, climbed on. The afternoon went so quickly. By the end, a total of three cats, six carp, one bullhead, three large fish lost.

1992: Madison, Wisconsin to Gentilly in northwestern Minnesota: Locust trees in Madison: branches heavy with flowers, their rich scent on the wind. Sweet rockets full all the way north, huge sunflower foliage, full canopy on the roadside trees, milkweed two to three feet, and some with first bud clusters. Spurge was full from Illinois to central Wisconsin. Crop stages similar between Yellow Springs to Madison, but becoming behind by Eau Claire. Minnesota wheat was six inches to a foot tall (starting to turn near Yellow Springs), first corn just sprouted, sugar beets the size of radishes, red-winged blackbirds nesting from Ohio to the Canadian border. Lilacs in bloom in Gentilly, iris full bloom in Ada, cottonwood cotton in the streets of Crookston.

1993: Poison hemlock at the height of its flower. Wild strawberries are ripe, red in the east garden and the lawn.

1996: As I went to the greenhouse at 4:45 a.m., the first cardinal sang in the yard. First three strawberries perfectly ripe in the garden. Raspberries very small and green. Last year's parsley sends up seed stalks. Young crow just out of the nest flew by me as I walked out the back door this afternoon, its parents watchful, loud for the next few hours.

1998: First heliopsis and first feverfew send out flower petals. First pink yarrow in the yard. Pyrethrum season is over.

1999: First orange Asiatic lily blossoms as all the blue flags end. Three peonies left, fragments of poppies, fragrant full bloom of the privet since the end of May, Catalpas full and falling. Snakeskins found along the garden rocks for the past two weeks, water willow blooming beside them.

2000: Back from Lake Erie: the Japanese iris in the pond is done now for the year. Water willow opening in their place. In the south garden, the pink achillea has begun its season. On Fairfield Pike, the catalpas are full bloom still; the yucca spikes are five feet tall. Daisies lanky now, ranunculus disappearing, bright yellow sundrops all blossoming against the south wall, a patch of orange lilies along the north garden. The south side of the yard is now almost completely sealed off from the world by the foliage of the red mulberry trees.

2002: Earwigs and green damselflies in the garden. A tiger swallowtail visited the sweet rockets this afternoon. Kousa dogwood is still in full bloom in the triangle park.

2005: To the far end of Caesar Creek with John today, fishing in deep water to 100 feet. Not a bite all day. Penstemon opens in the north garden. Flags all gone.

2007: Constant grackle conversations between parents and fledglings, in the bushes and back lot all day. The chatter has been going on for days, growing in intensity. The red-bellied woodpecker has been louder and more insistent, too – after a period of relative quiet. First scorpion fly seen in the yard.

2008: Returned from two days on the road and two days in Madison, Wisconsin. The two large koi, Emmet and Zelda, had been killed overnight by some kind of marauder. All the iris and Dutch iris are gone now, the peonies, sweet rockets, sweet Williams, and groundsel still full. Two tea roses bloomed: one yellow, one pink. Mock orange, locusts and honeysuckle are shedding hard, parts of the yard covered with flowers. The first cedar waxwings noticed in the white mulberry tree this afternoon. The first orange candy lilies opened near the trellis. In Xenia, stalks of yucca are waist high.

2009: Cardinal at 4:15 and 4:45. Red-bellied woodpecker at 5:15. Cold and gray all day. Catalpa flowers falling in Xenia. Faded chives flowers cut back. Wisteria gone, rockets very late, candy lilies full, three Stella d'oros, coreopsis seen, primrose and lamb's ear full, birds feeding heavily in the mulberry, giant alliums hold, earliest daylily gone, blue jay steady at the feeder, robins continue plentiful. Don's multiflora roses gone, his black walnut finally fully leafed.

2010: The first ripe raspberry picked in the garden. The first yucca flower opened on Davis Street. Daisy fleabane blossoming among the bamboo, the Japanese iris full bloom.

2011: Italy: In Spoleto at La Rocca, spring has faded to summer, even though large patches of yellow *ginestra* still flower up and down the valley. Poppies have faded here, and I didn't see the rugosa roses *Rosa canina*). A small-flowered campanula is open on the hillside, maybe *Campanula rapunculus*, and some new yellow sedum with tall stems and bright yellow flowers – like *Sedum nupestre*, and one four-petaled *Cardamine,* like a sweet rocket.

2012: Milkweed open at the edge of town, many yuccas in full bloom, first Shasta daisy in Liz's yard (and her yellow flowered, foxglove-like plant with long, pointed leaves and mallow-mullein kind of flowers. Corn is past knee-high in the fields on the way to Fairborn. Constant scrawing of starling babies, robins peeping orientation to their young. Mockingbird-like call, long and melodious now in the early to midmorning for several days. Long, black cricket hunter seen on the stones at the edge of the pond. Smartweed in bloom pulled up as I was weeding the zinnias. The great blue hosta at the west edge of the yard just came into bloom this afternoon.

Judy writes from Goshen, Indiana: "First of all, the gosling report. There is one family whose young ones are really pretty big--I'd say almost 2/3 the size of the parents. The other families are smaller, although they're coming along. I'll have to hike over to Westbrooke pond, where they hang out most of the time, to get a better picture, but I'd say the other little ones are almost halfway. They are so darned cute!! I love the parades just as much as the cats, and that's a lot."

2013: To Erise in northwestern Sicily throughout the morning, visited the ancient temple and theater of Segesta in the afternoon. Much greater variety of plants throughout the drives and walks. I took photos of a thistle or sow thistle with bright yellow flowers. There were many Queen Anne's lace in bloom - or a variety very similar.

2014: In Madison, Wisconsin, Tat's deep red peonies opened today.

2015: Tat's red peonies were opening last year on this date: they were full and drooping over the sidewalk from the rain when I arrived in Madison on May 29 this year. Grackles loud and excited in Don's maple trees as I walked by this morning. Comfrey full bloom at the Antioch farm, just budded at Tat's. White campion full here as in Madison.

2016: Spent flower clusters of the Osage tree falling on me as I walked past the shed (like on this day in 1990). In the north garden, a fine clump of bright yellow primroses had opened in the night. A few small quince fruits floating in the pond. At Peggy's, the pie cherries are ripening. Peonies down to one red flower, new wild daisies strong, two Stella d'oro blossoms (banks of them in the mall parking lot).

2017: Privet flowers completely gone, the earliest I have noticed through the years. Looking back, I can see that my peonies dissolved earlier than other years, as well. Serviceberries and late pie cherries deep red. Five Stella d'oro lilies flowering in the yard. The count begins. Winter wheat is a rich gold between here and New Carlisle (where I saw a yucca plant in full bloom. Small blue bell flowers/campanulas blossoming in the alley, still not open here. A tall, Christmas-tree shaped catalpa tree full bloom at Chris and Debbie's. In their woods, twinleaf foliage was yellowing.

2018: The flowers of several privet bushes along High Street have fallen, rusted, to the sidewalk like the honeysuckle blossoms of last week. Jill's mulberries, suddenly darker and sweeter, have started to fall to her driveway. Four Stella d'oro lilies open at home. At the local shopping areas, the Stella d'oros are in early full bloom. Throughout town, pink spirea is in full flower. Jill found a male tiger swallowtail on our walk this evening.

2019: Crisp and cool in the high 50s this morning, clear sky, grackle Pentecost continuing unabated. Jill's mulberries starting to come in. Returning to Spoleto from Rome (Italy), Neysa sent a photo of an orchid blooming in her yard.

2020: First daddy longlegs seen in the studio. And suddenly all the mosquitoes are here. Two days ago, even in the heat and humidity, not a single one. Now, it's almost impossible to sit on the back porch without being swarmed. In a Limestone Street yard, yucca stalks are up to my stomach. At the pond and in the alley, curly dock is blooming. Large pale blue-bodied dragonflies (*Libellula*) prowl the pond shoreline. One small, golden fold-wing skipper in the bamboo this afternoon.

2021: First primrose open in the north garden, Osage flowers falling by the studio, blackberries setting fruit on Davis Street, and the first red mulberry dropped to Jill's patio today.

2022: To Madison, Wisconsin, in sun for 500 miles: Canopies complete, wheat turning gray green, parsnips and hemlock and daisies common. In Madison, iris and peonies full early flower, the easiest markers.

*Harmonious knit, the rosy-finger'd Hours,*
*The Zephyrs floating loose, the timely Rains,*
*Of bloom ethereal the light-footed Dews,*
*And soften'd into joy the surly Storms.*

*These, in successive turn, with lavish hand,*
*Shower every beauty, every fragrance shower,*
*Herbs, flowers, and fruits; till, kindling at thy touch*
*From land to land is flush'd the vernal year.*

James Thomson

## June 4th
## The 155th Day of the Year

*Sweet day, so cool, so calm, so bright,*
*The bridal of the earth and sky....*

George Herbert

Sunrise/set: 5:07/7:59
Day's Length: 14 hours 52 minutes
Average High/Low: 79/58
Average Temperature: 68
Record High: 97 – 1895
Record Low: 42 – 1945

### Weather

The 4th is usually dry, with showers occurring just 25 percent of the days. Skies are clear to partly cloudy three days in four. Highs reach the 90s five percent of the time, the 80s thirty-five percent of the time and climb to the 70s a little more than half the time. Today is the second-last June day when a five percent chance of a cold afternoon temperatures in the 50s can be expected (the 12th is the very last day).

### Natural Calendar

May apples have fruit the size of a cherry. Buckeyes have half-inch burrs. Honeysuckle flowers have fallen, bridal wreath and snowball viburnum rusted. Timothy is ripe for chewing. Asiatic lilies, poison ivy, meadow rue, Indian hemp, and catalpa trees bud and bloom. July's wild petunia foliage is a foot tall. August's boneset has grown knee high.

Mulberry time begins for both the red and white varieties, and it typically lasts until the end of Early Summer – good for birds and good for pies! Tea roses and achillea are open in the garden, and the first foxtail grass ripples by the side of the road. Canadian geese are molting, now that all of their goslings have hatched. Mother grackles and robins are cleaning their nests, often depositing the white droppings of their babies in birdbaths or ponds.

## *Daybook*

1982: Some mulberries ripe along King Street. Sweet rocket gone except for a few cutovers.

1983: More fragments of May: sweet Cicely old, foliage turning a creamy violet color, yellow flowers of the golden Alexander gone to seed. Another piece of Early Summer: swamp valerian found on the way to Caesar Creek. Blackberries in bloom everywhere, snowball viburnum still prominent, white and red peonies and iris common throughout. Yellow sweet clover in the roadsides.

1985: Covered Bridge: Cabbage butterflies mating. Black damsel flies with white wing tips by the river, and pale tan moths. Mint is waist high, catchweed burs catching in my pants legs. Wingstem five and six feet tall, honewort full bloom, golden Alexander gone to seed, boneset three feet, lizard's tail with five leaves, corn salad and garlic mustard dying. At Middle Prairie maybe a dozen field crickets singing.

1986: Two small groundhogs, maybe six to eight weeks old, killed on the road this week.

1988: Iris flowers seem to have disappeared everywhere. Japanese honeysuckle and privets bloomed overnight. All snowballs and bridal wreath are gone. Chicory seen yesterday in Fairborn. Tiger lilies are budding.

1989: Strawberries peak in the north garden, cabbage butterflies spiraling, mating by the stone wall, catchweed burs catching on my pants. First chicory seen along the highway today, yellow sweet clover, purple vetch, crown vetch, multiflora roses, blackberries full bloom. First Japanese honeysuckle in the yard. In the woods, sweet rockets are in late flower, as blue waterleaf and ragwort decline. Daylilies have been out a few days, swamp orchids in bloom a week or so. Gold-collared blackflies are common, daddy longlegs everywhere. Cottonwood cotton floating down onto the streets. Watercress still full. Under the canopy, wingstem, touch-me-not, white snakeroot, wood nettle are huge. Avens is knee high, honewort is blossoming, apples an inch long.

1991: Campanulas opening.

1993: Parsnips full bloom.

1997: Into South Glen this coolest spring of the decade: Crickets loud. First multiflora rose in bloom, last wild geranium and white violet. Sweet rockets and maple leaf waterleaf on the down side of their bloom, garlic mustard almost gone. Corn salad full and white. Burs on the catchweed. Timothy emerging from its sheathes. Ragwort to seed. Wingstem, wild lettuce, wood nettle waist high. Scorpion flies are about, and gold collard blackflies. Teasel pants-pocket high. Lots of daddy longlegs. Orchard grass easy to pull, and sweet. Black damselflies. First white yarrow seen in south Dayton. Locusts full bloom along the freeway.

1998: Thimble plant heading up at the Mill. One blonde, one white domestic rabbit hopping around in the bushes. Several parsnips have gone to seed. Fire pink seen.

1999: Feverfew buds forming. Along the tree line as I drive, tall catalpa trees are white with flowers. The air is heavy with sweet privet and Japanese honeysuckle.

2000: At breakfast, I looked up at the tall locusts in the back yard. Their leaves were finally full, the last of the canopy. Later, feverfew seen in early bloom.

2001: The south garden fills with lamb's ear, dwarf geranium, spiderwort, late poppies, very late Japanese iris, water lilies, Stella d'oro lilies, primrose, daisies, rockets, buttercups.

2002: Another yellow swallowtail. Red mulberries falling in Dayton.

2003: Peonies, poppies, iris, blue flags, mock orange are completely done blooming today. Sweet Williams, cressleaf groundsel, daisies, peach-leaved bellflowers, and spiderwort keep the garden full of color. The very first water willow bloomed in the pond – beside five red water lilies and the last dark-purple Japanese water iris. Catalpas are in full bloom throughout the area.

2005: To the old catfish hole at Caesar Creek with John. The reservoir was a little low, and we had no bites during an hour of fishing. Only one small turtle was hooked near lunchtime. One good-sized crappie struck a walleye lure as we were trolling back to the landing. In the evening, John caught a goldfish, a catfish, two suckers and a chub at Sycamore Hole. First fireflies seen tonight.

2007: Loud, intense feeding of young grackles from before dawn until full daylight, then the activity lightened a little. Two young doves found in the garden this morning. They were maybe a third of full size, flew off rather agilely. In the alley, panicled dogwood in early bloom, pokeweed budding. In the yard, early orange and yellow Asiatic lilies anchor the garden now. Ranunculus season ends in the east garden except for a handful of blossoms. First buckeye butterfly seen in the yard this morning. Young sparrow being fed by its mother in the sweet Williams. Grackles continue to feed their fledglings – the whole woodlot is filled with their cackles. Jeanie reports fire pinks in full bloom at Clifton Gorge. Driving home from Beavercreek, we saw a roadside full of orange daylilies.

2008: Pink spirea seen in town today. Some peonies and iris still in bloom throughout the area – but no longer here in the yard. Cedar waxwings eating white mulberries in the back trees. Yesterday, a house finch was feeding a fledgling on the north trellis. Wisteria on the porch has just started to rust. Buds lengthen on the Japanese honeysuckle. Only three orange Asiatic lilies in bloom, ranunculus blossoms receding. Last night, a long line of thunderstorms moved through Yellow Springs, flooding the yard and the pond with at least three inches of rain.

2009: Most weigelas (Mateo's and ours) are done except the bright red one across the street. The pond iris has been completely gone for about three days, and the lizard's tails are getting fatter.

Starlings have replaced grackles at the bird feeder. The blue jay feeds steadily.

2010: Don's pie cherries are ready for pie. In the yard, our perennial salvia is done blooming, needs to be cut back to bloom again. The first heliopsis is just starting to unravel – not blooming yet. The Japanese iris in the pond (not the pale "pond iris") is still in full bloom. Jeanie heard and saw a few cedar waxwings today. Pink smartweed noticed as I was mowing the lawn. Wet, hot weather continues, corn way past knee high.

2011: Italy: Brief walk along the Spoleto bike path before a thunderstorm that lasted through the afternoon: Teasel tall and budded, great mullein starting to bud, dock (*Rumex acetosa*) red seeds, the *rosa canina* are fading, huge blackberry bramble with pink flowers, long patches of white achillea (*Achillea millefolium*), some white *Cardamine,* wide and deep fields of wheat tall and golden, lots of wild mallow, some dandelions, red clover, scarlet pimpernel, large patches of hemlock and thistles (probably the *Cardo mariano* instead of thistles) full bloom and some to seed. Hickory nuts full size on a pair of hickory trees near a small, family vineyard.

2012: Young robin accidentally swept from a honeysuckle bush while I was pruning, fully feathered, but unable to fly yet, hopped into the bushes, mother at its heels. One starling fledgling begging from its parent today. Competition picks up between hummingbirds at the feeder. A full portion of raspberries from the patch this morning. The year continues to bring plants into bloom well ahead of other years, but there is also plenty of overlap, too. One flower of the whirling butterfly gaura opened today. In the Phillips Street alley, a seven-foot sow thistle has been blooming since late May, leaves alternate, widely spaced, relatively thin. First chigger bite after working in the yard.

2013: Driving the countryside in northwestern Sicily: We stopped at the Crypta, a vast cement installation covering the remains of an entire village destroyed in an earthquake. Here there were butterflies, whites and sulfurs in abundance (perhaps spirits of the dead), whereas butterflies have been scarce throughout our visit.

2014: From Madison, Wisconsin to Yellow Springs (through heavy rain for miles and miles): Home to major changes: one deep purple pond iris has bloomed, and one bud is fat and ready. The bamboo has leafed out. Smartweed has pink flowers near the catmint. The first two orange Asiatic lilies, and three Stella d'oro lilies have opened. The clump of "ditch lilies" has sent up bud stalks. Jeanie's yellow tea rose and her pink tea rose have produced one large flower each, and the Knockout roses are starting to open on their new stems.  The penstemon, the Japanese honeysuckles and the yellow primroses have all come into bloom. The weigela and the ranunculus are still flowering, but they are in decline. Almost all the peonies are gone, old and beaten down by the rain. The wisteria on the porch has rusted. The Anna Belle, the "Indomitable" and the hobblebush hydrangeas have produced large bud clusters. Three alliums are still in bloom. Winter wheat was turning green-gold on the way to Xenia. One cabbage white butterfly seen as I was taking inventory – the butterfly population so meager that one cabbage white is an occasion. Rob reports, however, that at Cedar Bog this year all the species he had tracked before returned at the previously noted times.

2015: First cabbage butterflies in over a week seen this morning at home. Bird activity intense around the yard, fledglings eating and being fed. Catalpas and privets in full bloom, the latter with a heavy fragrance as I biked through town. First bi-color hostas noticed in bloom, and more hawthorns. Astilbes showing color, opening. Pond iris at their finest. A patch of daisy fleabane in flower noticed near the college.  Achillea has been coming in at Peggy's for several days. Her gray-headed coneflower stalks are up to my chest.

2016: Honeysuckle flowers brown on the front walkway, black mulberries falling to the sidewalk along Davis Street, one privet all shed along High Street. Two Stella d'oro lilies open in the east garden. More Osage flower stalks brought down by the wind. Cottonwood cotton lighter, it seems, more like dandelion or goat's beard seeds. Oakleaf hydrangeas in early bloom around town

Catalpas noticed flowering along Dayton-Yellow Springs Road, some petals blown down in this afternoon's hard rain.

2017: The Strawberry Rains are over, and the outlook for the week ahead is for dry weather. Four Stella d'oro lilies open this morning. Cottonwood cotton scattered along Greene Street. Black walnuts on Davis Street are the size of hazel nuts or large acorns, peaches the size of large walnuts. The first field cricket heard near Jill's shed this morning.

2018: Chilly morning in the 50s, clear and autumnal. Two Japanese iris, ten Stella d'oro lily blossoms, measuring the month. I saw my first orange ditch lily open a few houses down from mine on High Street. And the first white-spotted skipper in Jill's magnolia. Then Casey called at 10:20 a.m. with a bald eagle sighting!

2019: Mild and sunny. Grackles mostly quiet. Gold-collared blackflies, abundant this year, mating in the lily foliage. Jill and I saw our first firefly on the way home from the movies tonight.

2020: The pond has been foaming from bird fecal deposits for the past three days. First privet flowers on the sidewalk this morning. First buds seen on the milkweed, the pokeweed and the helianthus.

2021: Roses, Kousa dogwoods and pink spirea flowering throughout town, nine-bark and iris past their best. Along the highway, wild daisies and yellow sweet clover in full bloom. Downtown, the catalpa behind Tom's Market is heavy with blossoms. Stella d'oro lilies are open along Elm Street.

2022: Madison: In the woods near Maggie's house, blackberries, bishop's weed, waterleaf and Solomon's plume are in full flower. Locust trees are white with blossoms, poppies seen. In town, bridal wreath is full everywhwre.

*I must follow up these continual lessons of the air, water, earth,
I perceive I have no time to lose.*

Walt Whitman

### *June 5th*
### *The 156th Day of the Year*

*See, the sweet sun shines,*
*The shower is over,*
*Flowers preen their beauty,*
*The day how fair!*

Walter de la Mare

Sunrise/set: 5:07/8:00
Day's Length: 14 hours 53 minutes
Average High/Low: 79/58
Average Temperature: 68
Record High: 98 – 1925
Record Low: 41 – 1954

### *Weather*

Today's chance of a high in the 90s is five percent, and 90s are at least that likely in Yellow Springs until September 19. Fifty percent of the afternoons reach 80, and 30 percent are in the 70s. Chilly afternoons in the 60s come 15 percent of the time. A low close to 40 is more likely (five percent likely) to occur this morning than on any other June morning, and it is the last time that temperatures so cold can expected until September 6.

### *Natural Calendar*

When the canopy has closed above the woodland wildflowers, when winter wheat is a soft pale green, and the clovers and vetches are all coming in, then it's the best time of year for golden parsnip blossoms throughout the countryside. Catalpas and privets and hawthorns and pink spirea bloom at parsnip time, and the number of fireflies grows in proportion to the flowers on the day lilies. Yellow poplars (tulip trees) drop their multicolored petals (orange and yellow and green). The first raspberry reddens, and the first orange trumpet creeper blows. Bindweeds and sweet peas color the fences with pastels.

The peak of the parsnips in the fields is the high time for the wetlands' poison hemlock and angelica. In the shade, poison ivy, fire pink, and honewort are flowering.  At the edge of the forest, wild plants include blue-eyed grass, silver yarrow, yellow sedum, bright moneywort, fire pink, daisies, yellow sweet clover, wild roses, wild iris, dock, and smooth brome grass.  In the garden, the blue veronica, yellow coreopsis, deep purple loosestrife, and the first wave of the floribunda roses come into flower.

As the morning birdsong quiets, young blackbirds join their parents to harvest the ripening cherries and mulberries.  Cucumber beetles come to the pumpkins, squash, gourds and cucumbers.  Painted turtles and box turtles are out laying eggs.  The fearsome (but harmless) stag beetle waddles across your porch after dark.

### *Daybook*

1982: Stella d'oro lilies seen in town.

1984: The multiflora rosebush in the yard opened overnight, late locust blossoms rained down in a thunderstorm. Out to Caesar Creek: dock with small flowers, daisies, clover, blackberries, first yarrow, wild roses, Miami mist, yellow sweet clover, first blue and black damsel flies, first timothy emerging from its sheaths, swamp valerian, blue-eyed grass, cinquefoil, carp feeding at the shore, mating, grasshoppers drumming, flies pesky, bobwhite calling. First cobweb in my face. Wild onions getting seed bulbs, poison ivy ready to bloom. Fire pink seen. Spiderwort past its prime. When I sat on a log, I was covered with wood ticks. First brown wood toad seen, maybe an inch and a half long. Thousands of black tadpoles in the pools. *Juncus canadensis, Carex vulpinoide, Cares stipada,* and *Phragmites communis* collected.

1986: Catalpa flowers blew away today in the wind. Timothy was emerging from its sheaths at Middle Prairie, tender for chewing. The first black raspberries came in, one half a pint, covering the last of the strawberries in my colander. Several young raccoons killed on the back road, maybe six to eight weeks old.

1990: Tall meadow rue just starting to bloom at Clifton. Sundrops budding at the south wall, astilbe pink under the apple tree. Privet continues full bloom.

1991: To Jacoby from the Covered Bridge. The woods full of late honewort, some waterleaf still holding. July wildflower stalks chest high: touch-me-nots, wood nettles, wingstem. White cabbage butterflies, a dozen or so, clustered on a rock along the river. Maybe looking for salt in the urine of a dog or a deer that had passed by. Then more clusters of butterflies at mud patches higher up along the path. Large numbers of damselflies and monarchs. Lizard tail seed heads are out but not open. Daisy fleabane, Canadian and nodding thistles seen. Brome grasses, timothy, bottle grass peak. Flock of fourteen geese. No goslings. Panicled dogwood full. All multiflora roses long gone. Tall meadow rue, six feet, late full. Some angelica still full. A lot of moneywort. Yellow, red, white sweet clover full, all parsnips full. Men are working along the new bike path at Jacoby, and I think how Thoreau mentioned the outside workers, admired them and despised them.

1992: Most peonies have not opened yet in Crookston, Minnesota. Yellow sweet clover in bloom from Ohio north through Minneapolis and St. Cloud.

1993: Dutch iris more than half gone, scent of asparagus fern in full bloom has filled the greenhouse for days, delphinium early now, started a couple days ago. Iris three-fourths decayed in the village. Chicago peace rose is the first to open this month, then the Queen Elizabeth, then the Blue Girl, then the old-fashioned Rugosa. First striped cucumber beetle seen attacking the mums. Cottonwood seed in the wind: flurries of down across the highway south of town. Buds on the Virginia creeper outside my window.

1994: First garden primrose today. In the south garden, sweet rocket seed heads cut back for drying, goldenrod pulled, already five feet tall. Buds noticed on the hollyhocks, on the gay feather too. Most honeysuckle gone in the yard, mock orange three-quarters fallen. Downtown: bridal wreath has rusted, the pink spirea is open, privet is still budding.

1998: Frost in the North yesterday and today as a fierce front moves down from Canada.

2000: Early Summer grows more apparent: more roses, more achillea, late catalpas, the bright primroses, the soft gray and violet lamb's ears, the snapdragons and their pastels, the tall yellow yarrow heading up, the full blooming spiderwort beside the blue flax, motherwort blossoming, hollyhock buds heavy and leaning. In the pond, the pickerel plant opened. In Xenia, the first yucca flowers, and purple spirea in full bloom.

2001: First chicory and moth mullein seen open along the freeway in the late afternoon. More Canadian thistles. Coreopsis suddenly in full bloom along the entry to the interstate at Fairborn. Mulberries ripening.

2002: First chicory, first moth mullein, and first orange Asiatic lilies. Wild cherry bloom ends. Cottonwood full bloom, along with catalpas, privets, yellow poplars, and Japanese honeysuckle. Lizard's tails completely formed. Osage flowers falling now.

2003: Robins and cardinals loud at 4:30, dove joining in by 4:45. Song still loud at 5:00, quieting toward 5:30. At the pond near the shopping center, a huge flock of goslings –– maybe three dozen small birds – seen with eight adult geese.

2005: To the Ohio River with John: Cat fishing at the dam east of Cincinnati, full rigs with cut bait, no strikes, only one small drum was hooked. All along the road south, catalpas were in full bloom.

2006: Kelleys Island in Lake Erie: Cottonwood cotton flying everywhere, building up on the roads and sidewalks, hanging to the spent garlic mustard in the woods. Panicled dogwoods and poison ivy budded. "Canadian soldiers" everywhere; Casey says he hears them in the morning high in the trees. Here multiflora roses and blackberries are still in bloom, a few blue-eyed grass and wild onions flowering, daisies, a pale violet beardtongue-type plant, red-violet crane's bill. The dominant shrub, in full bloom throughout the quarry is ninebark, *Physocarpus opulifolius*. Stone habitats at the water's edge of fleabane and small cottonwoods and willows (the willows past bloom). A locust-like shrub with long purple blooms, most likely a false indigo or amorpha, seen flowering at the water's edge.

2007: The yard is quiet this morning – the grackle orientation of their young must have ended yesterday evening. Ninebark in the alley is completely done blooming. A black swallowtail seen before lunch.

2008: Mateo's weigela is shedding, and Don's multiflora rose. Peonies droop from the rain. Bright orange Asiatic lilies gather momentum in Peggy's garden and our north gardens. Honeysuckle completely gone, and most mock orange petals. Rocket here is disappearing. Jeanie continues to hear cedar waxwings. No grackles seen with fledglings yet today. The canopy seems complete, although the locusts have a little ways to go, as do the Osage. Cottonwood cotton continues to float on the wind.

2009: First red phlox opened this morning. Don's pie cherries and serviceberries reddening. Oakleaf hydrangea buds are opening, flowers young and green.

2010: At 5:00 this morning, robins and grackles startled me with how loud and pervasive they were, clucks and singsongs without interruption throughout the back trees. A little later when I sat on the porch, a small, pale hummingbird, the first I've seen this year, came to sip the penstemon. At the feeders yesterday and today, no fledglings seen begging for food. When I checked the garden around noon, I saw that our deer had eaten a good portion of the lettuce and had taken the top off of one tomato plant, then in the middle of the afternoon, the deer – a huge female - walked right into the backyard. Heliopsis is opening now, and the last of the Japanese iris are blooming in the pond. Near the church, a red oak has small acorns just emerging from their brown cores, maybe three-fourths of an inch across.

2011: Spoleto, Umbria, Italy: Chicory seen, tall and in full bloom on the way to the market near the Clitunno fountain. Peaches a third of their ripe size on Monte Luco.

2012: Linden trees fragrant, full bloom by the AME church. Avens and very early Japanese knotweed flowering in the Phillips Street alley, pokeweed with white buds there. Venus crossed the sun this evening, the last time for more than a century.

2013: Italy: The last two days spent riding through the Sicilian countryside, the sun hot, the sky without a cloud, the breeze cool. Yesterday we explored the north and south entrances to the national park, went swimming in the icy, clear water of the Mediterranean. Today, we drove south to the extensive ruins of Selinunte. So many new plants seen: teasel about three feet high but not ready to bloom (the same as Yellow Springs); giant thistles, some with violet blossoms, some the more usual pink, many thistles with sizeable yellow flowers - could be a type of sow thistle; also a very common small violet thistle, possibly a kind of knapweed; field after field of a plant with bright yellow *Ombrellifere*, reminiscent of Queen Anne's lace and parsnips; an angelica type plant, another *Ombrellifere*, tall and thick with its last year's stalk often standing beside it; a delphinium-like flower, tall and beautiful with large purple inflorescence, the *Acanthus mollis,* very common and seen two years ago near the Roman forum about the third week of May; English plantain (*Plantago laceola*ta); several tall wild *Malvacee* varieties; the large-petaled cactus, *Opoatia ficus indice L. Miller,* blooming throughout the area, as is the tall cactus with multiple long, straight branches; the pomegranate has red flowers; almond trees have set fruit.

2014: Snow-on-the-mountain still full bloom; few lily-of-the-valley bells still hold; waterleaf with white flowers, full – just like Tat's purple flowered waterleaf in Wisconsin. First pale pink astilbe noticed in the shade garden by the shed, and buds on the milkweed plants in the north garden.

2015: Two white-spotted skippers, four cabbage whites in randori play, a tiger swallowtail, one speeding red admiral in the garden today. Two heliopsis buds starting to unravel. A quick stop at North Glen: leafcup shoulder high and almost budded, wood nettle almost waist high, touch-me-nots covering the woods floor. On a jog through the village: catalpas, privets, old daisies, new astilbes, six-foot yucca stalks, early oakleaf hydrangeas, full red roses and pink spirea. At night, the steady, ghostly call of the Eastern gray tree frog (*Hyla versicolor*).

2016: Lizard's tail flower tails have appeared. Two Stella d'oro lilies. Yucca stalks seen about five to six feet. First gold-collared blackfly seen. The first ditch lily seen blooming on Dayton Street. Grackle babies continue to beg for food, fluttering their wings and scrawing (two seen chasing their parent). By the end of the day, I found the first blossom open on the pond iris.

2017: The only pond iris blossom withered over night. The first heliopsis bloomed. And there were thirteen Stella d'oro lilies open in the east and north gardens. Bright primroses still full flower. Grackles making a racket in the south honeysuckles this morning. Bamboo husks continue to fall into the pond.

2018: Five pond iris flowers this morning, eleven Stella d'oro lilies, and still full flower of the primroses.

2019: Matt reports that he thought he heard a cicada. We'll see. That would be pretty unusual…so early. No lilies to count today. Perhaps the rainy spring has delayed them a little… (and drove the cicadas from the ground?)

2020: Mateo's weigela is shedding. Jill's sweet rockets in decline. Purple barely showing on one pond iris bud. Bamboo husks falling. Dutch iris gone at Peggy's. Young rabbit, just a few inches long, seen in the north yard this morning.

2021: Large white/blue-tailed dragonfly seen in the garden.

*Contemplation of place brings an awareness not only of time but of self and of the evolution of the self, evoking the simultaneous presence of past and present versions of one's identity and thereby illuminating the full chronological depth of that identity with a new and poignant clarity.*

Kent Ryden

### *June 6th*
### *The 157th Day of the Year*

*Vast overhanging meadow-lands of rain,*
*And drowsy dawns, and noons when golden grain*
*Nods in the sun, and lazy truant boys*
*Drift ever listlessly down the day,*
*Too full of joy to rest, and dreams to play.*

James Whitcomb Riley

Sunrise/set: 5:07/8:01
Day's Length: 14 hours 54 minutes
Average High/Low: 79/58
Average Temperature: 69
Record High: 97 – 1925
Record Low: 41 – 1998/43 – 1894

### *Weather*
This is one of the four driest days in June (the 10th, the 25th, and the 26th are the others), and rain passes through only once or twice in a decade. Skies are clear 80 percent of the time, and the likelihood of temperatures in the 90s rises to 25 percent for the first time this year. Eighties occur 30 percent of the years, 70s forty percent, and there is only a slight possibility for cool 60s.

### *Natural Calendar*
In the shade, fire pink, and honewort are flowering. At the edge of the forest, wild plants include blue-eyed grass, silver yarrow, yellow sedum, moneywort, daisies, yellow sweet clover, wild roses, wild iris, dock and smooth brome grass. Oaks and black walnut trees and Osage orange have set their fruit. There are bud clusters on the milkweeds, buds on the delicate touch-me-nots, buds on the giant blue hostas, buds on the yucca, the purple coneflowers, the mallow, the balloon flower and the gayfeather.

### *Daybook*
1982: Old-field cinquefoil blooming now, vetch, lesser stitchwort, white campion, first Canadian thistle, bindweed by Ellis Pond.

Red-winged blackbirds still nesting in the wheat. By the swinging bridge, most of the watercress has gone to seed, replaced by wild forget-me-nots.

1983: Mill habitat: Sweet rockets and golden Alexander still dominate. Garlic mustard, ragwort, fleabane are gone, honeysuckles are fading, along with the tall buttercups. Nettles and grass waist high, tangled with catchweed (flowers turned to burs), make it hard to leave the path. Fire pinks still strong, clustered snakeroot full. Rockets, parsnip, clover, chickweed, and bright yellow goat's beard color the field. Some waterleaf and wild geranium still blooming.

1986: Peak of strawberries in the yard. First third of a pint of black raspberries picked.

1991: Balloon flower opens in the south garden. At Caesar Creek, the far fishing hole: one bass, one catfish, one bluegill.

1992: On the road: Peonies open in Madison, Wisconsin, not yet in Crookston, Minnesota, gone in Chicago. First crown vetch seen as I came south through Normal, Illinois. Throughout the lower Midwest, it's peak parsnip and yellow clover time. Uncle Bill reported hummingbirds had come to Gentilly, Minnesota, two miles from Crookston, the last week of May, pretty much on schedule.

1993: At four in the morning, birds quiet except twittering down the block. Cherries ripening a very little, some pale and yellowing, some a shade of orange. Mock orange petals dropping. Snow-on-the-mountain is full. Full sweet clover and wild roses, very first nodding thistle south of Kettering, the Canadian thistles about ready. White moth or butterfly (like a *Pieridae*) seen in the grass, then again on the front porch.

1998: Record low of 41 this morning. Early Summer stagnates.

1999: First black cricket hunter seen, last swamp iris bloom. First earwig in the bathroom.

2001: Catalpa flowers falling at Antioch School. Very last columbine in the east garden. Coral bells full bloom. Rockets, daisies and ranunculus fading quickly. Strawberries down to the last few pickings. Tadpoles, some with legs, released into the pond.

2004: Peak of mayfly hatch at the Santee Cooper reservoir in South Carolina. Blue-flowered pickerel plant in full bloom with the water willow. Learned that catfish mate when the water reaches 60 degrees and that they go on a feeding frenzy when the mussels die in the heat of early June.

2005: First pink spirea seen at school in Washington Court House. Pale-leaved spirea flowering downtown in Yellow Springs. First coreopsis and foxglove open at home, coreopsis seen full bloom along the freeway, foxglove just off Limestone Street. Wheat pale gold along the roads close to the Ohio River. Peonies declining, mock orange suddenly collapsing in the heat. Privets coming in. Spinach and radishes going to seed.

2006: Return from Kelleys Island, elderberries seen opening by the roadside in northern Ohio. At home, strawberries still not ripe, some rotting from the rain. Early panicled dogwood in the alley, full Japanese honeysuckle, lollypop lilies, white penstemon, privet. Some black mulberries starting to fall near Lawson Place and in the alley. Birds loud in the yard through the early evening, grackle families feeding together, the young – as big as the parents – demanding to be given food as they walk together in the lush grass. Lettuce holds in the garden, but the rhubarb is prostrate, the first crop gone, the second growth April size.

2007: Jeanie and I went strawberry picking today, got eight pounds. The man said the crop had started to come in just about ten days ago and that it would be gone in just a few more days. It was the hot weather, he said, that accelerated the season, cut it in half. Out in the countryside, the wheat was tall and gold-green. Some corn was knee high. In the back yard this morning, the grackles and sparrows were back, babies pursuing their parents, screaming for food.

2008: Japanese honeysuckle has been blooming about two days now. Osage flower clusters have been falling about the same length of time. Early privet along High Street, snow-on-the-mountain full at Gerard's, starting here. A definite change in the grackles' habits – the yard much quieter. Cedar waxwings still sing in the white mulberry tree. Cardinals and robins still call. Full catalpa blossoms along the highway north of town – catalpas and Japanese honeysuckle coming together. The pale violet pond iris is at its peak, will probably be gone tomorrow.

2009: Red-bellied woodpecker calls steadily. Early astilbe, white-flowered waterleaf, and coral bells at full bloom. Grackles and starlings clucking throughout the day. This evening, Rick told me about seeing grackles spitting out white fecal matter into the birdbath. Jeanie and I had seen the evidence of that but had not observed it. No cedar waxwings yet this year.

2010: Walking Bella this morning, I found an Osage fruit fallen to the sidewalk, maybe half the size of a golf ball, small adolescent hairs all over its bumpy skin. The deer came back twice today while I was working at the shop. Jeanie had to scare it away both times. Tonight we watched fireflies in the circle garden. Tornadoes in northern Ohio last night.

2011: Italy: Linden trees in Spoleto finally flowering.

2012: Finches have been feeding heavily and in considerable numbers this past week. Hemlock going to seed all along the road to Xenia, the year continuing to be ahead of almost all the other years. Bi-colored hosta blooms in front/east side of the house, and another blue on the north side. Near Lawson Place, cottonwood cotton fills the side of the road.

2014: Don's oakleaf hydrangea has started to open and a few of his pie cherries are reddening. All of the honeysuckle flowers are down and all of the catalpas are in full bloom throughout the neighborhood. A newly emerged orange polygonia visited the garden, and I found milkweed beetles mating on the two milkweed plants that Rick had brought last year. Wild grapes the size of BBs. Late Kousa dogwood noticed in the park. And Ann Randolf called this morning from Stewart Drive, reacting to my lament a few days ago about not seeing cedar waxwings in my mulberry trees and about the lack of butterflies in the yard: She had seen cedar waxwings last Friday (May 30th), seven on one serviceberry bush. On the 28th, she had watched as one waxwing took a berry, put it in the mouth of another, and the birds passed the fruit back and forth maybe ten times. She said she had seen them in pairs feeding throughout the last week of May. Then, she added that she had seen a monarch and a tiger swallowtail and a sulphur in the honeysuckles, and two brown thrashers after the rain on June 4th."

2015: Some of Peggy's pie cherries are ripe, nice and sweet. One heliopsis flower unraveling, catchweed burs catch on my pant legs, linden trees with berries. Measuring fruit time: peaches and apples at about a fourth, grapes bigger than BBs, local strawberries in the prime of their season. At the women's park near Glen Helen, long plantings of heliopsis and purple coneflowers have just begun to flower. A clump of baptisia has gone to seed, only a couple of blossoms left. Cup plant shoulder high. Timothy soft for chewing by the parking lot.

2016: Two bright yellow Asiatic lilies opened downtown. The pond Japanese iris is in early to middle bloom, deep rich purple as always. The hydrangea season has begun with the whitening of petals on the Annabelle and hobblebush, early bloom on the oakleaf, buds showing a little pink on the Indomitable Spirit.

2017: The first two ditch lilies seen this morning on Dayton Street. Early flowers noticed on the hobblebush, several oakleaf hydrangeas in flower, Indomitable Spirit hydrangea showing pink. Twelve Stella d'oros in bloom. Earliest chicory seen near the high school. Full bloom of Anna Belle hydrangeas along Dayton Street, catalpas mostly fallen on South College Street, yuccas tall and budded, daisy fleabane full bloom in Tony's field. A few more orange lilies this evening.

2019: From the foothills of Umbria, Italy, Neysa reports the ginestra bush (*Ginestra racemosa or Cytisus recomosus*) or Broom Plant is in full bloom and that its fragrance is wonderful. She also said she saw a family of wild boars crossing the road near her house: a mother, seven piglets followed by another large adult boar.

2020: First Stella d'oro lilies seen open across from the Village Artisans store downtown. On the highway north, a long drift of full-blooming yellow sweet clover. Cottonwood falling in clumps along North High Street. Near my studio, Osage leaves have finally formed and the Osage flowers trickle down to the hostas and the great burdock basal foliage.

2021: Only an occasional cabbage white butterfly seen so far this year in the yard, maybe one sulphur in May at the Glass Farm pond. Jill remarked that she had not smelled skunks all year, and I thought how I had had the same experience, and for several years.

2022: Return from Wisconsin: Peonies in the yard have wilted, and the bishop's weed is half to seed. Full Early Summer now. In the greenhouse, geraniums continue to keep their late-April and May blooming season.

## Community Summer
(for the *Yellow Springs News, June 6, 2020)*

At the end of the past month, "most migrant warblers passed through," wrote Leslie and Bruce. "Now resident wildlife settling down and concentrating on rearing young. Trees leafing out, full shade with sugar maples, some shrubs still blooming, grasses tall and blooming… perennials moving into early-summer. No longer feels like high spring with its bursting energy."

Still, new species continued to appear. Aida called to say "we saw our first pair of cedar waxwings on Sunday, May 31. Then Wednesday before the weather changed, we started seeing an influx of them, and today (June 5) they're everywhere."

The waxwings have arrived in late May to early June for many years, and they mate and raise their fledglings here. Scattered notes from several years attest to this pattern. Jeanie heard them in our high locust trees on June 3 in 2008 and 2010. On June 6 in 2014,

Ann called from Stewart Drive to say she had seen cedar waxwings in pairs feeding throughout the last week of May. On the 28th, she had watched as "one waxwing took a berry, put it in the mouth of another, and the birds passed the fruit back and forth maybe ten times." She added that she had also seen "a monarch and a tiger swallowtail and a sulphur in the honeysuckles."

Insects often do appear more readily as May becomes June. Rick reported that he "had the first visit to my knee-high milkweeds by a bright and new-looking female monarch" on May 26. Leslie and Bruce saw a tiger swallowtail butterfly on the 26th, as well. On May 29, they found water beetles in their pond, a damselfly and a 12-Spot Dragonfly on the 30th, a Diana butterfly and a zebra swallowtail on June 1, and  heard the first spring field cricket on June 6.

And Jill saw fireflies near Mills Lawn on June 2. It's really summer now.


*The word for "nature" in Chinese comes from Daoism and means "things as they are" or "things as they are spontaneously" So "nature" is a philosophical principle in a way rather than just the things you perceive in the landscape.*

Sunsook Hong Setton

### *June 7th*
### *The 158th Day of the Year*

*O for boyhood's time of June
Crowding years in one brief moon,
When all things I heard or saw,
Me, their master, waited for.*

John Greenleaf Whittier

Sunrise/set: 5:07/8:01
Day's Length: 14 hours 54 minutes
Average High/Low: 80/58
Average Temperature: 69
Record High: 95 – 1933
Record Low: 43 – 1910

### *Weather*

Skies are overcast more often on the 7th than on any other day of the month (55 percent of the time). Rain, however, comes an average of just one year in three. Temperatures are almost always above 70. There is a 15 percent chance of heat in the 90s, forty-five percent for a high in the 80s, thirty-five percent of 70s, five percent of 60s.

### *Natural Calendar*

The breakdown of Late Spring becomes more apparent as poppies, columbines, pyrethrums, lupines, peonies, iris and sweet rockets disappear. Strawberries are thinning as black raspberries start their season. The darkening of the golden winter wheat measures the steady advance of Early Summer.

Oaks, Osage orange, locust and black walnut trees have set their fruit. There are bud clusters on the milkweeds, buds on the delicate touch-me-nots, buds on the giant blue hosta, buds on the yucca and purple coneflowers, the mallow, the early daylilies, balloon flower and gay feather. Catchweed and chickweed die back, exhausted and matted. Watercress is pale, has turned underside up. May apple foliage is yellowing. Jack-in-the-pulpits are wilting. Brown seeds drop from the small-flowered crowfoot.

All the last, fragrant mock orange petals have scattered in the wind.

Large-flowered hydrangeas (like Anna Belle and the oakleaf) reach full flower. Daisies, golden Alexander, cressleaf groundsel, sweet rocket and common fleabane still hold in the pastures, but garlic mustard and ragwort are gone. Young toads plod across the sidewalks. White-spotted skippers, tiger swallowtails and red admirals sample the garden. Golden fold-winged skippers play in the sun.

### *Daybook*

1981: Fireflies began tonight.

1982: Squirrels are half grown, eating the new mulberries. Firefly season started tonight.

1984: First Canadian thistle seen in bloom today. Siberian iris completely gone (after just five days of flowering). Most locust flowers gone, peonies starting to wilt.

1985: Parsnip and angelica to seed, and first buds on the milkweed. Tall meadow rue blooming.

1986: Burdock ready to flower. Moth mullein common and full. Pokeweed in the yard is seven feet tall and has small flower buds. First tropical storm of the year forming in the Caribbean. For several days now, flocks of gold finches seen along Wilberforce Clifton Road and at South Glen.

1987: First black raspberry eaten, last quart of strawberries picked. Squirrels and groundhogs noticed half grown. White waterleaf still late bloom. Walked by the Mill at nine o'clock this evening: the field crickets were strong, frogs chanting. For the first time, mosquitoes were bothersome. Fireflies were common.

1988: Drought throughout Ohio and the Midwest is causing serious crop damage. Last poppies are blooming. Chicory opens in town. Daisies fading in the south garden. First raspberry eaten. Winter wheat turning more now; it pales at first, then becomes lighter and lighter green, then yellow, tan, gold, brown. Roadside smooth brome darkening, ripening like the wheat. Mock orange gone at home, still blooming in the Glen parking lot. No fireflies yet.

1990: Fishing at Caesar Creek, old fishing hole: one catfish, two perch, four carp in an hour and a half, mid to late afternoon, second quarter of the moon, muggy and hot. Frogs were loud, fish jumping everywhere. Carp sloshing along the shores. The catfish had been eating crayfish. On way home: wheat turning, mock orange almost gone.

1991: To Madison, Wisconsin: Yellow sweet clover the dominant flower throughout the whole trip. Crown vetch also full. Some bright purple cow vetch, yarrow, spiderwort. Peonies still late bloom in Wisconsin, mock orange full-flowered. Parsnips seen at the same level in both Madison and Yellow Springs. Chicory and meadow goat's beard in bloom most of the 500 miles north.

1992: Returning to Yellow Springs after a week in Wisconsin: peonies, all iris, ranunculus, sweet rocket almost gone. Pyrethrum cut back, roses and daisies full. First red-orange lychnis blooming, and coreopsis fully budded. Gay feather and evening primrose budded. Gray aphids take over the old rocket stems. Cucumber beetles and new red and black beetles eating mums. Astilbe color shows, but not in bloom. Lilies budding. Strawberries coming in, spinach going to seed, tomatoes a foot and a half high.

1993: The violet clematis is glowing in the sun, full bloom. More and more Siberian iris wither. Lupine holds late. Osage, mock orange flowers still falling. Peonies suddenly shriveling in the yard. Buds on the sweet peas, tiger lilies, hollyhocks, and south garden coneflowers.

1996: The rains continue, flooding and standing water everywhere. More than half the corn has still not been planted. East of the Mississippi, the crop will be light because of delays in seeding. In the West, dramatic drought. Here in the east garden the columbines are thinning as the astilbe reddens. In the north garden, the Siberian iris is dropping now, and the first garlic plants are starting to head up (down on Elm Street, wild garlic has had full tall heads for several days). In the west garden, the pyrethrums have passed their prime. Daisies have been beaten down by the rain; they are also fading. Sweet rockets have almost all gone to seed. First lamb's ear is flowering. This evening, the first primrose came into bloom.

1997: The cool spring continues: Siberian iris holding, sweet Williams approaching their peak. Daylilies budding in Xenia. Rockets are still late full. Daisies full. Pyrethrum past prime, but still all right. Spiderwort fat and lush this year. Pale columbine almost all gone. Mock orange holds at full, some petals falling. Peonies in the yard full and firm. Now the spinach is at its peak, radishes too.

1998: Baby robin on the front sidewalk, the second this week. Yellow swallowtails are coming to the garden regularly now.

1999: Zinnias planted. Loud crows and cardinals, full morning song at 4:45 a.m. First helianthus blooms in the south garden, totally full primrose.

2004: Santee Cooper, South Carolina to Yellow Springs: Red periodic cicadas were loud from 50 miles south of Cincinnati to about halfway to Dayton.

2005: The first purple coneflower and evening primrose opened today. Chicory seen in bloom.

2006: The Japanese pond iris was open this morning. Evening primrose is now in full bloom, along with the sweet William, lollipop lilies, lamb's ear. Throughout the village, pink spirea is common, but our bush is still only budding.

2007: Japanese pond iris continues full bloom. Some grackle babies still being fed in the lawn. Many purple coneflowers now in bloom. First "green-eyed" Susan unravels in the east garden.

2008: No Japanese pond iris yet, no coneflowers, no green-eyed

Susans. The yellow primroses have opened, though. Cedar waxwings and grackles, sparrows, and robins continue to feed in the mulberry tree – and mulberries are lush, thick this year (Mateo's tree heavy with berries ripening red). Red-bellied woodpecker calls off and on throughout the day. The pale, wild pond iris continues to flower in the pond, the pond taken over now by the tadpoles and a frog now that Emmet and Zelda are gone (but two fingerlings seen today instead of just one).

2009: The Japanese pond iris plant has two buds. Last night a deer came into the yard and ate the lower leaves off of the new cherry tree. Our red-bellied woodpecker continues to call throughout the morning, steady, insistent calls. Starling babies harassing their parents for food, whining in the mulberries. Robins were peeping this morning instead of singing.

2010: Cottonwood cotton on the ground near Lawson Place. A stag beetle attached itself to my shirt when I was working in the back yard. Along the road to Dayton, cattails seen full of pollen.

2011: Rome, Italy to Charlotte, N.C. and Yellow Springs: At the North Carolina airport, elderberries in late bloom, just like in Italy. A note from Ruby said that fireflies came out while we were gone.

2012: Adult robins still peeping steadily in the honeysuckles, orienting their young. Cottonwood cotton on the ground near Lawson Place. Rugosa roses, white sweet clover, hollyhocks, butterfly weed all seen in bloom on the way to Dayton, the white sweet clover in full bloom beside the yellow.

2014: The resident doe came into the yard this afternoon to eat lilies. I should set up a feeding station for it to distract it from the flowers. A red admiral at 3:30 in the north garden. Five different lily plants in bloom today, three deep orange Asiatics (Peggy has one, too.) and two Stella d'oros.

2015: After sunrise, steady peeping of robins guiding young or preparing for their summer retreat. Red-bellied woodpecker and a pileated calling in the back trees this morning. The Stella d'oros are way ahead of least year, almost early full. The orange Asiatics are at three, just like in 2014. Japanese pond iris is at the closing days of their season, also the white-flowered waterleaf in the far west garden. The last ranunculus by the pond is done. First buds noticed on the Shasta daisies. A red bindweed flower in the primroses this morning, the first I have ever seen in the garden. I discovered the deer in the yard yesterday afternoon, a day later than I did last year.

2016: In the wake of a brisk cool wave, the first re-blooming lily, yellow, flowered in the circle garden overnight. Three Stella d'oro plants in bloom, and the Japanese water iris. Common fleabane is ending by the pond, about the same time as the celandine. Smartweed in bloom is spreading around the lilies.

2017: A cool day in the 60s; next week: 90s forecast. Sixteen Stella d'oro lilies open this morning. One daddy longlegs noticed – the first time this year. White-flowered waterleaf is in very late bloom in the south garden. The red-bellied woodpecker has been quiet over the past week, perhaps the fledglings gone. A toad about two inches long was crossing the sidewalk as Jill and I walked home from the movies. First chigger bite of the year noticed on my leg.

2018: From Amherst, Massachusetts, Jill sends photos of peonies, poppies, rhododendrons. Wisteria, iris, early yellow re-bloomer lilies, the land there a full three to four weeks behind southwestern Ohio.

2019: The first Japanese water iris bloomed overnight. Gold-collared blackflies mating in the peonies. Pie cherries at Peggy's are fully ripe and ready for pie. Cottonwood cotton building up along Greene Street near Jill's house. Catalpas in full flower along Polecat Road.

2020: Most peonies cut back this morning. Smartweed blooming. Jeanie's yellow rose blossoming from a single stem that somehow has survived the decay of all the rose bushes and the invasion of the Japanese knotweed – and my clearing of the old garden area. In the afternoon, the first deep purple Japanese pond iris opened all the way.

2021: First nodding thistles noticed in bloom on the way from Fairborn. From Spoleto, Italy, Neysa reports ginestra fragrant and sweetening the wind. Here in Yellow Springs, Shep reports seeing the first firefly (eight or nine of them, he says) last night. And Matt Minde wrote: "Jen and  I were walking last night when I spotted my first firefly of the season. This was exciting, as it's an insect mating ritual which is NOT deafening, as earlier in the day we spent about two hours trying to hold conversations underneath trees covered with screaming cicadas. Honestly, my ears were ringing and my high-frequency hearing was greatly diminished, as if I'd been at a 'Who' concert without earplugs. So, to reiterate, it was nice to see the quiet blinking."

> *Not asking their names,*
> *Not trying to remember*
> *Wildflowers.*

James Luguri

### *June 8th*
### *The 159th Day of the Year*

*To loll back, in a misty hammock, swung*
*From tip to tip of a slim crescent moon*
*That gems some royal-purple night of June,*
*To dream of songs that never have been sung*
*Since the first stars were stilled and God was young....*

James Whitcomb Riley

Sunrise/set: 5:06/8:02
Day's Length: 14 hours 56 minutes
Average High/Low: 80/59
Average Temperature: 69
Record High: 96 – 1933
Record Low: 41 – 1901

### *Weather*

This is one of the sunnier June days, with a 90 percent chance of clear to partly cloudy conditions. Thunderstorms, however, occur about half the time. Temperatures are above 90 twenty-five percent of the years, in the 80s fifty-five percent, in the 70s twenty percent. Low temperatures remain above 60 degrees 40 percent of the nights. A cool dawn in the 40s happens ten percent of the time.

### *The Weather of the Week Ahead*

The second week of June always brings an increase in the likelihood of highs in the 90s, and the average percentage of afternoons in the 80s rises above the average percentage of 70s for the first time in the year. Highs in the cold 60s are rare, occurring just five percent of the days. This week also brings more sunshine than almost any other week so far in the year: 85 percent of the days have at least partly cloudy skies. And the week also contains the second-driest day of the month, June 10th, which brings a shower only ten percent of the years. The 13th and 14th are also usually dry, both having just a 20 percent chance of rain. The wettest days in the period are June 8th, 9th, 11th and 12th, each having a 40 percent chance of rain. Between June 8th and 11th, the average temperature rise slows to one degree in four days instead of Late Spring's one degree in three. Then, between the 15th to the 19th, it climbs just one degree in five days, reaching its summer zenith.

### *Natural Calendar*
*A wave for the sea,*
*Flower for fruit and fruit for tree,*
*A part for the whole,*
*A kiss for the soul,*
*Ambrosial lips: you for me:*
*Strawberry synecdoche.*

Those fond of classical letters might be familiar with the figure of speech called synecdoche (pronounced sin - EK - deh - key) in which a part of something is used to refer to the entire object – or vice versa. In natural history, this verbal device is even more useful than in literature, an isolated flower or scent or taste easily able to conjure whole seasons, call up memories that cross lifetimes.

In early June, strawberries are a single tip of summer. But with synecdochic power, their odor and flavor expands time and space, envelops a totality of events in its maturity. With strawberries come the longest days of the year and the completion of the forest canopy. The planting stars, Arcturus and the Corona Borealis, are overhead at night, Hercules not far behind them to the east, followed by the Milky Way, middle summer's Vega and the Northern Cross. July's Scorpius follows Libra across the southern sky.

One ripe strawberry implies all of the flowers of early summer: chamomile, clustered snake root, white clover, red clover, yellow sweet clover, yarrow, blue-eyed grass, angelica, prairie false indigo, hemlock, blackberry blossoms, wild roses, swamp iris, meadow goat's beard, feverfew, blueweed, black medic, daisies, wild mallow, fire pink, water willow, motherwort, white campion, parsnips, honewort, moth mullein, heliopsis, quickweed, lychnis, astilbe, swamp valerian, moneywort, scarlet pimpernel, catalpas, meadow rue, dogbane, sundrops, privet, spirea, poison ivy, tea roses, Miami mist, spiderwort, snow-on-the-mountain, day lilies, stella doro lilies, bindweed, thistles, sweet Williams, and crown vetch.

Strawberries are a sign that mulberries and pie cherries are getting ripe, black raspberries not too far behind them, a sign that quail are whistling for their mates, that box turtles will are laying their eggs, that spiders are weaving their webs across Glen paths, that the spring field crickets are mating, that fireflies are glowing, that skippers visit the garden, that maple seeds fall, that May apples are an inch across, that cattails and yucca stalks are four feet tall, that timothy is ripe for chewing.

The catalogue of objects and events could go on and on. And not only is each term in the list convertible from part to whole, from microcosm to macrocosm, the psychic possibilities for reminiscence or fantasy contained in each evocative fragment are beyond the reach of any kind of organization or reason. Overcome with the chaotic convergence of synecdochically charged spirit and matter, we reel under strawberry summer, feel lost, elated, nostalgic, confused, sad, excited, lonely, in love, full of regret and optimism.

### *Daybook*

1982: Clifton Gorge to Jacoby Road: Wild strawberries are red. Blue-eyed grass, yellow sedum, moneywort, sulfur cinquefoil, fire pinks, white violets (*Viola striata*), daisy fleabane, last rockets and columbines, a final ragwort, clumps of daisies, yellow sweet clover, yarrow, wild parsnip, angelica, wild roses, pepper plant, wild iris, poison ivy and pink hedge bindweed are flowering.

1983: Fishing at Jacoby, I caught a bluegill and a carp. Flies, mosquitoes and nettles bothersome. Sweet rockets and golden Alexanders provided color to the dark green undergrowth. Three very young wood ducks seen. Wild swamp iris full bloom.

1986: Madison, Wisconsin: Orange hawkweed just beginning. Leafy spurge, *Euphorbia esula*, in full bloom through the countryside, turning the fields yellow.

1987: Yucca and crown vetch full bloom. Smooth brome and

orchard grass becoming brown, red dock flowers complement their shades.

1988: First wild garlic blooms. Last white violets and sweet rocket. Chickweed has died in huge patches by the Covered Bridge, turning parts of the woods floor brown, catchweed yellowing beside it. Crown vetch full bloom, yucca not open. Woods dry from the drought, touch-me-nots and nettles wilting.

1989: Yellow Springs to Belize: Along the road to the Dayton airport, nodding thistles in early bloom, Canadian thistles only budding, and no chicory. Yesterday at South Glen along Grinnell, orchard grass was flowering and brome grass turning. It was full summer, the peak of all the first grasses. Tall meadow rue was unfolding. Blackberries and multiflora roses were completely open.

In Belize, the flamboyant trees were orange and red, full bloom. Mangoes and cashews, said the taxi driver, were just coming in. Hibiscus was blossoming throughout the capital. I saw the bright milkweed-like plant again, and yellow snapdragon weed, and low bindweeds. The rains have not started yet.

1990: First raspberry reddens, cherries turning.

1991: The paling of winter wheat in early June, then lighter and lighter green, then yellow, then tan, gold, brown, the smooth brome and orchard grass following, and dock's red flowers darkening the roadsides more. Dominance of parsnips, yarrow, honewort, sweet clovers, wild daisies, crown vetch, elderberry, honeysuckle berries, thistles, motherwort, clustered snakeroot, chicory, trefoil, yucca, hemlock, purple vetch, the very first great mullein. There are patches of dying catchweed and chickweed yellow and matted. The last of the mock orange and the best roses now, angelica past its prime, decline of strawberries, end of the watercress – pale and turned underside up, May apple foliage mottled and yellowing, multifloras done, first black raspberry ready: high tide of Early Summer.

1992: At Caesar Creek, four big cats, a carp, and a bullhead all from far hole between 1:15 and 2:30. The catfish are in, the summer starting. Warblers and finches strong, multiflora roses dense full bloom by the inlet.

1993: Into South Glen: First white-spotted skipper, first blues, first black swallowtail. Blue damselflies, florescent green ones, and black ones, the latter most common. First mosquito. First moneywort. White waterleaf full bloom, white violets still holding, the last of the spring flowers.

1996: Spent flower heads of the Siberian iris taken off today, pyrethrums and rockets cut back. The May garden is over. Rains continue. Osage flower stems fallen along Dayton Street and around the shed in the yard.

1997: Siberian iris in decline, last of the lupines. This year is becoming even later than last year, turning into the coldest spring and Early Summer in the past 19 years.

1998: Wheat is turning golden brown all the way up to Lake Erie. Catalpas are in bloom, daisies, sweet clover, elderberries, daylilies, and coreopsis, line the highways north. In Savannah, Ohio, 100 miles north of Yellow Springs, the landscape is a week behind home, peonies still holding late.

2000: Yesterday, Early Summer earwigs in the bathtub. Moneywort was in full bloom along High Street, dock full of its small red flowers everywhere.

2002: First firefly. Elderberries blossoming now.

2003: The white mulberry is heavy with fruit. The first Asiatic lily opened this morning, soft pink. Osage flower stems cover the roof of the shed.

2004: Oakleaf hydrangea at home has been blooming for three or four days. The first mallow and the first larkspur opened in the north garden. Zinnias are budding. Baby rabbit seen in the lawn. Baby robin in the woodshed; I had to lift it out on the end of a broom. Jeanie reports frogs calling along Corey Street during the daytime. At night, some kind of frog is calling from the trees across Dayton Street. Yellow evening primroses hold. Stella d'oro lilies full everywhere, Heliopsis full along the bike path, yucca full in town. Achillea is in bloom, the pinks, whites and yellows, in the north garden. This morning, the very first robins began to twitter at 3:40 a.m. The first cardinal sang at 4:25 a.m.

2005: Full bloom of roses, spiderwort, catmint, rockets, sweet Williams, dead nettle. Small coreopsis budding. Penstemon reaches early full. Most catalpas in bloom, but one tree on South College Street has started to shed.

2007: A few catalpas remain in bloom. All rockets are gone, have been for at last a week. Penstemon in the garden is in decline, most sweet Williams fading. Oak leaf hydrangea is more than half flowered. Baby rabbit seen in the vegetable garden. Pale-leafed heliopsis has been in bloom for at least five days. Wisteria has been gone about a week. Yellow primroses continue in the north garden.

2008: Catalpas full bloom throughout the area. Rockets holding at maybe a fourth. Full penstemon and wisteria. Nodding thistle starting in Fairborn. Don's oakleaf hydrangea has a few flowers. Wisteria suddenly gone on the back porch. Golden bi-fold winged butterflies are chasing each other now in the back yard in wild randori.

2009: Red-bellied woodpecker calls steadily from 5:14 in the morning. Full panicled dogwood and elderberry. Golden wheat. First chicory in bloom! Privet fading and burning bush flowers gone. Crown vetch and fields of small daisies along the freeways. Grackles clucking in the Danielsons' tree this evening.

2010: Linden trees at the triangle park are in late full bloom. Corn in some fields along the way to Fairborn is waist high. Milkweed seen completely open on the west edge of town. The first of Moya's black-eyed Susans is open.

2011: Back from Italy to the overgrown and deer-ravaged garden, only the catmint and the toppled penstemon in bloom. Robin chorus began at 3:45 a.m. Around the village, oakleaf hydrangeas have white flowers. In our north garden, purple coneflowers have buds, a few of the surviving daylilies are sending up flower stalks.

2012: One catalpa tree seen in bloom when we drove to Urbana this afternoon to purchase koi for the renovated pond. All the other local catalpas fell more than a week ago. Rugosa roses full at Ellis Pond.

2014: One large camel cricket in the tub this morning. The deep purple water iris in the pond are peaking today, the first ones decaying, five full beauties left.

2015: Pond iris almost exactly where they were last year, four full blooms remaining. Don's pie cherry tree completely ready for pie.

2017: Twenty Stella d'oro lily blossoms open this morning. Mosquitoes especially pesky. One water iris, only the second this year – and the last, is budding. At the library, oakleaf hydrangeas are in early full bloom. At the Island Park in Dayton, the season almost a week ahead of Yellow Springs: Stella d'oros and Canadian thistles are full, ditch lilies and nodding thistles early full, purple coneflowers starting, one bi-color hosta blooming. Parsnips bright yellow, aging hemlock, linden flowers to berries. Milkweed beetles on the milkweed buds. Three adult geese with three goslings the size of a big boot. In the afternoon, all kinds of grackle activity, clucking and cackling, fledglings begging everywhere: Grackle Pentecost every year it seems, the great enlivening of birth and spirit.

2018: First yucca seen in bloom.

2019: Goslings seen half size near the pond by Dayton Street. Chicory, parsnips, hemlock, wild daisies and yellow sweet clover color the roadsides to Cincinnati. At the monastery of St. Clare, pink spirea and a late Kousa dogwood. In the woods, May apples mottled, ramps budding. At the malls, Stella d'oro lilies are open.

Around Yellow Springs, sweet black fruit of the red mulberry trees stain the sidewalks. Tonight, after a windy day, and a mixture of cool and warmth, sun and showers, the back yard was full of fireflies for the first time this year.

2020: At John Bryan Park, the campground roadways are littered with withered tulip tree flowers. I woke up there to cardinals calling at 4:30. One small blue butterfly seen. Two pond iris opened this afternoon. Leslie and Bruce report the first tree crickets and a "mystery insect," whose sound was "buzzy and raspy and pulsing a bit, but not a cicada." The Ohio landscape service (BYGL) noted that some of the Brood X 17-year cicadas have been calling recently in Ohio. Early emergence may mean, according to that service, that a new brood is evolving and that climate change may also be influencing their unusual behavior.

2021: The first deep purple pond iris opened in the night. The first ditch lily seen in bloom across from the Covered Bridge. Stopped to listen to cicadas by the river: intense, dense calls surrounding me. This evening, Jill found a firefly blinking in the grass along High Street.

2022: The first deep purple pond iris is opening today. A cluster of Stella d'oro lilies has flowered along Elm Street. The bishop's weed clump has suddenly gone to seed, sweet rockets gone at home. I planted a bed of Dutch iris and reblooming lilies on Ranger's grave near the porch woodpile, and three pale-leafed hostas along the east fence garden. Several cabbage whites testing the kale today. Drain flies have appeared in the bathroom.

*Therefore am I still a lover of the meadows and the woods,*
*And mountains; and of all that we behold*
*From this green earth; (of all the mighty world)*
*well pleased to recognize*
*In nature and the language of the sense,*
*The anchor of my purest thoughts, the nurse,*
*The guide, the guardian of my heart, and soul*
*Of all my moral being.*

William Wordsworth

## *June 9th*
## *The 160th Day of the Year*

*And what is so rare as a day in June?*
*Then, if ever, come perfect days;*
*Then Heaven tries the earth if it be in tune,*
*And over it softly her warm ear lays:*

James Russell Lowell

Sunrise/set: 5:06/8:02
Day's Length: 14 hours 56 minutes
Average High/Low: 80/59
Average Temperature: 70
Record High: 94 – 1914
Record Low: 40 – 1913

### Weather

The sun almost always (90 percent of the time) shines today, and there is a 15 percent chance of a high in the 90s, fifty percent chance of 80s, thirty percent of 70s and five percent for cold 60s. Thunderstorms come one year in three, but an all-day rain only one in 15.

### *Natural Calendar*

It is the high time for cucumber beetles in cucumbers, for powdery mildew on the phlox and for potato leafhoppers in the alfalfa. Chinch bugs hatch in the lawn. Whiteflies attack azaleas. Weevils assault the yellow poplars. Rose chafers and two-spotted spider mites appear on rose bushes. Leafminers work arborvitae, birch, locusts, boxwood, elms, holly, and juniper. Eastern tent caterpillars leave their tents.

Inspired by all the insects, weaving spiders weave the first major network of cobwebs across the woodland paths. Long-bodied orb weavers set their webs across ponds and streams. Wolf spiders and toads hunt the fields and forest floor. Birds feast and feed their young with the great Early Summer insect hatch.

### *Daybook*

1982: First raspberry ripe today. First garden primrose unravels.

1983: Siberian iris bloom ends today.

1984: First two fireflies. First cucumber beetles seen.

1987: Wild multiflora roses gone by today. Staghorns noticed on the sumac, cherries ready to pick. Peaches half size. First great mullein and milkweed bloom. The 17-year cicadas are still singing. Blackberries have set fruit, red and orange berries coming out on the honeysuckles, elderberries full bloom, fire pink, Deptford pink full. First raspberries are coming in during the last days of the strawberries. Wild daisies strong, last long after those in the yard. First grasshopper seen. Two catalpas seen full bloom.

1988: Belize: Blackbirds whistle a half an hour after the first light on the horizon, half an hour before dawn, the same schedule as the cardinals in Yellow Springs. On the way to Altun Ha, the *milpas* have still not been planted with corn because the rains have not begun yet. Saw a few papayas turning red.

1990: First feverfew. First garden primrose.

1991: Doorweed, *Polygonum aviculare*, open in the east garden.

1992: Catalpas full bloom, cherries ripen.

1993: Only five or six Siberian iris left, lupines almost completely gone. Chives tattered, drooping and brown, the yesterday's perfect purple clematis shattered in the heavy rainstorm. The bright poppies gone, red pyrethrum becoming pale, decaying suddenly. First yellow sundrop (*Oenothera fruticosa*) opens its season. Catalpas seen in bloom on the way to Dayton.

1997: The first yellow primroses and the first lamb's ear bloomed today. Only four or five Siberian iris remain, and the peonies are beginning to lose their freshness. In the countryside, some locusts still hold their flowers. Along the bike path: blueweed in early bloom, the very first Canadian thistle, full Miami mist, fire pink, very late wild geraniums hold in the shade, burdock sending up giant stalks (at the same time as the yucca in town), dogbane budding (like the new gooseneck in the garden), blue-eyed grass, small-flowered and large-flowered cinquefoil. Rockets late but still dominant in South Glen. Parsnips and hemlock about equal with the number of flowers and seeds: maybe three-fourths still blossoming, the balance in green seeds.

1998: The first few black raspberries are now red.

1999: Yellow Springs to Utica, New York: Yellow sweet clover, crown vetch and daisies prominent along the roadsides. Near Erie, Pennsylvania, the very last locust flowers, iris, and rhododendrons seen, putting the lakeshore ten to fourteen days behind Greene County this year (but close to 1997 in Yellow Springs). All along the coast and into New York, grape vines with new leaves and parsnips, hemlock and multiflora roses in full bloom.

2000: Japanese honeysuckle still fragrant. The north garden's roses are all open, healthy, no beetles yet. The lilies are blooming just in one small patch, the two orange Asiatics and one yellow daylily. First yellow buds on the tall south-garden yarrow. The first firefly tonight.

2001: First violet water willow opens in the pond. Apples start to come down from the old tree. As we sat in the back yard this evening, we could hear mulberries falling to the north garden behind us.

2003: Tree lilac flowers are coming to the end of their bloom. Kousa dogwoods hold strong.

2004: First Frances Williams hosta has bloomed. Goosefoot has developed white flower buds. Lilies, achillea, roses, catmint, the new violet clematis, and astilbe transition the garden from Late Spring to Early Summer.

2005: First heliopsis and Japanese water iris unraveled overnight. Coreopsis is full now, another Asiatic lily starting (pale lavender), and the more delicate Turk's cap. Rockets have started to seed. Achillea has turned yellow. The neighbors' houses have pretty much disappeared behind the border foliage. Japanese honeysuckle coming in, just a few days behind the privets. Weigela suddenly gone. Yellow swallowtail seen.

2006: A cardinal woke me up at 3:55 a.m. Crows called in the back trees at 6:15, about the same time as usual. First monarch seen in the alley at 9:00 (Jeanie had seen one at school a week or so ago).

2007: First chicory open along Dayton Street this morning. Panicled dogwood and linden tree in full bloom along the alley. Lizard's tail about a third in bloom.

2008: In the pond, I saw the first tadpole with legs. First small bud on the pond's lizard's tail. First pale pink astilbe is coming in under the redbud tree. First pink smartweed seen in the garden. The first red early phlox opened overnight. White mulberries falling into the undergrowth. A monarch and a question mark butterfly seen in the yard this morning. Tulip tree is still in full bloom along Davis Street.

At South Glen, timothy and bottle grass sweet to chew, tall brome grass, chest high, with pollen, rockets almost gone, clustered snakeroot getting old, maple-leaved waterleaf and multiflora roses still in bloom, honewort flowering. Blackberries and black raspberries have set fruit, but it appears no raspberries will be ripe for a while. Wood nettle almost chest high. Along the river, one box elder tree has been uprooted, and the bottomland shows signs of major flooding after last week's rains, the water up as far as I've seen it. East near Indianapolis, whole towns have been under water. Loud chattering of grackles in the back yard trees throughout the day. Strong robin song at dusk. Tick found on my leg before I went to bed.

2009: Robins at 3:15 a.m. Later, a quiet morning in the yard. Grackles in the alley but not here. Small green berries on the bittersweet. All the bells gone from the lily-of-the-valley. Great mullein seen flowering in Wilmington. One Japanese iris blooming in the pond.

2010: The first flowers of the red phlox opened overnight. Some pink hollyhocks are blooming in the Phillips-Stafford Street alley.

2011: Robins at 3:45 a.m., doves at 4:30, cardinals at 4:40, sparrows at 5:30, with robins strong throughout the entire morning. A black spicebush swallowtail landed in the grass when I was moving the bird feeder, and a brown was resting on the shed door yesterday evening. But the yard and the village have little color. The fields, unplanted because of the rain, are dull. In the pond, a deep purple Japanese iris, the second to bloom, is open. The first two heliopsis flowers are coming in. Lizard's tail is forming in the pond. Fireflies in the wet evening.

2012: To the Monastery of Saint Clare near Cincinnati: Hemlock holding strong along many roadsides, some patches, though, all gone to seed. At the monastery grounds, ramps were fully budded, the first orange jewel weed and poke weed seen in bloom. At home, the starlings were "scrawing" (had been silent yesterday), and Jeanie reported young robins and starlings begging for food from their parents.

2013: Italy: Spoleto into the hills near Campello: birdsfoot trefoil; a violet flower with five petals, maybe up to an inch and a half across, large golden flower head, leaves curled, stem hairy, soft; wild mint and thyme and fennel; many ginestra plants, many having lost their yellow flowers, one seen with seed pods formed; varieties of small, yellow *composite*; a type of Japanese honeysuckle with large pink flowers (*Lonicera caprifolion*); a variety with flowers similar to crown vetch; a shrub with berries very much like elderberries, some starting to turn black; what appeared to be St. John's wort; a tree with elm-like leaves and hops-like, layered flower heads; the ubiquitous red and orange poppies; some bindweeds, pink or white; small, thick-leafed ferns attached to the stone cliffs; Queen Anne's lace.

And Judy writes from Goshen, Indiana: "It's raining

today, and the goose families just finished their waddle from one pond to the next. The goslings have morphed during the last week into miniatures of their parents--no more drab down but handsome little featherings that make them look even cuter. One family has only a single young one left, still wearing downy beige fluff; it is not as far along as its adolescent colleagues. I wonder what happened. Did a raccoon get the others, still in their eggs, or did they just have the single gosling?  In any case, it is a feisty little thing and hurries to keep up with its parents and relatives.

"Yesterday we went for a bike ride along the race and saw yarrow, wild roses, fleabane, lots of crown vetch, buttercups, wild viburnums and a lovely pink swamp flower that grows in clusters at the water's edge, maybe swamp milkweed? Very nice display. The Stella d'oro daylilies are blooming already, and mock orange, just as the peonies are fading."

2014: The deep purple Japanese pond iris are fading quickly now, only two flowers left. The iris at church were gone several days ago, but Moya's violet and yellow ones are still open. In the north gardens, six different lily plants in bloom, three orange Asiatics and three Stella d'oros. Three astilbes flowering in the southwest garden. The only weigela in bloom is the Danielsons' red one across the street. In the old north garden, Jerusalem artichokes are spreading and tall, may provide some screening this summer. The castor bean plants by the trellis are starting to take hold, well past two feet now. The bright yellow primroses and the spiderwort remain in full bloom.

2015: Three blossoms left on the pond iris. In the north gardens, the orange Asiatics and Stella d'oros are at the same stage as last year and the first yellow re-bloomer opened in the circle garden overnight. Mateo's weigela, the last one on the block, is gone. Spiderwort and primroses like last year. The very last peonies shriveled yesterday. In the rain last night, the first Osage fruit, the size of a large marble, fell to the sidewalk by the Lawson's. Six heliopsis flowers. White mulberries, blushing a little, falling to the weeds along the west property line. Penstemon lagging, last petals of the Japanese wisteria. Throughout the village, the standard blossoms, zeitgebers for the second week of Early Summer: pink spirea, catalpa, Stella d'oros, ditch lilies, panicled dogwood, oakleaf hydrangeas.

2016: Three blossoms on the pond iris, a few more buds. Eleven lily plants open today: three ditch lilies, seven Stella d'oros and one rebloomer. Peonies cut back two days ago, a disappointing year, the plants shaded and choked by the encroaching bamboo. Heliopsis not quite open yet, penstemon holding pretty well, a few pink petals of the north wisteria, all so much like last year (except no Asiatics this year), Jill's red mulberry tree shedding to her driveway. In the woods: honewort, clustered snakeroot, clumps of fire pinks, a few late white violets, budding hobblebush, mint tall and soft but not budded.

2017: The garden's lily run picks up now: twenty-one Stella d'oro blossoms, the first two yellow flowers on the reblooming lilies, the first two ditch lilies and the first Asiatic lily open. Heliopsis flowering: two. The last of the pond iris opened after lunch. Spiderwort and primrose full. The first black raspberries are ripe at the corner of Davis and High. A patch of feverfew wide open along Phillips Street. A few cabbage butterflies, one azure seen today. Once again, the grackles came together chattering and grackling in the back trees at the end of the afternoon, repeating their Pentecost pattern of Early Summer.

2018: To Cincinnati: Chicory, hemlock and tall cattails in the roadsides. Very late catalpa flowers. At the Monastery of St. Clare, gooseneck loosestrife was opening, ramps were budded. A constant static-like buzzing came from all around me, tree crickets. At home, a grackle heckled me when I worked in the zinnias, her young nearby. Not too far away, a robin parent was signaling its young. On the roof of the greenhouse, I saw the trumpet creeper was in bloom, the flowers almost lost in the sky. Cabbage whites came by as I worked replacing bricks on the patio.

2019: From Umbria in Italy, Neysa sends a photo of a Cream Spot Tiger Moth (*Epicallia or Arctia villica*), a large black moth with irregular white spots, and a large, metallic-green beetle. In the garden at home, the first heliopsis and the first large blue hostas have bloomed.

2020: Five pond iris are in bloom this morning, a small, deep purple center to the south garden now that the peonies are almost gone. At Don's house, the first buds of his oakleaf hydrangea have started to open. The buds on the heliopsis at home are straining but not open yet. One primrose (cut back by deer grazing earlier) has opened, and in the east garden, the first two Stella d'oro lilies have bloomed. One dark swallowtail butterfly glimpsed from the porch. Another young rabbit seen in the alley this morning; this year has produced more rabbits than I've ever noticed in town.

2022: Don's oakleaf hydrangea is coming into bloom. More lily buds showing up along the north garden. Three cabbage whites romping across the yard. Dutch iris and reblooming lilies planted in the northeast tulip area. The first chiggers felt on my ankles. At Ellis Pond, swallows sailed and swooped above the water and the new-mown grass.

> *Sleep not, dream not; this bright day*
> *Will not, cannot last for aye.*

Emily Bronte

### *June 10th*
### *The 161st Day of the Year*

*Now I may know the roughness of the tree trunks,*
*Rain on the willows, clover-sweet air.*
*Now I feel the life-burdened earth against my breast.*
*Now I may know the swift sweeping seasonal turn,*
*The four-quartered cycle of time.*

Janet Stevens

Sunrise/set: 5:06/8:03
Day's Length: 14 hours 57 minutes
Average High/Low: 81/59
Average Temperature: 70
Record High: 100 – 1911
Record Low: 43 – 1977

### *Weather*
This is typically one of the finest days in all of June, with rain and cloudy skies occurring just 20 percent of the time. Highs are in the mild 70s forty percent of the time, in the 80s twenty-five percent, in the 90s twenty percent. Fifteen percent of the afternoons are in the cool 60s - the last time for that considerable percentage until August 28.

### *Natural Calendar*
Wild multiflora roses often start to fade now, and the first bindweed goes to seed. Chiggers bite near this date; their season lasts through August in the North, well into autumn in the South. Most deer have been born by now. Raccoon and rabbit young are about half grown.

### *The Stars*
In the late evening, Arcturus in the constellation Bootes is the brightest light directly overhead. Scorpius is centered in the southern sky and dominates it until early July. Orion is high in the south at noon, promising the Dog Days.

## *Daybook*

1982: Chicory blooming. End of the mock orange. Mulberries are starting to come in, a few cherries ready to eat.

1984: Catalpas begin. Yucca stems are tall now, budding. Squirrel-tail grass seen along the freeway.

1986: First yucca flowers noticed.

1987: A light earthquake this evening around eight o'clock. Just a strange tremor, and then it was over. Could the 17-year cicadas have caused it?!

1988: Still no fireflies. Teasel and goldenrod knee high, wingstem to my waist. First black raspberry just turning. First moneywort seen, early blueweed. Red clover dying in the drought, flowers rusty, foliage withered. Blackberry fruit is set, last flowers falling. Angelica half to seed, stems red. Daisy fleabane and motherwort full bloom, meadow rue and dogbane budding. Bull thistles and yellow thistles, *Irsium horridulum*, are ready to blossom. Fresh, heavy sweet scent in the air, despite the lack of rain.

1990: Catalpas full bloom, iris and peonies all gone, air fragrant with the full bloom of privets, which replaced the mock orange in perfect sequence. Smooth nettle and first daisy fleabane coming in, very first mulberries falling to the street. Elderberries heading up. Most iris are gone now, some peonies still sighted. Goslings at Ellis Pond seem to be a fourth grown.

1992: First coreopsis today in the south garden. Lychnis early bloom. Evening primrose suddenly full bloom. Daisies still full, pyrethrum faded. First tall yarrow buds. Most all mock orange gone. First orange ditch lily opens along the north garden. Very last Siberian iris disappears. The last two regular iris hold on.

1993: First ditch lily opens in the yard, first veronica. Japanese honeysuckle early full bloom in the village. Very early Canadian thistles. First firefly of the year seen at the top of the apple tree in the back yard.

1998: Three new fish brought home for the pond today, a white mottled one with shining scales, a tan and orange with white pectoral fins, a fan-tailed gold. A young blackbird found dying in the lawn. Peak yellow sweet clover and hemlock. Beans planted a week ago break ground. Early hostas with white and green leaves are now in bloom, and the great blue hosta has white buds.

1999: Utica, New York to Bar Harbor, Maine: Leaving June behind, climbing into May. Bleeding hearts seen in New Hampshire. Orange hawkweed common throughout the Northeast. Lupines widespread. Lower Maine full of locust flowers, full bloom by the time we reached Augusta. Poppies, iris, peonies and lilacs throughout, especially as we came closer to the northern coast. Tall buttercups from Erie east to Bar Harbor. Parsnips and hemlock and wild roses, blackberry flowers, wild pink roses, spring gathering momentum the farther north we went.

2000: A third orange Asiatic lily bloomed today to the west of the yellow daylily. The very first hollyhock, a deep violet red, opened halfway. The first mallow bud was pink. The first ripe black raspberry eaten from the north garden. Red mulberries and white mulberries ripest now, falling to the street. Garlic stalks with fully developed seed heads. Great blue hosta ready to open, and another smaller variety in the hosta-astilbe bed.

2001: Ranunculus gone. Full mulberry time. Full yellow primrose and yellow Stella d'oro daylilies.

2003: At 4:45 a.m., the grackles had already joined the morning chorus, apparently up early for the mulberries.

2005: South Glen: Daddy longlegs everywhere in the shade, hunting on the ground and on top of the wood nettle. Gold-collared black flies mating, damselflies common near the river. Rockets mostly to seed, multiflora roses late, black walnut fruits about half an inch across, Osage flower stems covering the path. A pair of pileated woodpeckers seen working a branch in tandem, one on one side, one on the other. Red and white mulberries dropping to the ground. Pink smartweed blossoming in the garden. Final rhododendron and bleeding heart flowers wither.

2007: No privet flowers seen for a long time. No dark mulberries noticed in the village. Were they (and most of the privets) hurt by the April freeze? The birds are quieter in the yard this morning, and the pre-dawn chatter seems more subdued. Perhaps this is a molting time, a time after the turbulence of fledglings leaving the nest.

2008: The first pale yellow daylily bloomed overnight, and I saw the first gold-collared blackfly on the Jerusalem artichokes this morning. "Love bugs" mating on the lilies this afternoon. Birds continue loud, one robin vespers long at dusk. Red-bellied woodpecker continues to call off and on. Finches return to new white feeders.

2010: I watched a father downy woodpecker feeding suet to his fledgling this morning at 10:30. Peter said that he had seen two adult hawks teaching their baby to hunt a few days ago. This afternoon on a ride to Dayton, Jeanie and I saw great mullein starting to bloom along the road. Russian sage is open at Peggy's and at different locations around the area.

2011: Robins by 4:00, doves at 4:30 again, cardinals at 4:40. To Goshen, Indiana, driving through heavy storms: Many fields unplanted in southern Ohio, gradually filling with inch-tall corn and soybeans as we drove northwest. Yellow and white sweet clover, some chicory, some elderberry, a few patches of Canadian thistles, late hawthorns, full catalpas, fields of late hemlock and parsnips (hemlock all to seed south of town). Red-winged blackbirds still nesting, guarding their territories on the barbed wire fences all along the highway. At Goshen, the last of the peonies, full blooming primroses. In the alley at home, blooming panicled dogwood, black mulberries on the ground, and in the park, kousa dogwood. In front of the library, full oakleaf hydrangeas. The red weigela is flowering across the street.

2012: The green frog was croaking this morning at dawn, bullfrogs at Ellis Pond at sunset. In Wilberforce, one very late catalpa in full bloom, and the first orange trumpet creeper I've found so far this year, with many blossoms. Wheat is brown, appears ready to cut throughout the county. At home, the violet trellis clematis is down to just a handful of blossoms, two more Asiatic lilies opening, one yellow, one orange. Starling fledglings continue to beg for food.

2014: I couldn't sleep and got up to listen to the birds in the dark. The robin chorus began down the street at 4:18, had reached my yard by 4:23. The early morning was soft, sky overcast, barometer starting to fall, temperature at 60 degrees. I stayed outside waiting, saw my first fireflies of the year at 4:40, and finally heard the first cardinal call nearby at 5:06. A wren chattered at 5:21. If there were doves, they were drowned out by the growing volume of the robins. On the front screen door, a thin-winged moth, belonging to the *Pterophoridae*. The Japanese pond iris surprised me with seven deep purple blossoms today.

2015: It is the far side of daisy bloom now, and crab apples are the size of BBs, and serviceberries ripen and turn red as the cherries become perfect for pies, and mulberries grow soft and fall to the street. Catalpas have peaked and a few trees have lost their blossoms. Lily season has begun with Stella d'oros full bloom, ditch lilies gaining momentum, the first everbloomers opening, so many other varieties budding. Robins continue to guide their young with intense peeping. Sparrow fledglings sit by the bird feeder, flap their wings to beg for food. Coreopsis and low yellow sedum in bloom downtown. One huge elderberry bush in lush full follower at the edge of a property on Elm Street.

2016: Thirteen lily plants blooming this morning, all but three of them Stella d'oros. The heliopsis has one completely formed flower, two more coming. The Japanese pond iris continues with three blossoms.

2017: Measurements/inventory. Fourteen Stella d'oro blossoms, three ditch lilies, one Asiatic, three heliopsis blossoms, and the last water iris holds. In the pond, the lizard's tail stalks have collapsed, the bud clusters over two inches long, lying on the surface of the water. The great blue hosta is budding here by the northwest corner of the house and along Dayton Street. Throughout the village, the black mulberries are falling so quickly, and I see entire boughs collapsed into yards and streets with their sweet soft fruit. Leah reports more red-winged blackbirds at her property than she has ever seen. I think about repetition and repeating observations year after year, and I see how the more I see, the more each thing seen becomes.

2018: The first ditch lily opened in the night (the ones across the street almost all open), half a dozen Stella d'oros in bloom, the Annabelle hydrangea clusters whitening, and all around the yard, a Pentecost of grackles, what seems like an annual fledgling coming-out similar to what I've seen in the past, and similar in feel to the burst of sparrow chatter and flutter earlier in the month. The grackle young, like the sparrows, are loud and insistent, scrawing and whining, and the clucking, grackling parents fly back and forth trying to satisfy them. And about two this afternoon, a female Baltimore oriole came to bathe in the fountain. A half an hour later, the bright male drank from the hummingbird feeder.

Reading back over this day in 1999: the progress of the year Jeanie and I saw in the Northwest then is very similar to state of nature in  photos of Amherst that Jill sent me a few days ago.

2019: This year, the grackles were relatively quiet after their first day of excitement. From Italy, Neysa reports pie cherries are ripe, paralleling Don and Peggy's pie cherry trees here. In the west garden, three more Japanese water iris in bloom. Two astilbes flowering in front of the house. I begin the lily count for this year: one Stella d'oro and one mauve day lily open today. All day, the wind was relatively high, 10 to 15 miles per hour. Clouds dominated most of the day, and the temperature in the low 70s felt chilly. Leslie reports the more raccoon babies eating seed with their mother in her back yard. Her first raccoon baby sighting was on June 6.

2020: Cloudy and muggy: Tropical Storm Cristobal has moved straight up from New Orleans and is brining storms to the Midwest. In reference to last year on this date, Leslie reported her first young raccoon sighting on June 3. In the west garden, six pond iris in bloom, but just one Stella d'oro. Peggy's peaches are the size of acorns. John Blakelock found a cedar waxwing in his driveway with an injured wing, escaped, he thought, from the Copper's hawk that hangs around his neighborhood. After the thunderstorm and wind gusts late this afternoon, catalpa flowers lay all about along West South College Street.

2021: Theresa called to exclaim about the storm of cicadas near her house. And off I went into South Glen to look for them. Along the slippery path by the river, an overarching drone from the hills, newly hatched insects with big red eyes all about, delicate tan moths fluttering in the honewort and wood nettle, and my first daddy longlegs of the year. I drove over to the park and stopped where the buzzing was loudest, walked in to layers of sound, and uncountable cicadas flying back and forth through the trees, landing sometimes beside me in the clustered snakeroot. At home, a sulphur butterfly and a tiny blue, and the second deep purple pond iris. The very last peonies had withered.

*Summer reaches critical mass: so much color, so much new life, so much perfection that the weight of one more insect or the exotic scent of one more milkweed or the ecstasy of one more butterfly suddenly pierces the spinning ascension of time, and the season topples over of its own weight, the last infinitesimal addition pulling the vast Earth over, tilting it top-heavy into solstice.*

bf

## *June 11th*
## *The 162nd Day of the Year*

*Where'er you walk cool gales shall fan the glade;*
*Trees, where you sit, shall crowd into a shade;*
*Where'er you tread, the blushing flowers shall rise,*
*And all things flourish where you turn your eyes.*

Alexander Pope

Sunrise/set: 5:06/8:03
Day's Length: 14 hours 57 minutes
Average High/Low: 81/60
Average Temperature: 70
Record High: 96 – 1911
Record Low: 40 – 1972

### *Weather*

There is a ten percent chance of a high in the 90s today, 55 percent of 80s, thirty percent of 70s, five percent of 60s. The sky is clear to partly cloudy eight years in ten, but rain comes 50 percent of the time. The morning is cool (in the 40s or 50s) two thirds of the years; the last time the percentage is so high until September 15th.

### *Natural Calendar*

The violet heads of May's chives droop and decay. Tall buttercups recede into the wetlands. The blossoms of the scarlet pyrethrums, blue lupines and Siberian iris come apart. Nettles and grasses reach waist high and tangle with catchweed (the catchweed flowers turned to burs). Catalpa flowers fall in afternoon thunderstorms.

### *Chiggers and Japanese Beetles*

A survey of "first chigger bites" and "first Japanese beetle sightings" from June 4 through July 5 between the early 1980s and the early years of the 21st century offers a casual timetable for the onslaught of these two insects.

Easy markers for chigger and beetle season are red

honeysuckle berries, half-grown black walnuts and Osage orange fruits, ripening wild black raspberries, and sighting of the first stag beetle (a beetle which does no harm to humans or gardens). Since I began keeping records, the chiggers seem to be reliable visitors, but the Japanese beetles went from a plague at the end of the 20th century, to almost a rarity in 2017.

May 21, 2014: Shulamit reports her first chigger bite in Dayton.
June 1, 2018: First chigger bite in the yard.
June 4, 2012: First chigger bite today after working in the yard, the earliest so far – after a record-breaking warm spring.
June 7, 2017: First chigger bite of the year noticed on my leg.
June 10, 2022: First chiggers felt on my ankles.
June 11, 1986: First chigger bite in South Glen.
June 11, 1988:  First chigger bite.
June 11, 2011: First chigger bite on my ankle.
June 12, 2008: First chigger bite in the yard this morning.
June 13, 1998: First Japanese beetles in the garden roses.
June 15, 2021: First chigger bites from transplanting zinnias.
June 16, 2004: First Japanese beetles found on the ferns.
June 16, 2005: Jeanie got the first chigger bites of the year today, about five days later than the earliest years.
June 17, 2004: First chigger bites in the garden.
June 18, 1987: I'm full of chiggers after a day walking.
June 18, 2009: Jeanie reports the first chigger bits after working in the garden.
June 18, 2001: Chiggers have attacked me!
June 20, 2012: First Japanese beetles found: in the zinnias.
June 21, 1998: Five Japanese beetles in the roses.
June 21, 1999: A few Japanese beetles in the roses.
June 21, 2004: Home from southern Wisconsin: Japanese beetles have eaten the roses.
June 22, 2017: First Japanese beetle, quite small, in the north garden.
June 25, 2001: First Japanese beetle found in the roses.
June 25, 2010: First chigger bite when I mowed the lawn.
June 26, 2003: I got my first chigger bites today; Jeanie was attacked yesterday.
June 27, 2016: First Japanese beetle found in the lilies.

June 29, 1982: First chigger bites from walk in the woods.
June 30, 1993: First Japanese beetles found in the roses, have probably been out a couple days.
June 30, 2003: First Japanese beetles found in the roses.
July 1, 1996: Japanese beetles arrived on June 30th.
July 2, 1983: First chigger bite of the year.
July 4, 2021: First Japanese beetle found in the Japanese knotweed.
July 5, 1997: First Japanese beetle found on the roses.

## *Daybook*

1982: End of catalpa flowers.

1983: Bluegills still guard their nests at the Bletzingers' pond.

1984: A few peonies, the medium pink, hang on in the village. Motherwort bloomed today. An indigo bunting seen, the first ever.

1985: Yucca blooming today.

1986: At South Glen, smooth brome had droplets of yellow pollen. Teasel heads were three-fourths of an inch long. I got my first chigger bite of the year. First wild petunia seen. Water willow full bloom in the Little Miami River.

1988: No fireflies yet. First teasel head found, three fourths of an inch tall. Timothy emerges from its sheath. First chigger bite noticed.

1989: Belize: west to the Guatemalan border. The land dry throughout until Benque Viejo, where it had rained six hours straight on the 10th. North into the outcroppings of stone, the horizon was gray from field fires. A resident told me the milpas were burned beginning around May 15th, the corn and beans planted after the first soaking rain. At the ruins of Benque Viejo, the sky was identical to last year's here on the 23rd, dramatic, high cirrus sweeping up over Guatemala. Returning to Belize City, I saw water lilies blooming in the river.

1991: First hollyhocks open in the yard. First large dish of black raspberries picked; some reds will be ready in a few days. Our tree of heaven completed its flowering today.

1993: At home, first deep orange lychnis opened, first motherwort. Red astilbe color shows clearly now. Along the way to Caesar Creek, the catalpas were in full bloom, their white flowers replacing the locusts, exotic, tropical. The sky was divided, clear to the north, mostly cloudy to the south; I fished exactly between a cool front and a warm front for most of the day. The lake was sweet with the smell of multiflora roses and boxwood, loud with the sucking and splashing of carp, boisterous flicker calls, the brow, brow, brow of bullfrogs, steady jumping of small and large fish across the water, whine of catbirds.

A curious red admiral butterfly rested on my cooler, unafraid as I got bait and moved about the boat. He flew away after a while, came back in 20 minutes, then he was replaced by a persistent blue that landed on my shirt, tasted the sweat. Then later, a brown visited, like the one that stayed with me at the other catfish hole two years ago. Water bugs mating, swallows hunting back and forth across the lake. A pair of flickers came to the dead Osage above my bobbers. They courted, kissed for a minute, then the male mounted, they mated a few seconds, and they were gone. Three large catfish caught in five hours.

1997: The coolest year on record so far: mock orange petals three-fourths fallen, with the locust leaves a third of their summer size, the last Siberian iris blooming, the full bloom of sweet Williams and lady's mantel, the early days of privet. On the way home from school, the first yellow daylily seen along Grinnell Road. In the garden, spinach is going to seed and radishes hot, peppers and tomatoes in flower, lettuce and kale getting body. Thyme and parsley are ready to use. At the Cascades, there were tiny locust petals and fragments of tulip tree flowers scattered across the path. On the forest floor, only the white violets and the waterleaf were in bloom.

1998: Grackles have been chattering steadily all morning, the ritual of the young leaving the nest and the ritual of the feasting on mulberries and raspberries. Large white buds grow more prominent on the great blue hosta. The Francis Thompson hosta planted just a week or so ago has opened almost all the way, and the variegated hosta is fully stalked and budding. Yuccas are high, but none seen blooming yet.

1999: Acadia National Park, Maine: Full young rhododendrons, roses, bluets, blue-eyed grass, bunchberry, swamp valerian.

2000:  This morning when I got home from work, I found that a pink Asiatic lily had bloomed overnight, west of the latest orange. Along the freeway this afternoon, hemlock two-thirds to seed, maybe a fourth of the thistles. In Dayton, some hollyhocks and hosta seen in early full bloom; at home, two hollyhocks have emerged, and the great blue hosta is opening. The first pale violet mallow flower came in too. First purple coneflower seen in the village. More fireflies are out tonight.

2001: Common ditch lilies finally starting along the roadsides. Astilbe full bloom at home.

2003: The first orange Asiatic lily opened today, and the first Shasta daisy unraveled. First trumpet creeper seen. Full bloom time for primrose, achillea, white penstemon, sweet William, spiderwort, peach-leafed bellflower. Now the Stella d'oro lilies are starting to come in throughout the area. The robin chorus was light at 4:00 a.m., and grew steadily for an hour and a half. Doves joined in at 4:40, a few cardinals and blackbirds near 5:00.

2004: This year, the white penstemon and the peach-leafed bellflowers are now almost done.

2005: The dark-purple water iris hold for a second day. The spirea bush in the back yard and one orange daylily in the northwest garden, one astilbe under the redbud tree all opened last night. Oak-leaf hydrangeas are starting to produce petals. Pie cherries and serviceberries are ripening on Dayton Street, pacing the mulberries.

2006: Fully grown camel cricket found in Jeanie's teacup this morning.

2007: Monarch butterfly visits the sweet Williams in the late morning. Young grackles still being fed in the yard this afternoon.

2008: The second daylily, a pale pink one, bloomed overnight. The new green frog that has been at the pond for several weeks croaked this morning for the first time at 5:07, croaked again in the middle of the afternoon. Stella d'oro lilies are in full bloom in Xenia; the transplanted ones in the north garden just came in today. A young fawn, its spots still very prominent was feeding in Moya's back yard this afternoon about 4:00. Yucca seen in bloom in Xenia. Jeanie is renovating the circle garden now, cutting back the hyacinths, flax and violets, getting ready to put in whirling butterflies, butterfly bushes and more herbs.

2009: Oakleaf hydrangea getting more white petals. Sweet Williams fading. Anna Belle hydrangea opening. One full purple larkspur plant, three heliopsis flowers, several Asiatic orange lilies and one Turk's cap, in addition to the earlier full candy lilies. In the alley, a couple of black raspberries ripening. Grackles feeding their young in the Stafford Street maples. Waning privet blossoms hold here and there on the Limestone Street hedge.

2010: A ruby-throated hummingbird looking for nectar in the sparse penstemon blossoms before dawn. As he turned toward me, his deep red throat flashed in the twilight. Only one of the Japanese iris remains in bloom now in the pond. Eleven raspberries picked this morning from last year's growth – our biggest harvest so far. The deer has switched from lilies and lettuce to peas. Endless summer hydrangeas have large white and pink flower clusters.

2011: Osage fruits, hairy and an inch or so in diameter, down on the sidewalk this morning, victims of last night's storm. The last Japanese iris has wilted in the pond. First white-spotted skipper near the apple tree, a large dragonfly close by. I had the first chigger-like bites in the garden this afternoon. The earliest monarda is opening.

2013: Sardinia: Portoscuso: Perfect weather in the 80s with a sea breeze. We drove the coast from beach to beach, along the shore all types of thick-leafed perennials, fully conditioned to their habitat by the steady mild winds.

Many of the familiar landmarks that I saw in Sicily and around Spoleto: the yellow ginestra; oleander shrubs in pink and white and violet along the roads and streets; the large-petaled cactus, *Opoatia ficus indice L. Miller,* with yellow blossoms; Queen Anne's lace in abundance; orange poppies; a variety of thick, maritime angelica; figs ripening; roses flowering; grains and roadside grasses all golden brown; haying underway throughout the island – as it was in Umbria and Sicily; olive groves in bloom; vineyards strong; some blackberry bushes setting fruit; cottonwood cotton in the wind; teasel tall but not flowering yet; tall hollyhock-like mallow common in reds and pinks; bindweeds and knapweeds with their soft violets.

And beach after beach with pale sand and the ocean so perfectly clear, turquoise, some waves high from the wind, some sheltered places still and benign. Where we waded or swam, the water was still chilly, but sometimes I could stand on mossy rocks, just a few feet underwater, that had been warmed by the sun.

2014: Privets and catalpas falling now, many mulberries and pie cherries ready for pie, strawberries at Alice's coming in strong for over a week, garden rhubarb almost too ripe, great mullein budded, orchard grass and wild onions and catchweed going to seed in the alley. The garden is beginning to show more color now, the Stella d'oros and the orange Asiatics giving patches of brightness here and there, the primroses (*Oenethera*) holding, spiderwort and catmint adding purple and violet, and all the zinnia sprouts beginning to color the soil with green.

2015: To North Glen with Rosemary and Chris: One small polygonia, one unidentified polygonia-like butterfly with pointed wings, and a white moth with a black cross on its "back," a very early *Clymene*. Dominant foliage: touch-me-not to four feet, wood nettle almost ready to bloom, some ironweed and wingstem to five feet. Honewort seen in flower, common, in a two-hour walk. A few scraggly white violets in one small patch. Several wild onions flowering. Along the river, privet flowers were falling. One micrathena seen in its circular web. The very first yucca flower opened on Fairfield Road. The yard at home is almost the same as last year. This year, though, I have noticed that the monarda has started to head up.

2016: Seven ditch lilies this morning and eight other lily plants, seven of them Stella d'oros and one everbloomer. Four heliopsis flowers open, summer well underway now. Primroses and spiderworts complement the new blossoms. The lone astilbe from years ago has poked its flower head out from the weeds under the redbud tree, indomitable. At the corner of Davis and High Streets, three ripe black raspberries.

2017: Four chigger bites counted this morning. Twelve Stella d'oro lily blossoms, two rebloomer blossoms and two Asiatic blossoms, no ditch lilies in the yard. The last pond iris holds. Except for three heliopsis blossoms instead of four and a small variation in the lily count, the season runs parallel to last year's and to 2015's and 2014's. First yellow touch-me-nots just off Stafford Street. First yucca flowers along North West College Street. Heat now settles in across the Midwest, 90s here and in Madison, Wisconsin.

2018: The first heliopsis is unraveling. The grackle Pentecost, the coming out, graduation, whatever…continues.

2019: At the Covered Bridge, the river high and fast from all the rain, the woods a habitat of late honewort, many plants to seed, with wood nettle and touch-me-not foliage climbing past my waist, and bottle grass with pollen. No lilies in the garden today, but two in the Glass Farm area. One Queen Anne's lace plant heading up there. One of the Endless Summer hydrangea shrubs in the north garden has the first flower cluster in several years. Leslie reported a monarch butterfly, a hackberry butterfly, a great spangled fritillary and a wood satyr butterfly, house wren fledglings and a tiny American toad "smaller than a black field cricket, and smaller than my little fingernail."

2020: Six Stella d'oro lilies open, five pond iris. Anna Belle hydrangea coming in. Yucca full height and budded on Davis Street. Parsnips and hemlock full bloom along the rivulet near Ellis Pond. One firefly seen yesterday evening, only the fifth so far this summer. A second yellow rose appeared on the remnant of Jeanie's last rose bush. White waterleaf flowers declining, but still prominent, all around the pond and the south garden. Looking back over almost forty years of today's notes, I can see that the land is about a week late this year, but that the sequences are in what seems like perfect order.

2021: One checkerspot butterfly at the radio station entrance, Canadian thistles blooming and to seed there. One blue, the second so far, in the honeysuckles. Cicadas dead on the sidewalk and street. Also cicada bodies on the asphalt near the grocery store. Don's oakleaf hydrangea is in early bloom. The koi are more active, perhaps stimulated by the chemical change from fecal sacks being deposited there by birds.

*Doubtless God could have made a better berry, but doubtless God never did.*
Dr. Boteler (in Isaac Walton)

### *June 12th*
### *The 163rd Day of the Year*

*Among the crooked lanes, on every hedge,*
*The glow-worm lights his gems; and, through the dark,*
*A moving radiance twinkles.*

James Thomson

Sunrise/set: 5:06/8:04
Day's Length: 14 hours 58 minutes
Average High/Low: 81/60
Average Temperature: 70
Record High: 95 – 1902
Record Low: 42 – 1888

### *Weather*

A cold and rainy June 12th can occur once in a decade (that happened in 1985: precipitation and a high of only 52), and thunderstorms pass through half of all the years. But the sun still shines at least a little three days in four, and highs reach above 90 on 15 percent of the afternoons, are in the 80s fifty percent of the time, in the 70s thirty percent. A minimum of 100 frost-free days remains in the growing season of the Ohio Valley.

### *Natural Calendar*

Sawfly larvae eat the leaves on the mountain ash. Head scab and glume blotch develop on the winter wheat. Lace bugs cause yellow spotting on sycamores, oaks and azaleas. The first generation of sod webworms is often born near this date.

### *Daybook*

1983: First orange daylily noticed along Grinnell.

1984: First daylily seen on Grinnell. First raspberry turning red.

1986: Thimble plant and hobblebush blossoming. Wood nettles dominate the undergrowth, with clovers, elderberries; panicled dogwoods still full bloom along the roadsides. Tall meadow rue is still open at South Glen. Angelica and parsnips have as many seeds as blossoms. Milkweed is budding, timothy full bloom, cherries and black raspberries are reaching their best. Only a few sweet rockets are left. First chigger bite this afternoon.

1987: First hemlock is rusting.

1988: Worst drought since 1934. All the northwest Ohio crops are ruined. Lawns and pastures are drying up, thistles wilting by the side of the road. More animals have been run over on the highways. Few insects about, no water available besides the rare morning dew. At home, the strawberry peak is over, yucca is budding. Lizard's tail is developing small bud heads along the river.

1989: Caye Caulker, an island one hour into the reef off the coast of Belize in the Caribbean, at the beginning of the rainy season: 18 wild flowering plants, seven different shrubs and trees found. Familiar horseweed starting to bloom a month before it comes in at South Glen. I wandered along the mangroves, swam in the hot, clear water at the southern tip of the land, collected what appeared to be *Verbenaceae, Eleusine indica, Fabaceae,* and *Ageratrum conyzoides*.

1993: First carnation, and garden lily, last pyrethrum. Hawthorns are in full bloom throughout Yellow Springs and Wilberforce. On an oak branch fallen in the wind, acorns have set tiny green nuggets. Pink spirea shrubs are in full bloom. Silver olive flowers gone.

1997: Flickers call throughout most of the morning in the woods behind the yard. Cardinals are quieter now. Robins still chirping near dawn. Mourning doves calling, too. At the village pond, goslings half size, the size of adult ducks.

1999: Acadia, Bar Harbor, Maine: A late pink lady slipper found by the campsite. A local writer says they come out around the 1st of June. Lambkill/sheep laurel identified, , four petal moss flower, haircap moss. Blueberries: some still flowering, and some have set fruit. Tall meadow rue up but not flowering. More plants: tall Robin's ragwort, three-toothed cinquefoil, columbine, wild flags, spreading dogbane, beach pea, white Labrador tea, pink herb Robert, witherod *(Viburnum cassinoides)*, yellow-flowered bush honeysuckle, wild strawberries, mountain laurel budded, yellow water lily, pink marsh cinquefoil, snowball viburnum, bridal wreath spirea, and full poppies (almost exactly 30 days behind Yellow Springs).

2000: To Springfield, then John Bryant Park: Wheat is rich green-gold. Chicory is finally open. Trumpet creeper seen blossoming on a telephone pole. Yarrow and elderberry full bloom. Orange honeysuckle berries under the canopy, leafcup and hobblebush ready to bloom. Last of the old maple-leafed waterleaf and clustered snakeroot. Full-blooming honewort. Black swallowtail seen.

2001: Yucca in the yard, planted years ago, finally blooms, the first yucca in town, from what I can see. Elderberry seen open on the way to Chillicothe, forty miles southwest of Yellow Springs. Tall cressleaf groundsel dying back in the fields near Jamestown. In the countryside, parsnips and hemlock dominate, although the hemlock around Yellow Springs has come to the end of its cycle. In the water garden, lizard's tail has formed its flower.

2002: First heliopsis bloomed in the north garden. Honewort full bloom in the North Glen.

2003: First chicory seen in bloom along the freeway this morning. First black raspberry eaten. Tattered, dark pink peonies still hold on the west side of Mrs. Lawson's old house on the corner of High and Dayton Streets. No fireflies seen yet this cool Early Summer.

2004: Greg told me that the first butterfly plant (not bush) bloomed in his yard today. Very last cressleaf groundsel cut back in the north garden. Many Canadian thistles to seed along Dayton-Yellow Springs Road. Yucca full bloom in Xenia.

2005: The first monarch butterfly seen in the sweet Williams today. In the pond, the Japanese iris reached full bloom, and then were beaten down by rain. The first water willows were open beside them. In the north garden, the first yellow daylily came in overnight and the first tall mallow flowers. John reported that mayflies emerged today at the Santee Cooper reservoir in South Carolina. He added that catfish were only biting on the flats, not in the channel.

2006: First fireflies in the cool evening.

2007: Last night was the first night of more than just a few fireflies. Today, the perennial yellow primrose is declining quickly. Monarda is heading up in the north and south gardens. Birdsong continues to change: doves still call, and the grackles are loud and steady, but the cardinals have stopped singing after dawn. First pink mallow bloomed by noon. Japanese iris finished their season with yesterday's blossoms. This afternoon several young robins and fledgling grackles enjoyed the water from the sprinkler in the back yard. Adults continue to feed both the baby robins and grackles. One milkweed plant opening near the park this evening.

2008: The first Japanese iris opened overnight. The oakleaf hydrangea reached early bloom. The third daylily, a freckled orange, flowered. Panicled dogwood is coming in and Mrs. Timberlake's feverfew is in full bloom along the Stafford Street alley, Don's multiflora rose completely done, and his pie cherries showing some reddening. The first three red hollyhocks opened in the alley by the church, kousa dogwoods full bloom along Xenia Avenue. Some catalpas still in bloom. Ellen said she had found three cicadas when she dug the grave for her cat that died this week. She said she put the cicadas back where she found them. I got the first chigger bite of the year on my ankle this morning. I sat outside after dark, the robins singing strong until about a quarter after nine, and then the back yard was full of fireflies. They must have started mating at least a week ago – I just wasn't there to see them.

2009: A hairy Osage fruit, about an inch in diameter, fallen to the sidewalk. Grackles still active in the alley trees. First flowers on the pokeweed. Groundsel flowers gone. Sudden bloom of tall, orange "ditch lilies." Oakleaf hydrangea early full, wild onions headed. Some bright yellow Asiatic lilies open.

2011: First red raspberries noticed at home, the few that escaped the deer. The east hedges are filled with full-blooming Japanese honeysuckle, flowers covering up the forsythia and the vines underneath. Pink spirea is full behind the peony bushes. Daylilies and purple coneflowers are budded in the southeast garden, and dahlias that I planted in early May are two feet tall among them. Privet flowers are gone along High Street.

2012: Yellow garden primrose, pink spirea, sweet Williams, astilbe, Heliopsis, Stella d'oro lilies, catmint, roses, all the hydrangeas (pink and white), spiderwort, Rugosa roses, still full bloom. I cut webworms cut down from the redbud. A monarch (or maybe it was a viceroy) came to the butterfly bush. Gray tree frogs calling from the honeysuckles. More day and Asiatic lilies slowly coming in. Starling fledglings still being fed, the yard loud with bird calls, especially the scrawing of starlings and the peeping of robins orienting their young. More zinnias transplanted, hellebores transplanted.

2014:  A small fawn, maybe just a weeks old, legs so thin and delicate, wandered onto the front sidewalk from the south edge of the property, then into the east garden, ran when it saw me. Its mother has eaten almost all of one of our oakleaf hydrangeas. In the north garden, the hobblebush has put out its first white side flowers. At Ellis Pond, panicled dogwood (*Cornus racimosa*) in full bloom.

2015: The very first two sundrops *(Oenothera fruticosa)* opened overnight. Great spangled fritillary on the Anna Belle hydrangea at 7:30 this morning, a viceroy crazy in the west bushes at 8:45. The north garden's hobblebush has all its white side flowers this year. Penstemon cut back, all its flowers suddenly gone. Catalpas coming down all along Polecat Road. Canadian thistle blooms soft and purple. Wild black raspberries about half ripe. First great mullein flower seen pacing the first sundrops. Deer in and out of the garden much more than usual today.

2016: Twelve lily plants blooming today, the Stella d'oros nine of those, two ditch lilies and one everbloomer. First purple daylily seen behind Jill's house. First Canadian thistles along East Enon Road. One great mullein starting to flower off Talus Drive.

2017: Thirty-one Stella d'oro blossoms, two everbloomers, three Asiatics, five ditch lilies. The last pond iris has withered. Sundrops/primroses hold, bright yellow patches in the north garden. The Anna Belle hydrangea has half of its flowers, hobblebush full. The pink-blossomed Indomitable Spirit hydrangea is reaching full bloom. Walking down Dayton Street I saw a Great Spangled Fritillary, the only butterfly other than cabbage whites that I've seen in over a week. In the evening, the local woodchuck feeds on the grass near the west end of the yard. Once in a while, an opossum hurries by along the giant hostas. . On the road to Xenia, hemlock definitely fading.

2018: Thirteen Stella d'oro blossoms, three ditch lilies, three pond iris still budded, wild daisies and yellow primroses still full, one heliopsis unraveling. The Indomitable Spirit hydrangea is just starting to show red, Shasta daisies trying to open.

2019: Two ditch lilies seen in town this morning. John Blakelock called to say he was seeing robins eggs on the ground, a second brood of nestlings, he thought.

2020: Seven pond iris in bloom. First gold-collared blackfly seen in the bee balm. The first canna lily plant bloomed this morning, the root having been wintered over in the greenhouse.

2021: Two pond iris in bloom, two more budded. The first canna lily blossom has been open for four or five days. At the Saint Anthony Friary in Cincinnati, a large-flowered magnolia was in bloom, the 17-year cicadas loud and flying around throughout the campus, many dead on the driveway. Oppressive heat in the afternoon, 90 degrees. One checkerspot butterfly seen at home in the hostas. On an evening drive, a flock of starlings seen rising from a newly sprouted soybean field. The wheat was golden. Along Hyde Road, a row of catalpa trees was in full bloom. No mosquitoes at the back porch, and I remember wondering where the carpenter bees had gone the past few days.

2022: Five deep purple pond iris in bloom today. Milkweed budded. Robins peeping steadily. Several cabbage white butterflies exploring, No pesky mosquitoes yet in the back yard. More bulb planting, including some tall cannas, in the north garden. Suzy brought over a young rabbit, just a little bigger than my extended hand She had saved it from her cat, and the kit seemed uninjured, scooted right into the protection of the bishop's weed when I set it in the garden. Early afternoon, I thought I heard a screech owl's soft, descending call. First ditch lilies seen in flower. From Vermillion Lake in northern Minnesota, John sends a photo of a type of wild cherry tree in flower.

*Sweet June, dear month, while yet delay*
*Wistful reminders of a dearer May;*
*June, poised between, and not yet satiate.*

Vita Sackville-West

### *June 13th*
### *The 164th Day of the Year*

*Then let us, one and all, be contented with our lot;*
*The June is here this morning, and the sun is shining hot!*

James Whitcomb Riley

Sunrise/set: 5:06/8:04
Day's Length: 14 hours 58 minutes
Average High/Low: 81/60
Average Temperature: 71
Record High: 95 – 1902
Record Low: 42 – 1903

### *Weather*

Today, the 14th, and the 15th are the June days most likely to produce highs in the 90s (there's a 30 percent chance of 90s) and the 80s (a 40 percent chance of those). The remaining percentage falls to 70s (25 percent chance) and 60s or high 50s (just once in a third of a century). Skies are mostly clear to partly cloudy (completely overcast conditions coming only 15 percent of the time), and rain falls one day in four.

### *Natural Calendar*

Painted turtles and box turtles are laying eggs. On Lake Erie, walleye fishing is usually at its best. Winter wheat in the Lower Midwest is almost all headed by this date, and about a third of the crop is turning from green to gold. The first cut of alfalfa hay is almost complete in an average year along the 40th Parallel east of the Mississippi. Most of the corn, soybeans and sunflowers have been planted. In the fields, bottle grass and timothy are sweet. Acorns have formed on the oaks. Droopy lizard's tail flowers in ponds and streams.

### *Daybook*

1980: Multiflora roses have completed their bloom.

1981: First raspberry eaten today (the season lasted 28 days this year). A few final strawberries: their season lasted 17 days.

1983: The end of the mock orange flowers, a three-week season.

1984: First great mullein flowers along Grinnell and Wilberforce-Clifton Roads. Family of woodchucks seen, the young maybe two months old.

1985: Deep Summer already here, mosquitoes biting full force in the yard, angelica fading at Middle Prairie, watercress lying toppled over like a tangle of dead snakes; wild petunia, bedstraw, hobblebush, Indian hemp are open, Deptford pinks in bloom, last of the daisies, first of the black-eyed Susans, leafcup budding. White beardtongue, *Penstemon digitalis*, found, has been blooming maybe a week.

1987: Birds quieter before dawn this morning, then pick up about seven o'clock. Pie cherries coming in all at once. Black raspberries ripened overnight for a first bowl at breakfast. Roadsides are bright with yellow sweet clover, chicory, red clover, bird's foot trefoil. Trumpet creeper seen, has been out maybe three or four days. Yucca is in full bloom, great mullein getting ready, along with the milkweed. Orchard grass and volunteer wheat are brown. Mosquitoes biting in the yard at night, fireflies all here.

1988: First black raspberry is just ready. No fireflies yet.

1990: First chicory seen today.

1991: Identical to my notes this week of 1987.

1993: The grackles are here to eat the cherries and mulberries, the yard full of the sound of their wings and calls. First sweet pea opening. Fireflies came out of the high canopy tonight, a few blinking in the yard.

1998: Mallow opened today in the south garden. The first centipede of summer appeared on the bathroom wall, the first Japanese beetle in the garden.

1999: Maine: Full peonies throughout the area, plain green-leafed snow-on-the-mountain (bishop's weed) in bloom: southern Ohio May.

2000: Faint robin chorus at 4:30 a.m., then by 5:20, the cardinals are coming in.

2002: Water willow bloomed in the pond today. The first violet Asiatic lily opened in the north garden. The first Frances William hosta blossomed, too.

2003: At the entry to South Glen beyond the Covered Bridge, past the only buckeye fruit on a small tree, I came on a colony of blooming wood nettle, almost as high as my waist, that spread out around me hundreds of yards in all directions. Innocuous and lying close to the ground a few weeks ago, the nettle had taken over this entryway to the Glen, making an idyllic but stinging barrier to the river on the right and the hills on the left. Only a few pale moths, daddy longlegs, and a green-bodied damselfly navigated the surface of the new floral hegemon. Only the licorice seeds of April's sweet Cicely, a few struggling honewort, and black snakeroot were visible in the mass of rough, toothed nettle leaves. I could remember the layers of this past spring beneath them: wild ginger, blue cohosh, cut-leafed toothwort, violets, hepatica, large-flowered trillium, bloodroot, violet cress and early meadow rue. But they were as inaccessible as the periodic cicadas that lay a little further down waiting for May.

2004: Around the yard: Mid-season hostas are budding. The first Japanese iris unravels. Lizard's tail, water willow, astilbe, oakleaf hydrangea are full. Sweet Williams and lamb's ear very late. First foxglove, early gooseneck, trumpet creeper. Ironweed and butterfly bush are up to four feet, Joe Pye past six feet. Black swallowtail seen.

2006: Cardinals and robins still strong early. Crows at 4:55 a.m. Walk in the cool morning: Honewort in the dark woods, touch-me-nots waist high and climbing, one late mock orange near the river, one Kousa dogwood not far away, mulberries falling throughout town, pie cherries ripe along Dayton Street.

2007: Grackles still feeding their young in the back yard. Pink smartweed is blooming in the front garden, hollyhocks in the far alley, trumpet creeper along Limestone Street. Lots of fireflies tonight.

2008: The red-bellied woodpecker still calls.

2009: Red weigela across the street is gone. The mulberries are black and sweet on Gerard's tree along Dayton Street. Fading panicled dogwood flowers, fading penstemon. Many candy lilies have disappeared. The yellow rose flowers have ended. Pink rose full bloom. Late pink clematis. Ramps fully budded under the mock orange bush.

2010: The first lizard's tail buds opened overnight. The bicolor hosta started coming in, too. Tall buds on the standard hostas we got from Kate years ago – they usually bloom in July. A ripe black raspberry noticed in a yard on Davis Street.

2011: The canopy is complete and the iris and mock orange and honeysuckles and peonies are done blooming. I ruminate about the dependency of each phase on its markers, the emptiness of the May spaces. The weakness of the garden plan uncovered by the lack of replacements, sequences suddenly ended, the signs interrupted, gaps opening in time, in season, within borders that had defined the progress of the year by their changes, now rich and green but flat and silent. Yellow swallowtail in the Japanese honeysuckle at noon. Great blue hosta in early full bloom at Greg's, just starting at home. Orange ditch lilies becoming common now, and Shasta daisies noticed, too.

2012: Tufted titmouse fledgling removed from the bindery this morning. Caught sight of a bird, gray, large, that is such a songster these mornings, maybe a mocking bird.

2014: The first local chicory flower seen today, but all the other chicory plants have only their tall stalks.

2015: The first lizard's tail opened beside the pond overnight. A bright orange Asiatic flowered in the middle of the east Stella d'oros. Mulberries drop to the day lily foliage. One Shasta daisy has a bud, and buds are forming on a few of the zinnias.

2016: Over thirty lily blossoms today, mostly Stella d'oros, but the ditch lilies are up to a dozen. And the first violet – pink day lily opened overnight in the circle garden. Heliopsis blossoms up to five. Sparrow fledglings fluttering and chasing their parent for food. The wild daisies are almost gone, the first Shasta daisy bud barely starting to unravel. The great blue hosta at the west side of the property is just starting to bloom, the first time it has flowered since I divided and moved it several years ago. Two yellow roses in bloom on Jeanie's old rose bush, part of the rose garden from decades ago. I cut one and placed it by her ashes. On the sidewalk past the Lawsons' yard, several Osage fruits fallen, the largest about golf-ball size. Downtown: one Queen Anne's lace in bloom.

2017: Lily count: Ten ditch lilies, twenty Stella d'oros, five pink tiger Asiatics. A thunderstorm knocked down the spiderwort. Heliopsis: five blossoms. Along King Street, early trumpet creepers are blooming, and gooseneck loosestrife is in full flower. Several large-leafed hostas and bi-color hostas blooming. One hackberry butterfly in the honeysuckles. Panicled dogwood with berries. News reports suggest that 2017 will be a bumper year for ticks that may carry Powassan virus.

2018: Four ditch lilies, four Stella d'oros, one heliopsis.

2019: Cold in the low 60s today, a rare occurrence for June 13. One day lily flowering, many lily buds. Oakleaf hydrangeas and Annabelle hydrangeas are reaching full flower around town. Wild raspberries reddening along Davis Street. Pokeweed bud clusters visible in the north garden. Strong winds with occasional gusts throughout the day have stripped leaves from the trees all around the neighborhood.

2020: Another relatively cool day in the 70s. The storm of last year on this date occurred two days ago, the June 10 high-pressure system quite strong and wide. Five Stella d'oro lilies in bloom, no ditch lilies yet. At the pond, elderberries are just ready to open.

2021: Heat wave building. Cabbage butterflies more common today outside my office window. The second pre-hurricane low is forming in the Caribbean. Only one ditch lily open. The pond was especially foamy this morning, and the koi unusually excited. The fish seem to have become more active as the foam increases from fecal deposits from grackles or other birds. Sitting on the back porch talking to Maggie this afternoon, I saw three cabbage whites, one blue, one fold-wing and one of the 17-year cicadas (a rarity in the neighborhood).

2022: First day in the year with 100-degree heat index. Three cabbage whites playing in the garden. A fallen apple from Peggy's overgrown grove was maybe half the size of a golf ball. Heliopsis has small buds. Jill brought over a small bowl of red mulberries for snack. Constant robin peeping. Once again, I heard several calls from a screech owl.

*Nothing that is can pause or stay;*
*The moon will wax, the moon will wane,*
*The mist and cloud will turn to rain,*
*The rain to mist and cloud again,*
*Tomorrow be today.*

Henry Wadsworth Longfellow

### *June 14th*
### *The 165th Day of the Year*

*Taste the sugar berry sugar purple berry*
*sugar wild hot sugar sunning sugar berry*
*sugar in the sun.*

Leon Quel

Sunrise/set: 5:06/8:05
Day's Length: 14 hours 59 minutes
Average High/Low: 82/61
Average Temperature: 71
Record High: 94 – 1895, 95 – 2022
Record Low: 46 – 1978 and 2019

### *Weather*

Today is a hot day in a typical year at average elevations along the 40th Parallel (40 percent chance of 90s, fifty percent of 80s, just ten percent chance of 70s), with a 90 percent chance of sun, and a 30 percent chance of a passing thunderstorm. Cool mornings in the 40s or 50s occur just twice in a decade, making this the first time so far this year that the chances of lows in the 60s reach 80 percent.

### *Natural Calendar*

Orchard grass is getting brown and old, English rye grass full bloom, exotic bottle grass late bloom, brome grass very late, some timothy still tender. All across the nation's midsection, there are hedges of white elderberry flowers, roadsides of violet crown vetch, great fields of gold and green wheat.

Hemlocks and thistles have gone to seed near St. Louis. Sweet clover has almost disappeared in Memphis, and the blackberries there are turning red. In the Deep South, Queen Anne's lace blooms, wild lettuce and horseweed, too, and elderberries set their fruit. The wheat fields are bare along the Gulf of Mexico, the roadsides full of black-eyed Susans, pennywort, thin-leafed mountain mint and Mexican hat. Deep in Central America, the sugar cane crop paces the sweet corn in Iowa.

## *Daybook*

1980: Mulberries ripening, falling to the street and to the undergrowth.

1982: Young starlings in the yard, trying to fly.

1984: First raspberry ripe today.

1988: First tall violet mallow bloomed today along the south wall. Goslings, a third to half grown, were crossing the highway south of town with five or six adults. I saw a painted turtle laying eggs in the path near Mill Dam and found the first wild petunia in bloom. At sundown, carp lay near the surface of the low river near shore, drifting listlessly as though the heat and the drought had drained their energy.

1990: Some of the mulberry crop is gone now. Blueweed is in full bloom along the railroad tracks.

1991: Mulberries peak, fall to the street purple. They came in early, stayed just two weeks in the warm, dry weather. To Columbus: parsnips and sweet clover still bright, crown vetch rich, trumpet creeper seen full bloom.

1995: To St. Louis: Through Indianapolis, the land lush with yellow sweet clover, trefoil, purple cow vetch, pink crown vetch, poison hemlock, wild parsnips, yellow moth mullein. The wheat is golden green. At about 180 miles southwest of Yellow Springs, the first white sweet clover comes into bloom, the first sign that we are driving deeper into summer. About 250 miles from home, the first milkweed opens, and cattails are twice as tall as they are at Jacoby. Wheat browns rapidly as we approach St. Louis. Yucca is in full bloom, and half the white hemlock flowers have suddenly turned to seeds. Nodding thistles, still fresh and full in Greene County, begin to break apart, more than half of them to thistle down along the Mississippi. In eight hours, how far have we gone? A week for sure, more like two, placing us at early July in Yellow Springs Time.

1996: Summer finally settling in now. The rains that lasted through April and May and the first week of June are finally letting up a little bit. In the woods, everything is fresh and moist. The river is still high but starting to subside. Honewort, fire pink, white violets are common in the undergrowth. Parsnips and goat's beard full bloom along the highways. Catalpas dropped some of their flowers in the thunderstorm this afternoon. Butterflies are common, fireflies (which first appeared on the 9th) obvious now after dark. The first lilies were late, but appeared with the fireflies. Along the west border of the yard, first bloom of the giant white-flowered blue hosta.

1999: Maine: Middle May of Yellow Springs continues. First robin birdsong at 3:00 a.m. Flowers seen: Alpine azalea, field sorrel with reddish dock-like flowers and arrow shaped leaves, blue ocean lungwort-type of plant growing in rocks along the shore. Wide vistas of orange hawkweeds and golden buttercups.

2000: I got up late, about 5:30, the morning quiet, no chorus, no cardinals.

2001: Last bowl of strawberries from the home patch. This morning in the sun, dozens of red admiral and question mark butterflies, along with several buckeyes and fritillaries, clustered against the far west garden. This afternoon, soft pale lizard's tail flowers opened. Tonight, the first fireflies.

2002: Very last strawberry. Very first mallow.

2003: Larkspur opened yesterday in the north garden. By 6:00 this morning, only a few grackles calling in the back yard. First two fireflies of the year seen tonight about 9:30.

2004: First centipede appeared in the bathtub!

2005: First moonbeam coreopsis opens. New daylily, peach color, opens in the northeast garden. Birdsong vibrant and loud at 4:30 a.m. Full bloom: great blue hosta, heliopsis, coreopsis, oak-leaf hydrangea, sweet William (declining), penstemon, spirea, privet, candy lilies.

2007: Catbird heard in the back yard before sunrise. Raccoon or skunk dug up five coleus plants from around the redbud tree overnight. Also broke into the garbage can and scattered food around. In the shed, it shredded the thistle seed bag and scattered seeds on the floor.

2009: Great blue hosta flowers opened today.

2010: Some corn is up to my chest on the way to Xenia. Another dozen raspberries this morning! One butterfly bush on the corner of Davis and High Streets is in bloom, but our bushes are only budded. Peas ready to eat in our garden, lettuce holding. The tips of the spring growth on the raspberries have wilted on many plants, but there is no sign of a fungus or insects.

2011: Crickets have been calling ever since we got home on June 8th, the first year I've noticed them this early in town, local northern spring field crickets most likely. As I prepared the north side of the house for paint touchup this afternoon, I found two praying mantises, about an inch long, thin as ichneumons, running across the siding.

2012: Robins and starlings taking care of fledglings through the morning and afternoon, cardinals calling all day, and at dusk. Five squirrels squabbling over a hole in the box elder tree at the back of the house. Along Dayton Street, Peggy's Russian sage is blooming now, probably about a week since it started. Midseason hostas (which often bloom just after July 4, have budded. Apples half size in the alley. Only a few of Don's pie cherries are left, very dark red. In the yard, the yucca holds at late full bloom. Half a dozen dahlias have opened so far, and the zinnias are at about a full dozen. Along Dayton-Yellow Springs Road, most of the thistle blossoms have turned to down.

2014: The yellow (rebloomer) daylilies in the circle garden are just starting to come in. Along Dayton Street, the serviceberries are turning red at about the same rate as the pie cherries. Several hosta, large and small, budded, one ready to open. Queen Anne's lace also budding. I continue to transplant zinnias and lilies into the circle garden.

2015: A little after sunrise, the sparrows came flocking to the feeder, several dozen, chirping and chirping. The far-west, deep orange daylily bloomed overnight, two of the huge Orientals in the north garden by the peach tree, and another pale yellow rebloomer in the circle garden. Nine different patches of lilies starting to come in now: the count begins. The great blue hosta buds are ready to open at the northwest corner of the house. The surviving two hibiscus plants, one on each side of the porch, are a couple feet tall. The scraggly amaranth patch near the pond is finally filling in, could end up being lush and beautiful.

2016: Large camel cricket in the tub this morning. At least fifty lily blossoms this morning, another pink and violet day lily, numerous Stella d'oros, at least a dozen ditch lilies. The penstemon was about gone this morning (still strong in some village gardens), and the insects had returned to the phlox despite the dusting. Riding to Jill's on Davis Street, I looked up to see black walnuts the size of cherries – reminding me that I had seen buckeyes a little bigger than that a few days ago. And I saw the first yucca opening, early white campion open. Along Greene Street, cottonwood cotton in the street, tucked against the curbs by the wind. Yesterday, a catalpa tree by the Xenia bike path was still in full bloom, but all the catalpas in Yellow Springs have dropped their flowers. Fireflies abundant in the back yard tonight, the air humid and warm.

2017: Storms circling. Forty Stella d'oro blossoms, seven Asiatics. Half a dozen small bumblebees working the spiderwort this morning.

2018: One red admiral butterfly at the hummingbird feeder, circling and circling and then landing and drinking a long time. The very first milkweed flower opened today, ditch lilies multiplying to 18, Stella d'oros 13, rebloomers 2, pale pink

Asiatics 3. On Elm Street, buckeyes are the size of the end of my thumb. Grackles and sparrows continue their Pentecost feeding and calling. A red housefinch seen pursued by two of its fledglings. Brad Roof reported that he saved a large mud turtle from the middle of the road last week. Peter Hayes said he'd stopped to save a box turtle in similar circumstances. Static from tree crickets from first light through the afternoon.

2019: Sun and near record cold this morning. One mauve day lily, two Stella d'oros, one ditch lily unraveling. The birds feed steadily now, fledglings begging.

2020: Another cool day, high barometric pressure remaining unusually stable. Ten pond iris, seven Stella d'oro lilies in bloom. Birds feed steadily, but few fledglings seen. Small green-gold bottle flies, an occasional bee fly and bumblebee, numerous honeybees explore the spiderwort. Only a couple of cabbage white butterflies throughout the day. Large-leafed early hostas seen in bloom along Dayton Street.

2021: Cool morning in the upper 50s. Lily counting season has begun: five orange ditch lilies, four Stella d'oros. Three pond iris in bloom and two azure butterflies seen, several cabbage whites, two daddy longlegs. Small, hairy, marble-size Osage fruits fallen to the sidewalk.

2022: Heat wave deepens. Severe thunderstorms last night, record high of 95 today. Sierra's ditch lilies are opening across the street, mine still holding back.

*In such moments, as today's, when you've been called upon to map an hour of time, you must remember that everyone else is here in the city with you. There is no one flying overhead looking to rescue you, or orient you, or to later provide you with a map of an aerial view. There is no one to make a note of it if you give up and remain lost. You are the witness. You.*

Bonnie Nadzam

## *June 15th*
## *The 166th Day of the Year*

*Instinctively summer is accepted as the normal condition of the earth, winter as the abnormal. Summer is 'the way it should be.' It is as though our minds subconsciously returned to some tropical beginning, some summer-filled Garden of Eden.*

Edwin Way Teale

Sunrise/set: 5:06/8:05
Day's Length: 14 hours 59 minutes
Average High/Low: 82/61
Average Temperature: 71
Record High: 96 – 1897
Record Low: 47 – 1933

### *Weather*

Temperatures remain hot most of the time: four years in ten bring highs in the 90s, and five in ten bring 80s. Cool temperatures in the 70s or 60s share the remaining ten percent. The heat may contribute to making today one of the three June days most susceptible to a thunderstorm (the 2nd and the 20th are the other two). Rain falls 55 percent of the time. After the showers, the sky clears up eight years in ten.

### *The Weather of the Week Ahead*

The likelihood of rain diminishes this week of the year, and the period brings at least four days that historically are favorable for field work. Chances of completely overcast conditions decline to less than 20 percent. The 16th, 17th, and 18th have a very low incidence of rainfall (just 20 percent chance of showers), and chances on the 21st are only 30 percent. Two days this week are often rainy; however,; today and 20th have better than a 50 percent chance of thunderstorms. Temperatures are usually warm, with only 35 percent of the afternoon highs remaining below 80 degrees. Hot 90s occur at least 20 percent of the time. Lows are in the 60s the majority of nights, but nighttime 50s and 40s occur up to 40 percent of the time.

## *The Natural Calendar*

As Early Summer deepens, the days are the longest of the year, and mulberries and black raspberries are sweetest. Milkweed beetles look for milkweed flowers on the longest days; giant cecropia moths emerge. The first monarch butterfly caterpillars eat the carrot tops.

Damselflies and daddy longlegs are everywhere in brambles along the rivers when mulberries and black raspberries come in. Mosquitoes, chiggers, and ticks have reached their summer strength in the deep woods. Long, black cricket hunters hunt crickets in the garden.

Two out of three parsnips, angelicas and hemlocks are going to seed. Multiflora roses and Japanese honeysuckles are dropping petals. But wingstem and tall coneflower stalks are five feet high. Virginia creeper is flowering. Canadian thistles and nodding thistles are at their best. Blackberries have set fruit. The very first trumpet vines sport bright red-orange trumpets, and the first yuccas, Deptford pink and first great mullein come into bloom.

## *Daybook*

1982: Hail, some up to an inch in diameter, fell today in a storm.

1983: First firefly.

1984: At Wilberforce, chicory is finally open. South Glen: Most white-flowered waterleaf is suddenly gone. Seed clusters have formed on the Jack-in-the-pulpit, and white violets are disappearing. First moneywort seen, first tall meadow rue. Timothy is sweet and tender. There are bud clusters on the milkweed. Some parsnips have rusted, gone to seed. Geese seen with big fat goslings. Small box turtle on the woods path. Buds on the touch-me-nots. Brown seeds falling from the small flowered crowfoot. Wild ginger still in bloom. Young woodchuck, frightened by my approach, climbed a tree to escape me, hung there above my head looking at me like a raccoon.

1986: Red berries on the King Street honeysuckles now.

1988: Very last strawberries from the garden eaten today, and a dozen black raspberries. First firefly came out tonight, delayed by the drought.

1990: Cherries and mulberries ready for pies. My mouth waters, and I am excited.

1993: Most garden daisies in Yellow Springs and most hawthorn flowers are past their prime. The wild thin-leafed daisies in the pastures, however, are still in full bloom. Full bloom of coreopsis throughout town. First carnations open, first chicory and Queen Anne's lace blossoming along the southern highway, first catnip on Dayton Street, first tall blanket flower in the south garden. Yellow tiger swallowtail in the pink sweet Williams. Daisy fleabane under the cherry tree is in full bloom. Peppermint found along the high path at Clifton Gorge, has been out for weeks, beginning to fade. Large patches of fire pink along that walk, and orange poison ivy flowers.

1995: St. Louis to Salina, Kansas, heading west towards Columbia, Missouri: The roadside vegetation remains relatively stable, generally "Midwestern" (a week or two ahead of Yellow Springs) with Queen Anne's lace, yellow and white sweet clover, crown vetch, daisy fleabane, yellow and white moth mullein, dogbane, milkweed, chicory, white bindweed in full bloom. Huge compass plant, four to six feet tall, seen near Columbia and beyond. Into Kansas, the landscape changes quickly, the number of trees and clovers dwindling, and the vegetation becoming predominantly grasses. The green of the wheat starts to pale as we drive west, and crops were still being planted throughout the Plains.

1998: Queen Anne's lace opens. Neysa reports tadpoles swimming in the water at the Alhambra in Granada, Spain.

2002: First yellow daylilies coming in. Big blue hosta blooms. The first pale-leafed Japanese iris and the first lizard's tail blossoms in the pond.

2003: First Frances Williams hosta, first big blue hosta, first Heliopsis, first red lilies flowered today.

2004: The first purple coneflower is opening in the north garden today. They have been blooming at the Women's Park for about a week. Mallow now in full bloom, and lilies gathering momentum. Oakleaf hydrangea anchors the northwest corner of the garden with its white flowers. Hollyhocks are out throughout the village. Kousa dogwood flowers disappearing in the triangle park.

2007: Blue jays feeding their young in the back yard today – grackles, sparrows, robins and jays all with fledglings in the second week of June.

2008: Red-bellied woodpecker called early in the morning. The first mallow opened overnight. The first wild orange lily and the first chicory seen on the way from Clifton. At Clifton Gorge, honewort was going to seed, clustered snakeroot mostly gone to seed, a few white waterleaf flowers (most gone), berries on Solomon's plume, just a few white violets left, some fire pink seen in bloom.

2009: To Santee in South Carolina: Hemlock all to seed below Cincinnati. Trumpet creeper in bloom near Lexington, Kentucky. Mimosa trees blooming from central Kentucky south. At Santee, maybe a hundred miles from Charleston, the corn was tall and lush, ears fully formed, the first time in several years the crop has looked so good when we arrived in middle June. Watermelon festival announcement heard on the radio. We have driven down into the middle of Yellow Springs July. Heal-all blooming along the dock, mayflies everywhere, especially at dusk. Two geese with four fuzzy goslings (boot-size) swam by a little after 8:00.

2010: First avens seen flowering in Mateo's yard and in the alley this morning. First mallow opened in the north garden, and a few monarda blossoms are developing. Very last primrose by the roses. Trumpet creeper vine seen in full bloom along Dayton-Yellow Springs Road this afternoon. Storms in the night, the yard soggy, standing water in some the properties along Dayton Street.

2012: Yucca drooping now, Stella d'oros past their peak. All Don's pie cherries gone. Monarda reaching early bloom. Primroses hold full.

2013: Spoleto, Italy: The fragrance of jasmine in full bloom fills the entire city, has been growing stronger and stronger since I arrived at the end of May. Behind Neysa and Ivano's studio, a small pie cherry tree is full of cherries that are getting soft. There have been no birds here to eat them. Beside the cherry, a persimmon tree with small fruits about half the size of an acorn. Ivano said that the fruit is ripe after all the persimmon leaves have fallen in the autumn.

2014: Snow-on-the-mountain almost completely seeded now. The first ditch lilies (*Hemerocallis fulva*) coming into bloom at Petty's and Moya's, the latest I think I have recorded the start of their season. Heliopsis seen full early bloom as I drove down Corry Street. At South Glen: Leafcup budded, honewort aging, lush jewelweed, wood nettle dominating the forest floor, getting ready to flower (nettle and honewort sharing the landscape, the rough and the delicate), aging violet-flowered waterleaf, a daisy fleabane, a few scattered sweet rockets. Pales moths flutter from the foliage as I pass. At home, only two cabbage butterflies, two blues and a glimpse of a black swallowtail.

2015: In the middle of days of heat and rain, the annuals surge. The first orange tithonia (sprouted up in the attic during February) opened in last night's storm. Webworms are crawling around in their webs on Peggy's cherry tree. The castor bean has grown a foot in 48 hours. The reluctant amaranth and the hesitant zinnias no longer hold back. Eleven clumps of lilies in bloom: mostly Stella d'oros, ditch lilies, rebloomers and trumpet lilies. One blue chicory seen on the way to Beavercreek, drifts of Canadian thistles fresh and pink, a few more great mulleins.

2016: Walking with Emily from 6:30 in the North Glen, robins and cardinals and doves and house wrens filling the air as I walked out of the house. At the Glen parking lot, I heard a screech owl, and when Emily arrived, she found it in her binoculars, and I saw my first one, so blue in the trees. As we made the loop around the yellow spring, we heard green frogs, and many different birds including chipping sparrows, Carolina wrens, red-bellied woodpeckers, pileated woodpeckers, chickadees, indigo buntings, pee-wees, a red-shouldered hawk and we got close to an Acadian Flycatcher – my very first. Its call was so distinct, a firm and sharp two-note song.  In the undergrowth, moneywort was in full bloom near the river. Honewort was going to seed. One ragwort still had a few flowers. Along the road south to Xenia, some hemlock already gone to seed, new bright birdsfoot trefoil, banks of crown vetch, parsnips nodding.

2017: Thirty-three ditch lily blossoms, forty-three Stella d'oros, seven Asiatics, four everbloomers. A few cabbage whites, a handful of small bumblebees with legs gold with pollen. The purple coneflowers in the northwest garden are barely starting to unravel. Several Osage fruits have fallen to the sidewalk from the wind and rain. Small black beetles with black wings flying near the porch. In the countryside, the wheat is a rich orange brown. A long patch of nodding thistles in bloom, some to seed, past Fairborn. The lawns are white with clover now, and the great blue-leafed hostas are in full bloom.

2018: Tree crickets buzzing all around today. The red admiral has come for a second day of sugar water from the hummingbird feeder. And around 10:00 this morning, I saw my first female Eastern black swallowtail of the year, shyly moving in and out of the honeysuckles. Another swallowtail seen briefly this afternoon. The birds seem quieter today, far less of the frantic chirping and scrawing of the past few days.

2019: Only three Stella d'oro lilies open today, no others in the garden. On Davis Street, we found the yucca plant in full flower. Buckeyes on the tree near the grade school are the size of a marble. From Madison, Wisconsin, Tat sends a photo of a large turtle laying eggs near the lake and said she saw one crossing the road about ten days ago.

2020: Thirteen Stella d'oros today, nine deep purple pond iris. When I was cutting back bamboo near the south wall, I surprised a sizable grass snake that had a fat, male American toad halfway in its mouth. On the way to Ellis Pond, I saw great mullein in bloom by the side of the road.

2021: Sixteen ditch lilies, four Stella d'oro lilies in bloom. Two pond iris. And a great spangled fritillary came by, the first large butterfly I've seen this year. A young rabbit, the size of a small kitten, explores the north yard these mornings. I got the first chigger bites of the season this afternoon. Honeysuckle flower-drop is over now.

2022: Elderberries full flower on the way to Fairborn. The great blue hostas are blooming in the dooryard and by the back porch. From Goshen, Judy reports: "We had TWO geese parades this morning: one early, with little ones ranging from advanced fluffball to nearly-feathered, and one just now, with adolescents very nearly grown and looking very pleased with themselves. A treat! 22 in the first parade, 14 in the second. I talked with them, of course, and they seemed pleased with the praise."

*On earth and only on earth are sunset glow, green leaf, and eyes to see them. Here is all we know of reality, all-sufficient to our destiny, our thoughts and passions.*

Donald Culross Peattie\

## *June 16th*
## *The 167th Day of the Year*

*The day, immeasurably long, sleeps over the broad hills and warm wide fields. To have lived through all its sunny hours seems longevity enough.*

Ralph Waldo Emerson

Sunrise/set: 5:06/8:06
Day's Length: 15 hours
Average Hi/Lo: 82/61
Average Temperature: 71
Record High: 96 – 1897
Record Low: 42 – 1908

### *Weather*
Today is clear to partly sunny 90 percent of the time, with rain arriving one day out of four. Today is also the first day of a three-day period on which relatively little precipitation occurs. Highs are typically in the middle 80s (65 percent chance), with hot 90s occurring 15 percent of the years, 70s fifteen percent, and cold 60s just five percent. After today, chances of a high below 70 drop to less than five percent (except for three scattered days in July and August) at average elevations along the 40th Parallel until the first week of September.

### *Natural Calendar*
Inside the four major seasonal categories lie clusters of hidden parallel and interlocking seasons that measure and define time inside of time, creating by their colors and shapes and sounds and tastes and smells the broader temporal landscapes.

The final floral and faunal constellations of the Sun's residence in Gemini collect fragments of Late Spring and Early Summer, foretell Deep Summer and the sign of Cancer. Each fragment is a landstar, a separate season within galaxies of objects and events.

Late May's clovers still sweeten pastures and lawns. Meadow goat's beard and chicory stand by the roads. The first wild daisies give way to Shasta daisies that last to July. Gaunt yuccas compete with new great mulleins. Common fleabane cedes to daisy fleabane.

The orange day lilies (ditch lilies) are the crown of June, easy transitions to the Asiatic and Oriental lilies and the multicolored day lilies that bloom under the Dog Star, Sirius. Pink spirea and an assortment of hydrangeas last beyond the longest days. Smartweed replaces chickweed between garden furrows. Queen Anne's lace and black-eyed Susans foretell the heat of August's Leo. Milkweed opens for the deliberate, venal milkweed beetles. Lizard's tail dips to the rivers and ponds. The compass plant follows the Sun, spreading its blossoms above the nettles.

All these creatures are glimpses of a homely universe as well as reminders of what is not visible or is not noticed. A land star metaphor is less an exaggeration or distortion than a suggestion about an astronomy and astrology of place. The space and time between Sirius and lilies, like the space between lilies and spirit, is not as great as it might seem. As above, so below. As below, so above.

### *Daybook*

1980: Some cherries red enough for pie. Raspberries are turning now.

1982: Yucca stems tall, buds large. Chicory is finally ready to open.

1983: Catalpas full bloom along Fairfield Pike and the north highway. Japanese honeysuckle noticed in bloom.

1984: Mock orange completely gone. Yuccas open in Cincinnati, catalpas done there. No chicory flowering in Yellow Springs, gradually coming into bloom about 30 miles south of here.

1986: Some Canadian thistles going to seed, an occasional burdock ready to flower. First webworms noticed in a crab apple. First scarlet pimpernel found.

1987: Canadian and nodding thistles starting to seed.

1988: On the road east and then south, miles of blue chicory. Milkweed, only budding in Yellow Springs, was open on the other side of Indianapolis. Great mullein coming in south towards the Illinois border. Butterfly weed full bloom in southern Illinois. All thistles gone to seed below St. Louis. First blackberries were starting to turn in southern Illinois, red in northern Georgia. Elderberries, in flower all across the Midwest, were setting fruit near Atlanta. Wild lettuce was in bloom from there all the way to Florida. Horseweed open in Jacksonville, cattails completely developed.

1990: Red monarda seen in bloom throughout town.

1993: First pale-leafed hosta open on Stafford Street. Hawthorn blossoms deteriorate all at once. First carnation blooms. Yellow tiger swallowtails visiting the bright sweet Williams.

1995: From Salina, Kansas to Rawlins, Wyoming: The flat high prairie continues as we climb from 1,000 to 5,000 feet into Denver. The Midwestern flora gives way to sagebrush and yucca. Yucca is blooming in Salina as well as in Denver (like in Yellow Springs now). But we found a patch of dandelions at a rest stop near Denver: the first sign so far of seasonal regression (two months!) due to altitude.

1996: First bright orange lychnis opened in the south garden this afternoon. Cherries ripening on the dying cherry tree (its leaves yellowing and thinning now). Black raspberries still hard and green.

1998: The garden chard has fully developed as the last of the spring lettuce is used up. Twelve feet of it is giving us three times what we can use. Yucca is blooming now. Foxglove flowers end. First magenta fringed loosestrife opens. Asiatic lilies starting. Pink hollyhocks opening.

1999: Maine: Lupines getting old here and there. Privet budding in Bar Harbor.

2001: Blue Asiatic dayflowers open this morning at Susi's. First black raspberry ripe in the garden. First heliopsis opened. Purple veronica coming in. Full bloom of tea roses, yucca, primrose, water willow, yellow daylily, pink achillea, late lamb's ear, violet Asiatic lilies.

2003: First hollyhock, pale pink, opened today. Yucca stalks tall but not open yet. The dusky blue peach-leaved bellflowers have ended their season at the same time that the sweet Williams are quickly seeding.

2004: The month-long wet spell continues, showers almost every day or night. First Japanese beetles found on the ferns. First rust noticed on the ferns along the north wall. As I walked down High Street with Bella, a small, green Osage fruit, maybe two inches in diameter, fell from a tree onto the sidewalk and broke in half.

2005: Jeanie got the first chigger bites of the year today, about five days later than the earliest years.

2007: A few black raspberries seen in the far alleyway.

2008: From Yellow Springs to Santee-Cooper Reservoir, South Carolina: Thistles and hemlock seeding near Lexington, Kentucky. Mimosa trees flowering from middle Kentucky all the way to Santee, thick as redbuds in April along I-26 in some places. A few last large-flowered magnolias in Carolina, full white crepe myrtles in full bloom at a rest stop below Columbia, full rose of Sharon throughout. Wheat has all been cut at Santee, and roadside grasses have turned like the wheat south of the mountains, corn crop shriveled in the reservoir, mocking birds singing through the day.

2009: Santee, South Carolina: Osprey feeding young in the cypress. Black tadpoles in the shallows, violet star grass, pond lilies or floating heart (small-flowered water lilies). Narrow leafed willow herb on Ferguson Island. A four-petaled white houstonia/bluette, madder family, sprawling, opposite, entire, four long pistils. Geese with a flock of half-grown, fully marked goslings. All the catfish full of roe, the exuberance of the habitat, overbrimming with death and life. The night so loud I kept waking up, toads calling, shrieking. At the campground, five-petaled, yellow water primrose, alternate entire leaves, closes at dusk.

2010: The first blossoms opened on the butterfly bush in the circle garden overnight. The first purple coneflower is unraveling in the north garden. Black raspberries are dark and sweet in the alley.

2011: The first purple coneflower is unraveling in the north garden, and the first pink smartweed is in bloom by the lilies. At the park, the linden tree is in late full bloom, and catalpas still blooming throughout the area. The butterfly bush is budded but not close to opening. The first two hummingbirds visited the feeders this afternoon. Several yellow swallowtails and hackberry browns in the high trees. Rob said the browns have just come out. Across the countryside to Columbus: wheat is golden green. The few planted fields show corn two or three inches high. Hemlock is almost all to seed in the roadsides, yellow sweet clover full, parsnips still bright. Some privets in bloom along High Street.

2012: The yuccas are gone now, here and throughout the village. In the east garden, the Stella d'oros are almost done. More purple coneflowers coming in, Queen Anne's lace full, very tall. Alley knotweed eight feet and full bloom. A few raspberries still coming in, blackberry fruit set, mulberries still hold. Peas should have been picked last week. Astilbes are still providing color between the hostas. Red phlox, the earliest of the summer phloxes, are opening. Primroses holding. More dahlias coming in, huge splotches of color at random along the garden wall. Zinnias reaching early bloom, starting to provide a balance to the loss of the blue salvia. Wheat dark, still not being cut here. Some cardinal and sparrow fledglings during the day, cardinals singing, some starlings scrawing, but overall, the day was much quieter than yesterday. Cottonwood cotton season seems to be over at Lawson Place. On my evening walk, a field sparrow was singing, but the robins and cardinals weren't calling. First earwig found in the house about a week ago.

2013: Spoleto, Italy: A walk with Neysa and Ivano in a river valley, lined with high cliffs, along a bike path made from the old Spoleto-Nurcia rail line right-of-way. A lush habitat of wildflowers, including the first time in Italy that I have seen yellow sweet clover, and catchweed all to seed (just like in Yellow Springs); clematis vines (without flowers or buds); many stinging nettles and a variety of wood nettle; one germander plant in full bloom; many blackberries budding and flowering; a variety of thistles, including *Silybum Marianum Gaertu* and many small-flowered *Cirisium vulgare ten* or *Cirisium arvense scop*; a delicate *Ombrellifere*, very much like caraway, probably *Anthriscus cerefolium Hoffm*; a type of vervain budded, just starting to open; an abundance of bluebell *Campanulacee;* numerous pale violet *Hellanthemum cistacaeae;* linden trees with seeds, and exuding sap on top of Ivano's car; walnut trees with half-inch to inch- size fruits, looking very much like the fruits of Yellow Springs black walnuts – and at the same stage of development. On the way home, I noticed a catalpa tree in full flower. And as I walked, I was surrounded by flowers I didn't recognize, framed by the plants that I did know, everything fitting in, with or without a name, around the landmarks from home.

2014: The first ditch lily opened in the yard overnight. The first yucca flowers seen along Fairfield Pike, must have just opened today. Black walnuts are an inch in diameter, bittersweet berries the size of BBs in the alley. Eleven lily plants (Stella d'oro, Asiatic and "Ditch") flowering. Wild onions, three feet tall, seed bulbs unraveling. Serviceberries red and falling, pie cherries almost gone.

2015: Yellow Springs to Santee-Cooper Reservoir, Santee, South Carolina: An almost immediate change as my nephew John and I drove southeast this morning. Near Chillicothe, dark wheat, pink spirea losing color, full bloom potentilla, elderberry bushes mostly gone to berries, cattail spikes more prominent among their leaves, roadsides of chicory and daisy fleabane. Parsnips and hemlock mostly gone to seed, large round bales of golden hay in several fields.

Into West Virginia, the vegetation returned to Yellow

Springs levels, then quickly moved into Deep Summer in North Carolina: Mimosa trees and crepe myrtles were in full bloom in central North Carolina. Teasel was tall, milkweed in full bloom. There were fields of ditch lilies and many Stella d'oros, Queen Anne's lace, horseweed, nodding and Canadian thistles, black-eyed Susans, trumpet creeper and bright butterfly weed as we drove farther toward Charlotte. When we reached Santee, I found the corn fully developed, peanuts maybe eight inches high. At the canal, I found my first greater coreopsis. Heat to 103 degrees late in the afternoon, water temperature 76. Mother mallard and two ducklings (about a fourth grown) swam by our fishing spot.

2016: To Xenia: Moth mullein, sow thistles and chicory were in full bloom along the roadsides. I must have missed them days ago. I saw the first Shasta daisies open south on Xenia Avenue, and the first one of mine has just stretched out a couple of petals. A milkweed plant along Dayton-Yellow Springs Road seen with pink flower heads. Twenty-four lily plants in bloom this morning, Stella d'oros and ditch lilies with two everbloomers and one violet-pink standard day lily. One earwig floating in the birdbath.

2017: Stella d'oro lilies and ditch lilies at twenty-nine blossoms each, three bright yellow everbloomers, still nine Asiatics. Milkweed buds showing color. One monarda open here and at Jill's.

2018: Jill found the first purple coneflower and the first monarda in bloom on our evening walk. Down High Street at about 7:00 this evening we came upon a noisy flock of grackles around a small, solitary hawk, perhaps a red-shouldered hawk or Cooper's hawk. After a few minutes they drove it away and followed in pursuit. A humid evening walk, crescent moon high in the west, sky aquamarine, Venus in the northwest, fireflies all about.

2019: More heavy rain throughout the night. Two robin fledglings seen on my walk with Ranger before sunrise. Five Stella d'oro lilies open this morning, no day lilies or ditch lilies, and the heliopsis is unraveling. I noticed that the drooping buds of the lizard's tail have formed near the pond. Several purple coneflowers noticed blooming in town. Half an hour north of Yellow Springs, the rolling hills around Troy have wheat fields all golden. One field seen with corn knee high – but there were many patches where the corn had been lodged by the wind and rain.

2020: High pressure continues, barometer at 30.35 for the fourth day, mild and breezy. Thirteen Stella d'oro lilies open this morning, five Japanese pond iris, the first two ditch lilies and the large blue-leafed hosta in the west garden bloomed in the yard, and the first heliopsis flower unraveled all the way. First milkweed bug found in the milkweed. Very small rabbits seen in the Limestone Street alley, and two at home in the yard. Fireflies flickering after sundown through the neighborhood.

From Goshen, Indiana, Judy sends the following: "Writing to say that we had a parade of nearly 20 geese this morning, and it's now difficult to tell the young ones from the parents. Some of them are quite aggressive, snaking their necks out and trying to bully the others."

From pairing off in early March to having fledglings almost adult size, the geese have progressed right on schedule.

2021: Thirty-five ditch lilies, three Stella d'oros and only one water iris this morning, and the first yellow heliopsis bud opened all the way in the night. As I walked the garden, a large orange butterfly sped past me, a fritillary or a *Poligonia*.

2022: The night is humid and warm. I am not able to hear crickets (that must be there), but the yard is full of fireflies, more than I've seen at one time in years.

*I stood there watching the wind ripple and wave through the grain, a sea of green animated with constant, unceasing movement, swirling about my waist as if alive, following no pattern of movement but waving now this way, now that, filled with an eternal surging restlessness, a great stirring of life, rustling in its undulations, and I thought of it as a symbol of life itself: the heavy heads holding the staff of life, bending and swaying in the warm south wind.*

August Derleth

## *June 17th*
## *The8th Day of the Year*

*Trompin' home acrost the fields: Lightnin'-bugs a blinkin'*
*In the wheat like sparks o'things a feller keeps a think-in.*

James Whitcomb Riley

Sunrise/set: 5:06/8:06
Day's Length: 15 hours
Average Hi/Lo: 82/61
Average Temperature: 72
Record High: 96 – 1936
Record Low: 43 – 1899

### *Weather*

Today is generally a mild day with a good chance of a high in the cool 70s, the second greatest chance (50 percent) all month. Eighties come 40 percent of the time, 90s ten percent. Rain falls just one year in four on this date, and the sun appears nine years in a decade.

### *Natural Calendar*

Now mulberries, plump and sweet, fill the last days of Early Summer. It's high noon of the year, the peak of Black Raspberry Season, Goose Molting Season, the commencement of Corn Borer Season, the center of Timothy Season and Fledgling Season, the end of Asparagus and Rhubarb Seasons, the first of Sweet-corn-tassel Season.

Delphinus follows Cygnus in the east after 10:00 p.m., Altair, the bright star of Aquila shining below them. Just ahead of Cygnus, Vega leads the Milky Way west. Overhead, Arcturus moves into the western half of the sky, the Corona Borealis coming in to take its place. Libra lies due south, July's Scorpius right behind it.

Early risers see the sky the way it will look on a late September night: the Milky Way overhead, the Great Square covering most of the southeast, huge Cygnus shifting west, following bright Vega. June's Corona Borealis will be setting now, and the first sign of winter, Aldebaran of the constellation Taurus, will have just emerged in the northeast.

### *Daybook*

1982: First red berries noticed on the honeysuckle.

1983: First Queen Anne's lace seen on Dayton Street. Strawberries coming in steadily. First black raspberry.

1984: Panicled dogwood blooms on King Street. A few last bleeding hearts remain at home. First small dish of black raspberries picked from our brambles. First sow thistle blooming in the alley. Purple cow vetch open now in a field.

1986: Mullein and pokeweed bloomed today in the yard. First yucca opened in the village. A question mark butterfly, wings stretched out to the sun, sat on the garden wall. There are two or three generations of that species born each summer; this is one of the first. At Jacoby, the first leafcup has opened, first dogbane and black-eyed Susan seen. Deptford pink found. Enchanter's nightshade was budding. The great skunk cabbage, so lush and heavy a month ago, was weathered, eaten by insects. Watercress sprawling, pale, in the pools. Old yellow garlic mustard colored the woods floor a dull gray-green. Deep Summer's avens full bloom in the sun.

1989: Catalpas still keep their flowers. Chicory open in places. Only one or two fireflies. Blueweed and feverfew noticed in full bloom.

1990: The last of the strawberry crop at home.

1991: Caesar Creek: Today a blue butterfly followed me, sat on my hand, two small orange spots on its exterior wings, one orange spot on the inner edge. Only a few of the red periodic cicadas (Brood XIV that had emerged in much of the Ohio Valley) were left. I saved one from the water about 2:30. Large pink wild roses were in full bloom at my fishing hole.

1992: First black raspberry and last strawberry eaten. The front garden changing. Astilbe has its color now, and the blue veronicas are coming in, the purple coneflower three feet tall and budding. In the south garden, the coreopsis are all open, solid gold, the red-orange lychnis full beside them, mallow tall and budding, balloon flowers, zinnias, and gay feathers budding. The first cosmos opened completely. The first lilies are opening along the north hedge. In the village, catalpas still hold.

1993: All strawberries gone, first black raspberry reddening.

1995: Rawlins, Wyoming north to Yellowstone Park in the northwest corner of Wyoming: Lilacs and iris seen blooming at 6,100 feet in Lander. Fields of dandelions appeared between 7,000 and 7,600 feet, the higher the elevation, the better the April Yellow Springs bloom. Blue upland larkspur common at 7,000 feet and above. At a rest stop, 7,800 feet, heartleaf arnica found, like a yellow bloodroot. Small-flowered buttercup here too, and my first scarlet globe mallow. Wild strawberries blooming at the lodge in Yellowstone. All around the park, huge yellow sunflower-like flowers on a short plant with big leaves: mule's ear wyethia.

1998: Astilbe has lost its color quickly. Flickers and blue jays calling. Cardinals and doves still sing before dawn. I am getting up too late to check the morning robin chorus.

1999: Asticou Gardens, Maine: Azaleas lingering, rhododendrons already gone. Columbine, forget-me-not, pink spirea starting, delicate cutleaf *Stephanadra incisa*, blue speedwell, white water lily, the end of the thin-leafed red bleeding heart. Coral bells in bloom. At Jordon Pond, yellow loosestrife, *lysimachia* and blue *baptisia.*

2001: First mallow shows pink. First buds on the gooseneck. Last year's parsley gone to seed. Francis William hosta and great blue hosta come into bloom.

2002: Arrowhead leaves are starting to form at the edge of the pond.

2003: More lilies starting: a pink one on the west end of the garden, another orange on the east end.

2004: Periodic cicadas are still calling but are dying in greater numbers now along the bike path. In the north garden, the mid-season hostas are budding, the August Moon hosta has bloomed, the Joe Pye is heading. Maybe this year – because of the heat and rain, and the plants being at least a week ahead of schedule – the annual cicadas will come out just as the periodic cicadas all die off. First chigger bites in the garden.

2006: Tree of heaven is in full bloom throughout town, dropping flowers, spreading pollen. Yesterday, the first of the pale yellow Asiatic lilies opened. A few serviceberries noticed, some red, some black. On the high branches of the spruce trees in the alley, pine cones about five inches long. Panicled dogwood flowers gone.

2007: No Japanese beetles or chiggers yet. Yarrow full. Primrose completely gone. Full oak-leaf hydrangea, lizard's tail and great blue hosta. A few monarda plants becoming red at the top. Purple coneflowers gathering momentum, green-eyed Susans full bloom and strong. Yuccas full bloom in Xenia. Parsnips still golden in the fields along the bike path. First earwig seen yesterday. A monarch butterfly came to the garden at noon. Japanese honeysuckle still fragrant. Great mullein flowering in Fairborn, hemlock going to seed quickly in the roadsides.

2010: Trumpet creeper vines in full bloom throughout town and countryside. The wheat is a deep gold along Grinnell Road. First hackberry butterfly and another admiral seen today.

2011: Cardinals, doves, robins, jays, sparrows, grackles through the morning. One skipper, one hackberry brown, one hummingbird by 9:00 a.m.

2012: Soft rain shower at 7:30 this morning, the air thick and warm. Highs in the 90s forecast for today and every day of the week ahead. In the evening, some standing water at Don's yard after several thunder storms passed through. At Peggy's, early purple coneflowers parallel the bloom of early Russian sage. Lamb's ear there is holding but getting old. In the countryside, black-eyed Susans common, thistledown increasing from the Canadian thistles, but bull thistles are still pink. Clustered bellflowers disappearing quickly. In the roadsides, all the hemlock pale and gone to seed, the hemlock perhaps as good a marker as any of the end of Early Summer. From Madison, Wisconsin, Tat says here monarda is in, and all her lilies in bloom – evidence that the warm year has treated Wisconsin like it has treated Ohio.

2013: Spoleto, Italy: Walk down the bike path for three hours: *Gallium verum (rubiacee)*; *Cirsium vulgare (composite)* and *Silybum marianum gaerti (composite)* positively identified, most plants gone to seed; scarlet pimpernel (*Annagallis arvensis*) found, some with orange flowers, some with blue, a similar, purple flower found on a plant with alternate, toothed leaves, similar to wild geranium leaves; chicory and burdock found, not blooming; sweet pea and an early variety of virgin's bower climbing and flowering through the undergrowth; curly dock full of orange seeds; two real dandelions; coriander: other unidentified flowers: a summer cress with four white petals and alternate toothed leaves; soft violet puff ball flowers, about an inch across, leaves short, alternate, slightly toothed; small daisy-like *Asteraceae* with thin, string-like leaves; yellow *composite* with large center, short petals, basal leaves only; tall (three feet), prickly plant with five-petaled, pale violet flowers, alternate, pointed leaves – prickly like the stem, narrow pyramidal shape like a prickly foxglove.

2016: To Gethsemani near Louisville: Departing Yellow Springs at the height of ditch lily bloom, my plantings and all the plots around town coming in at once. The trumpet creeper that has climbed all across the porch and up to the roof of the greenhouse has bud clusters. The large hosta in the east garden has produced white flowers overnight. Across the countryside, some corn was neck-high. The orange ditch lilies at their peak remain a constant. Along the Kentucky highways, the wheat is no longer golden, there are many drifts of daisy fleabane in full flower, strips of white sweet clover, long rows of hemlock dying back (considerably ahead of southern Ohio), occasional black-eyed-Susans, a few blooming mimosa trees, and the two chestnut trees in the monastery enclosure full of starburst-like blossoms. Some wild daisies still in bloom here near the church.

2017: Stella d'oro lily blossoms and ditch lily blossoms tied at thirty-nine each. An abundance of fireflies tonight, the air warm and humid, the slightest breeze.

2018: The red admiral haunts the hummingbird feeder for the third day now. The grackles are still protective of their young, but the flurry of the past week seems to be over, the graduation or avian Pentecost complete for now. More purple coneflowers seen, these on Davis Street. In the yard, some Shasta daises and one deep orange day lily (the one in the far west portion of the garden) came in overnight. Strong buzzing of the tree crickets and an occasional field cricket chirping this morning. Throughout the village, deep orange butterfly weed is in full bloom, hydrangeas heavy, fat, white, melon-like. A bed of cup plant with foliage fully developed, stalks five-feet high, massive planting. This evening, Monk killed a young starling.

2019: More rain, no lilies blooming today.

2020: Three ditch lilies, nine Stella d'oro lilies, seven pond iris in bloom. One checkerspot butterfly, one cabbage white. One yucca plant in a Davis Street yard is full of blossoms.

2021: The counting-timing of summer continues: Thirty-eight ditch lilies, three Stella d'oros, no pond iris. The first hackberry butterfly of the season appeared in the garden this morning. Several azure butterflies passed through. Wheat is becoming dark brown on the way to Fairborn.

2022: Starlings are raucous this morning, chattering and flying back and forth, fledglings scrawing, another Pentecost coming-of-age celebration. On the sidewalk: black walnuts the size of acorns, fallen in the rain. In the east plantings, four Stella d'oro blossoms, the first lilies of the year in my yard. Quickweed is flowering around the new raspberry bushes. Two pond iris flowers open, the clump overrun by spreading phlox. Trumpet creeper with prominent buds above the porch. Cabbage white butterflies active in the north gardens. Webworms noticed in the trellis vines. A brief glimpse of a yellow tiger swallowtail as I sat on the back porch. Small thuja trees arrived in the mail, placed in wate; I was seduced by their soft juniper foliage, look forward to nurturing them in the greenhouse. This evening, I heard my first field cricket chirp in the spiderwort.

*I sense the adequacy of the world, and believe that everything I need is here. I do not strain after ambition or heaven. I feel no dependence on tomorrow. I do not long to travel to Italy or Japan, but only across the river or up the hill into the woods.*

Wendell Berry

## *June 18th*
## *The 169th Day of the Year*

*The heaven is now broad and open to the earth in these longest days. The world can never be more beautiful than now.*

Henry David Thoreau

Sunrise/set: 5:06/8:06
Day's Length: 15 hours
Average Hi/Lo: 82/61
Average Temperature: 72
Record High: 98 – 1944
Record Low: 47 – 1903

### *Weather*

Indicative of summer stability and the dominance of high pressure at this time of year, 65 percent of June 18ths are without rain, and the sun appears 90 percent of the years. Temperatures are mild: in the 70s thirty percent of the time, in the 80s sixty-five percent of the time, with just a five percent chance of 90s. Evening lows are usually in the 60s, with cold 50s occurring 30 percent of the years. A tornado threatens one year in 50 on this date.

### *Natural Calendar*

Some multiflora roses and Japanese honeysuckles are dropping petals now, but August's wingstem and tall coneflower stalks are five feet high. Virginia creeper is flowering. Many Canadian thistles and nodding thistles start to go to seed. Orchard grass is getting brown and old, English rye grass full bloom, exotic bottle grass late bloom, brome grass very late, but some timothy still tender. Throughout the Lower Midwest, winter wheat is gold or browning. Clustered snakeroot and honewort are seeding as avens and wood nettle begin their seasons. Bamboo grass has fresh growth, and July's wood mint is budding. In the Southeast, the kudzu vines are ready to blossom.

### *Daybook*

1982: Last pint of strawberries picked. First small dish of black raspberries. At South Glen, parsnips, angelica, yarrow and tall meadow rue still dominate the fields. Milkweed is starting to flower, first milkweed bugs discovered. Blueweed found in bloom along the railroad tracks, water horehound flowering in the swamp. Honewort strong in the woods.

1983: First black raspberry turning a light shade of red. Chicory bloomed today. Mulberries ripening. Quickweed is open in the garden. Peak of privet blossom. Three young groundhogs, maybe eight weeks old, seen along Grinnell Road.

1986: Cardinal sang at 4:04 a.m. First pokeweed opened.

1987: The 17-year cicadas disappeared as suddenly as they came, the woods quiet. In the yard, all the strawberries are gone, black raspberries peaking. North along the railroad tracks: first catmint seen in bloom, poison hemlock going to seed, leather flower identified – *Clematis viorna*, lush. At Caesar Creek three carp caught up the channel at Far Hole. Wild petunia seen at South Glen, timothy bearded with pollen, hemlock going to seed, water willow full bloom. Young geese half grown, moving in an extended family, four adults, five goslings. Groundhogs seen by the side of the road, a third grown. One indigo bunting identified. And I'm full of chiggers after a day walking.

1989: Walking South Glen, I left the path and wandered from one small glade to another. I felt a sense of intimacy with myself in those enclosures. The sun so hot, air still a little cool, but no breeze inside the hollows with their timothy and bottle grass, surrounded by thick Osage and honeysuckle. I was relieved to be isolated, out of sight, private in the sudden absence of the outside network, in the liberation of protecting woods.

1990: Veronica, astilbe, and coral bells full in the east garden. Four lilies have opened so far. One broccoli plant ready to eat. A few strawberries left. The very first black raspberry ripe. Privet flowers are gone. Primroses hold. Mallow is budding.

1991: Purple loosestrife blooms in the yard, probably a week earlier along the Ohio River in Switzerland County. First stag beetle came to the porch after dark.

1993: Black walnuts half an inch to an inch in diameter. Osage fruit, blown down in the storm last night, is maybe a fifth of its autumn size. Bing cherries found ripening at the south end of town.

1995: Yellowstone: Low elk thistle, field chickweed, cow parsnip, woodland strawberry, western cressleaf groundsel, glacier lily, water hemlock, common yellow monkey flower, violet goosefoot. Aspen leaves the size of my thumbnail.

1999: Bangor, Maine: Potentilla, tansy, early pink spirea open. Foxglove budding. White campion seen, strawberries ripening (their festival is June 26th, three weeks later than a Yellow Springs festival would be). In Vermont: deep green wheat.

2000: Portland, Oregon, and to Astoria and Cannon Beach, June 18th through the 21st: Litany of plants telling time: mid-season cow parsnip, Scotch broom (yellow pea-flower shrub) in full bloom. Tall pussy toes everywhere, tall buttercups, peonies and poppies at the ocean, late rhododendrons (Pacific rhododendrons) along Highway 26, full roses, clovers, alliums, small-leafed dock, yucca not blooming but ready, cattails just emerging, full yarrow, coastal thistles six-feet tall and budded, elderberry – many with fruit set, common purple vetch, seacoast lupine and wild purple foxglove very prominent, California poppies, chicory, redwood sorrel found, but not in bloom, goat's beard, early catalpas, Rugosa type "Wood's rose" full, thimbleberry shrubs in bloom, maybe a third had set fruit, full blackberry flowering season, *Rubus ursinus* and *Spirea densiflora* full, early teasel without blooms, white sweet clover, full moth mullein, Canadian thistle, Queen Anne's lace.

2001: First purple loosestrife, first avens. First pale blue-bodied dragonfly at the pond. Chiggers have attacked me!

2004: To Madison, Wisconsin, the day clear and cool: The

landscape is uniform throughout the trip: parsnips, chicory, elderberry, crown vetch, yellow and white sweet clover, trefoil, milkweed, hemlock, daylilies, wheat all turned, corn about knee high everywhere, red-winged blackbirds still sitting on the fences, guarding their territories.

2007: Small white bindweeds blooming in the alley yesterday and this morning. Jeanie heard the first cicada this morning, short, intermittent calls. The birds were quiet today, only one grackle baby being fed by a parent, very few birds around. A few chigger bites have appeared on my legs – the first of the year.

2009: Jeanie reports the first chigger bites.

2012: One monarch this afternoon in the zinnias. Seventeen varieties of lilies in bloom today. Pink spirea color starting to break down. All the yucca flowers gone, large seed pods in their place. Some corn up to my armpits along Dayton-Yellow Springs Road. A very quiet walk this evening - not a single bird song heard.

2013: Castelluccio, Italy: We arrived at the beginning of the first phase of the annual wildflower bloom, two weeks after the time we came in 2011, but too early for the best flowering. Still, there was plenty to find: field after field of lintels in their yellow and yellow-green bloom; drifts of orange poppies (*Papaver commune rhoeas*); the tall blue *Fiordaliso* (cornflower or *Cyanus segetum Hill*); common daisies big as the cornflowers; a variety of the six-petaled, white star of Bethlehem, most likely an *Omithogalum umbellatum*; the single flowers of the *Bistorta officinalis Delarbre* that look like puffy, pale violet plantain stalks; *Campanula rapunculus*; *Verbascum longifolium*, a lanky giant mullein; the ubiquitous ginestra; red clover, white clover; the divided white five petals of the *Cerastiums (Caryophillaceae* family); buttercup: *Ranunculus brevifolius;* a pink *Anacamptis pyramidalis (Orchidea permidae)*; a forget-me-not type flower with heavy, hairy, entire, toothed leaves; and iris were in full bloom in the Castelluccio town square.

2014: The first heliopsis is unraveling.

2015: Santee-Cooper, South Carolina: In the middle of a heat wave, highs in the 100s. One yucca plant noticed at about the same stage as yucca in Yellow Springs. Where we fished, I found fine-leaved sneezeweed (*Helenium tenuifolium*) full flower, and the large violet kudzu buds just starting to open (the vines having covered all the hillsides and shoreline area on both sides of the canal).

2016: A brief walk at Gethsemani in Kentucky: No wildflowers in the woods, one white-spotted tick picked up, one tattered black swallowtail seen. The dramatic part of the walk: The first five of dozens of white American Lotus buds were completely open, big as heads of lettuce, at one of the small lakes here. Returning to photograph the flowers, I saw a younger black swallowtail.

2017: Along Limestone Street: black walnuts fragrant, rough-hulled, an inch and a half long, fallen peaches the size of black walnuts, buckeyes the size of marbles. The Stella d'oro bloom in the yard is in retreat, twenty-two in bloom this morning, the majority from a new clump on the north side of the house. Ditch lilies open: fifty-three blossoms, but the foliage in the dense patch of ditch lilies is dying back from lack of sun and overcrowding, Nine Asiatics, no rebloomers. The monarda is rapidly coming on, On Dayton Street, pink spirea plantings have completed their season. On Elm, golden coneflowers in full bloom.

2018: A male Eastern black swallowtail came to the hummingbird feeder this morning around 8:00 a.m., the morning so humid and warm, tree crickets so strong, the red admiral of the last days having ceded to the swallowtail.

2019: Finally, the lilies start to come in: nine Stella d'oros this morning and three ditch lilies. And a dozen heliopsis flowers round out this new season of summer. A black walnut the size of a cherry tomato on the sidewalk, fruit of days of rain.

2020: Mating cabbage whites. The first silver-spotted skipper. Another checkerspot butterfly. Three Stella d'oros, four ditch lilies. Pale brown starling twins begging from their parent, who dug out suet for them. Nodding thistles full flower along Dayton-Yellow Springs Road.

2021: A large fritillary butterfly and a hackberry butterfly and an azure in the garden before this morning's storm. The last zinnia sprouts planted. One yucca plant seen in full flower, leaning from the rain. Forty-nine ditch lilies in bloom, no pond iris, two Stella d'oros, two heliopsis blossoms. Two very small rabbits haunt the garden. Tropical Storm Cynthia strikes New Orleans as evening thunderstorms pummel southwestern Ohio, with even a tornado sighting east of Dayton. The Brood X cicadas are still chanting in the park.

2022: At Ellis Pond, the six ducklings of this spring were all full grown and sitting together on the rock they used to sit on when they were little with their parents.

*I am owner of the sphere,*
*Of the seven stars and the solar year....*

Ralph Waldo Emerson

### *June 19th*
### *The 170th Day of the Year*

*These long days are all the promise we are given.*

Peter Davison

Sunrise/set: 5:06/8:07
Day's Length: 15 hours 1 minute
Average Hi/Lo: 83/61
Average Temperature: 72
Record High: 96 – 1933
Record Low: 46 – 1909

### *Weather*

Today is another mostly sunny day (95 percent of all June 19ths are at least partly clear), but storms rise from the heat 35 percent of the time. Highs reach into the 80s sixty percent of all the years, and the chances of temperatures above 90 increase to 20 percent. Milder 70s come one year in five.

### *Natural Calendar*

For the next week, the length of the day holds steady near fifteen hours all along the 40th Parallel, the sun's declination varying only six hundredths of a degree. Fledglings continue to haunt the honeysuckles, adult robins continually guiding them with staccato peeps. Orange and pink Asiatic lilies and the ubiquitous ditch lilies reach full bloom. Yucca is fully open. Summer primroses, roses, heliopsis, foxglove, pink and yellow achillea, gooseneck loosestrife, late daisies, purple and white spiderwort and blue speedwell shine in the garden.

Today is an early date for starting the second cut of alfalfa in the Lower Midwest. Commercial broccoli and squash harvests are underway throughout Ohio and Indiana. Six to eight leaves have usually emerged on the field corn. Tobacco is almost all transplanted in Kentucky. Strawberries are about half harvested along the 40th Parallel, but that season is just beginning on the Canadian border. Cherry picking is taking place throughout the East. Wheat and oats are almost ready for harvest, and the Dog

Days are just around the corner.

### *Daybook*

1984: First chicory seen in town. Deptford pink found at Grinnell Swamp. The last bleeding heart disappeared in the east garden.

1989: Jacksonville, Florida: Some elderberry and yucca still in bloom. Daylilies open west of the city. Wild lettuce gone to seed. Arrived in Belize this afternoon: yucca blossoming, at the same time as in Florida and in Yellow Springs. Flamboyant trees and spider lilies in full bloom, like in Miami

1990: On the way to Madison, Wisconsin: orange ditch lilies full, Canadian thistle purple for over three hundred miles, bright blue stripes of chicory all the way north, patches of daisies, yellow sweet clover, Japanese honeysuckle, fields of daisy fleabane, hedges of white elderberry, waysides yellow with parsnips, hillsides of violet crown vetch, wheat golden across Indiana and Illinois, the roadsides and fields basically unchanged from Yellow Springs to above Chicago, land, time, space blending in the heat.

1991: Mulberries almost all gone, cherries completely ripe, mid-season hosta budding. Carnations gone today, some yucca done blooming too. Flickers still calling in the morning.

1992: First cherry pie from our tree.

1993: Yellow Springs to Houston, Texas, 6:00 a.m.: White sweet clover has started in a few places near Yellow Springs, and a few hemlocks are dying back. Chicory opening at dawn. Elderberries, and nodding thistles still full bloom near Cincinnati. A few thistles gone to seed just south of the Ohio River, first milkweed seen then, about 90 miles south of Yellow Springs, then in a few more miles, milkweed everywhere in full bloom.

Orange trumpet creeper is open below Warsaw, Kentucky, about 115 miles from home. Cattails with pollen at 130 miles. Hemlocks, which are still pretty green and stable in Greene County are yellowing, many gone to seed near Louisville. Teasel twice as tall there as at home. Now fence rows full of trumpet creeper. First dogbane and first great mullein seen open at 220 miles, Virginia roses full bloom, fields of thistles, clover, fleabane. Most tobacco leaves are six to ten inches long throughout Kentucky.

Near Bowling Green, Kentucky, 285 miles from Yellow Springs, most thistles have gone to seed. Sweet clover mostly gone by Nashville, about 340 miles. First bright orange butterfly weed open at 375 miles. Clovers and thistles disappear from the landscape at 400 miles, replaced by Queen Anne's lace and fleabane. Elderberries start to set fruit 100 mile north of Memphis, at 450 miles. Watermelons are coming in throughout southwestern Tennessee, fresh peaches at 580 miles, new horseweed plants and old wild lettuce becoming the only roadside foliage.

Then horseweed in bloom in Arkansas, rice fields bright green, trumpet vines continuing to dominate the fence rows. All wheat fields cut, seems relatively recently. Hemlock holds at half to seed all the way through Arkansas.

At 700 miles, false bishop's weed takes over from the Queen Anne's lace (false bishop's weed is short, maybe six inches, but has a similar flower head), and black-eyed Susans become dominant to the coast, sometimes fields of them throughout Arkansas.

Large white magnolia flowers, at the end of their season, seen in southern Arkansas, and hold through to Houston, yucca full bloom to the ocean. White egrets appear in a field near Marshall, Texas, 920 miles from home, elderberries continuing half set throughout, wild lettuce full bloom mid Texas. Pennywort in bloom in Houston. Thin-leafed mountain mint, Mexican hat *(Ratibida columnaris)*, thin-leafed dayflowers, *Coreopsis tinctoria*, identified in Houston, the latter common throughout eastern Texas and into Arkansas.

1995: Blackfoot, Idaho, 4,600 feet: flax, yellow sweet clover, black medic, and full red and white clovers, salsify, full lupine, tall pink balloon flowers. Iris and peonies seen in south central Idaho at about 3,800 feet. Pelicans, white and black, soared above the Snake River.

1996: Another turtle in the middle of Grinnell Road this afternoon, the second turtle in a week. Are they out so late to lay eggs?

1999: Bennington, Vermont to Yellow Springs: Deep green wheat near Rutland. Black-eyed Susans and parsnips full bloom, cattails and great mullein blooming toward the New York state border, full elderberry blossoms, chicory, blueweed, peonies, white sweet clover, haying from Albany west (and strawberries coming in with the first of the hay) hemlock done, catalpas still full, milkweeds, bright orange butterfly weed. A swarm of 17-year (or 13-year) cicadas near Canton, Ohio.

2001: To Madison, Wisconsin: early-summer fare throughout the 500-mile trip: crown vetch, parsnips, trumpet creeper, Queen Anne's lace, chicory, elderberry, purple vetch, milkweed, white and yellow sweet clover, trefoil, coreopsis, daisy fleabane, black eyed Susans. Canadian thistles – full of down in Yellow Springs – showed  the progress back into the first week of Early Summer, turning violet as we went north. Parsnips became brighter too, hemlock stronger.

2002: Very end of privet bloom. Only scattered peonies, sweet Williams, late dogwood, and cressleaf groundsel left from early June. Some black raspberries reddening. Pink spirea, heliopsis, and the pale Japanese iris are in full bloom. Mulberries still falling into the undergrowth. One whistling cricket heard this afternoon.

2003: Dianna Mathews called: the kids found one red cicada.

2004: Tat's garden in Madison seems about at the level of the first week of Yellow Springs June – her beginning primrose perhaps the best gauge. In the arboretum, prairie false indigo is in full bloom, spiderwort, heliopsis and purple coneflowers coming in. Throughout Madison, *Syringa reticulata*, the dramatic Ivory Silk Japanese lilac, is at various stages of bloom. As I walked through the park with Maggie, I pulled fresh timothy to chew. I saw cottonwood cotton drifting across the fields.

2007: Robinsong began softly at 4:25 this morning, but it was nothing like the strong springtime chorus. One cardinal sang at

4:45. Doves a little later. A blue jay at 5:00, red-bellied woodpecker at 6:20. In the north garden, lilies gradually coming in, daylilies and Asiatics. The earliest Asiatics (what I called the candy lilies) have already completed their seasons. Mallow, astilbe, yarrow and heliopsis are now at full bloom. One young grackle being fed by its parents this evening. Summer squash flowering but not setting fruit, perhaps because of the lack of bees.

2009: Santee, South Carolina to Yellow Springs: The entire countryside is lush, deep green, no sign of drought or decay anywhere throughout the full 650-mile trip.

2010: Cottonwood continues to shed near Lawson Place. Tall ditch lilies at their peak throughout town. Heliopsis and mallow full now. Richard Zopf brought over a quart container full of black raspberries, just picked.

2011: Zinnias, primroses, red achillea, penstemon, herbs all transplanted today. A few raspberries picked, left over from the deer. Damselflies seen in the yard and around the pond. Many daylilies are budding now, and the monarda is showing color (two of Peggy's large monardas are bright red). Heliopsis is in early bloom, spiderwort full, Annabelle hydrangea, oakleaf hydrangea, first purple coneflower, late salvia. Moya's campanulas are in the middle of their season. Hollyhocks in early bloom at various locations about town.

2012: The pink "Indomitable Spirit" hydrangea is losing some of its color. The mocking bird-like songbird is singing steadily outside the greenhouse this morning. I didn't hear him yesterday. The tree frog was calling at 7:00 when I went outside. A very small Savannah or song sparrow at the feeder today, very tame. Twenty lilies in bloom, blue salvia coming back after being deadheaded. Robins peeping off and on, guiding their young, cardinal singing at dusk, but a quieting of sound throughout the day, the longest days of the year creating some kind of new summer space. Starlings and grackles have disappeared from the yard, contributing to the absence of spring sounds. Three fritillaries and a polygonia seen today, many frolicking cabbage butterflies. Chiggers getting worse!

2013: I read through the inventories of past years, reminded of the different phases of our gardening, the spreading and disappearing of varieties, the continual shifting in the land's priorities and in the intensity of our work.

2014: The first two blossoms on the large blue-leafed hosta by the back porch opened over night. Snow-on-the-mountain all to seed now. The early bright orange Asiatic lilies have faded in the last couple of days.

2015: Santee-Cooper, South Carolina: John and I fished the canal starting at 5:50. Only two small cats caught. Light wind throughout the morning. First cicada heard at 8:30. Rose of Sharon noticed in full bloom near the highway, and one catalpa tree had long seedpods.

2016: Gethsemani, Kentucky: First robins heard at 4:25 a.m., the same time as in Yellow Springs in 2007. Doves and song sparrows were loud outside the monastery by 5:00, crows joining in from the hills nearby. Driving home, I saw many orange butterfly weeds and teasel heading. At home, at least thirty-two lily plants in bloom, including a pink and yellow day lily and a pink and violet one. The first two Shasta daisies had opened in the past two days, and two monarda flowers were completely out.

2017: Fifty-three ditch lily blossoms again this morning, fifteen Stella d'oros, seven Asiatics, three everbloomers. No standard daylilies yet. The first flowers opened on the milkweed, aroma deep and rich. Trumpet creeper flowers above the greenhouse roof are climbing higher each year. A cabbage butterfly and a great spangled fritillary around 10:00 a.m. Steady robin peeping in the honeysuckle bushes all around the yard. Grackles continue to feed, but starlings have stayed away for weeks. Jill saw the first small murmurations of starlings this evening on the way to Fairborn. Walking down Wright Street, I found an ancient basswood tree shedding its flowers.

2018: Neysa's ancient peach tree and the pear tree on Greene Street have fruit the size of large marbles. The red quince fruits are twice that size. The Osage fruits fallen to the sidewalk are golf-ball size. This afternoon, a hard long rain beat down the milkweed and the Mexican sunflowers. Late this afternoon, a hackberry butterfly visited the hummingbird feeder, sat entranced with sugar as I approached it. In the evening, the hummingbird came by, too.

2019: To Hopewell, Virginia with John: clouds and sun, gilded wheat and hay fields, blue chicory, full bloom of ditch lilies (as opposed to those lilies just starting at home), one large-flowered magnolia tree, various thistles, all the hillsides rich deep green throughout the drive.

2020: The wheat fields on the way to Cedarville are a golden brown, corn up to my calf, not quite knee high. Great mullein in early bloom. Tree crickets at the falls park near Cedarville. At home, the starling fledglings are now savvy enough to compete with their parents for suet. Blue jays in constant motion. Cardinals and grackles, a downy woodpecker and sparrows all taking turns. A few cabbage whites, one silver-spotted skipper. Eight ditch lilies, three Stella d'oro lilies, two pond iris open. The bright yellow primroses and the blue-violet spiderworts continue to give solid color to their garden patches. On Greene Street, the cottonwood still has cotton, the street sides full of fluff. A few catalpa trees still hold flowers.

2021: More storms and regional flooding. Sixty-four ditch lilies in bloom. The first monarda/bee balm blossoms show color. Milkweed has opened, and the first milkweed bugs are scouting their plants. Brood X cicadas still chanting.

2022: Nine ditch lilies in bloom, five Stella d'oros, one pond iris. Like last year, the first color is showing on the monarda. Butterfly sightings: several. cabbage whites, one hackberry, one silver-spotted skipper and a glimpse of an orange butterfly. Gladiolas planted: 40.

*Observe the daily circle of the sun,*
*And the short year of each revolving moon:*
*By them thou shalt foresee the following day,*
*Nor shall a starry night thy hopes betray.*

Virgil

## June 20th
## The 171ˢᵗ Day of the Year

*From brightening fields of ether fair-disclosed,*
*Child of the sun, refulgent Summer comes.*

James Thomson

Sunrise/set: 5:06/8:07
Day's Length: 15 hours 1 minute
Average Hi/Lo: 83/62
Average Temperature: 72
Record High: 100 – 1888
Record Low: 47 – 1980

### Weather

Rain occurs a little more than half the time on June 20, making this the day with the greatest likelihood for precipitation since June 2. Clouds completely cover the sky three years in ten. Chances of highs in the 90s rise to 25 percent; 80s come 35 percent of the years, 70s thirty percent, 60s just one year in ten. The odds for a cool night in the 40s or 50s remain steady at the mid-June level of three in ten.

### Natural Calendar

Throughout the Midwest and East, milkweed bugs appear for Milkweed Blooming Season. In the mild nights it is Giant Cecropia Moth Emerging Season; throughout the days it is Monarch Butterfly Caterpillar Season. Across the countryside, the last week of Early Summer brings Wild Black Raspberry Season, Golden Wheat Season. Garden seasons include Great Blue Hosta Season, Gooseneck Season and Russian Sage Season. Damselfly Season and Lizard's Tail Season reach their peak by the water. Elderberry Blooming Season and Yellow Sundrop Season and Black-Eyed Susan Season are visible from the freeways. Enchanter's Nightshade Season joins Honewort Season in the dark woods. Chigger Season and Mosquito Season and Tick Season make outside activities more challenging.

## *Daybook*

1981: Wild black raspberry season began in the yard today.

1983: Scarlet pimpernel found at Wilberforce today.

1984: First yucca seen in bloom (held back by the cold spring).

1986: Milkweed bloom is well underway now.

1987: Night walk: only a handful of crickets chirping, fireflies no thicker than at home, small moths crossing my way, no mosquitoes. It was warm and close in the woods, cold and wet out in the open fields of Middle Prairie. Mist became much thicker after eleven o'clock. Full moon rising in the southeast, Arcturus overhead, Regulus and Leo west, Spica in Virgo, Vega behind Hercules, then Altair, Deneb with Cygnus. Wingstem, blackberry, ironweed, daisy fleabane, soapwort, elderberry, all easily identified under the moon and stars. Timothy was sweet: I pulled and chewed the entire walk.

1990: Madison, Wisconsin: Peonies late full bloom, mock orange, coral bells, primrose, catalpas, snow-on-the-mountain, all the clovers, spurge, nodding thistles, honeysuckles, panicled dogwood are in the middle of their seasons, two to three weeks behind Yellow Springs. In the late morning, I drove up into northern Minnesota: the wheat (which is nearly all gold in Ohio) hasn't started to turn yet, and sugar beets are six inches high.

1995: Boise, Idaho to Portland, Oregon: As we drove west, the landscape became richer, and more like the Ohio fabric. Cow parsnips, yarrow, late potentilla, moth mullein, yellow sweet cover, milkweed, great mullein, and Canadian thistles were in full bloom (the thistles at early June Ohio levels). Boise's wheat was half turned, even green in some fields, like the wheat around Yellow Springs a week ago. Late iris near Boise, iris done close to Portland. Blackberries in full flower from Portland down to the coast.

2001: Madison, Wisconsin: For the most part, this Wisconsin

season is close to Yellow Spring's this year. Potentilla, spirea, hosta, daisies, tall meadow rue, yarrow, white-flowered waterleaf, spiderwort, honewort, daylilies, snow-on-the-mountain all close to southern Ohio level. False prairie indigo common, full bloom. Avens are open here, as are Asiatic dayflowers. Still, I saw one peony bush still in flower, one Solomon's seal, remnants of Late Spring. Poke milkweed identified in Tat's back yard, flowers just starting.

2002: Robin chorus strong when I got up at 4:15 a.m. The first cardinal sang at 4:28, the first doves at 4:30, first titmouse at 4:41, blue jay at 4:45, wren at 5:00. By the time the bees came out at 6:30, the robins and cardinals were silent. By noon, the robins were clucking their mentoring sound. In the North Glen, avens and yellow touch-me-nots are in bloom. The cohosh has pale blue-green berries. The mood of the woods is quiet and dark. The first pink hollyhock and the first purple daylily opened in the north garden this morning.

2003: The first tall pink mallow opened in the north garden this morning.

2007: Several monarda plants have fully developed flowers this morning, and several of the red phlox buds have opened. Young robins and doves feeding in the yard, some robins opening their wings in the sun, stretching them out on the lawn as if to dry them. The finch feeders are full of golden finches. Small white bindweed flowers have disappeared in the alley, replaced by a mound of purple morning glories.

2008: Throughout the Glen, tall wood nettle, honewort, waterleaf, wingstem, ironweed, weathering May apples, and touch-me-nots have obscured the web of spring, all the trilliums, the violet cress, the ragwort, the purple phlox, toothwort, Jack-in-the pulpit and bluebells.

In my garden, giant hosta leaves have covered the foliage of snowdrops, aconites, crocus and scilla. Pigweed, creeping Charlie, wild violets, waterleaf, dandelions and amaranth have filled in all around the remnants of the April windflowers. The stalks of hyacinths, daffodils and tulips have fallen over and are ceding to the next planting of zinnias and Mexican sunflowers.

Listing of those flowers is like a recitation of historical facts. Like dates or events in human history, they are lost or do not make sense unless they are recreated in my mind. Memory and imagination tell the stories, fill in the setting with details of sound, taste, texture and color and odor, connect the stories to other stories.

The meaning of natural history, like the meaning of human history, is dependent on my reenactment of what I saw happen or of what I believed happened. Without the thinking of or the telling of what has occurred, things lose their place, become disconnected, make no sense. So I go back over what has taken place in the woods and garden. I relive as best I can the steps that brought me here, review their sequences pulled from underneath the overgrowths of previous phases.

The sediment of passage dissolves so quickly. Natural science only goes part of the way. It is I who must move beyond the names and dates, defend imperfect memory and insufficient data with fantasy, fill in the past with my own truth. I am, like Emerson might suggest, "the owner of the sphere," and I am responsible for not only my own narrative but for that of the world around me.

2009: First large cobweb from a long-bodied spider seen above the pond. Pale violet shading on the garlic mustard leaves and seedpods as they age. Some panicled dogwood holds in the alley, the alley overgrown with bamboo, honeysuckle, mulberry, tree of heaven.

2010: A Father's Day ride to Chillicothe and then south and back home, maybe 200 miles: Wheat all deep brown throughout, one field cut. The roadsides were full of trefoil and red clover, black-eyed Susans, Queen Anne's lace, butterfly weed, sweet clovers, mulleins. The corn was shoulder high or better in all the fields. Only a few washed-thin soybean fields showed signs of the heavy rains that had moved through so often earlier this month. The entire landscape was lush and verdant, the peak of Ohio Early Summer.

2011: Wheat is golden brown in most of the fields around Yellow Springs, corn three to four inches. Catalpas are shedding, linden trees very late bloom, first trumpet creeper flowers noticed on Limestone Street, some of the blossoms already fallen.

2012: I just noticed that Moya's rose of Sharon has burst into bloom, the earliest I've ever recorded the flowering of that shrub. It must have come in several days ago, and I walked right by it without noticing. In the zinnias, the first Japanese beetle found. Coming home from the mall, we saw farmers harvesting their wheat. On my evening walk, I found Don's rose of Sharon opening, and another with first flowers in the alley. Tremendous heat wave across the East, record highs in New Hampshire and Vermont. Temperatures in the 90s here for several days.

2014: Just south of town, wheat is a rich brown. Hemlock almost all to seed. Parsnips still yellow, moth mullein full near the Little Miami River. Corn and soybeans are lush and tall throughout the area. At home, the north garden color gathers momentum from the red roses, the orange ditch lilies, the blue and violet spiderwort, the Anna Belle and the hobblebush hydrangeas, the late full yellow primroses, the newly transplanted pink spirea, the first peach Oriental lily, the first full blossom of the heliopsis. The cream-colored leaves of the variegated knotweed offer an anchor at the west end. Milkweed buds are blushing, ready to open. Japanese honeysuckle vine, climbing the fences and through the forsythia and honeysuckle bushes, adds fragrance and texture to the southeast corner.

2015: Return from South Carolina: The landscape in southern Ohio is similar in color and strength to that of last year, but the yard and garden, sodden from the daily rains while I was gone, is much further along. Now the monarda is red, the Joe Pye with tight small buds, the primroses almost gone, the ditch lilies and heliopsis completely full, the Stella d'oros on the way down, all the hydrangeas full, especially the Anna Belle and the red-pink "Indomitable Spirit." The deer have eaten at least two-dozen lily buds from various parts of the garden. The roses, stunted badly by the last two winters, are overgrown by annuals and perennials this year. And so the era of roses that Jeanie began thirty-five years ago is coming to a close, covered and replaced by more recent plantings. So many hostas have put out flower spikes while I was gone, the Great Blue beautiful in early bloom. And the trumpet creeper that Jeanie gave me put out its first orange trumpets.

2016: This morning I found that the deer had eaten many lily buds, a couple of primrose buds and half of the decorative amaranth tops while I had been gone over the weekend. Just like last year! I guess I forgot to spray again! In spite of that, there were twenty-eight lily plants in bloom this morning, down just a few from yesterday evening. A great spangled fritillary visited the garden this afternoon.

2017: Sixty-five ditch lily blossoms, fifteen Stella d'oros, seven Asiatics, two rebloomers, and the first standard day lily, a pink one – beginning the full day lily season – and  then in the evening, a small rust-colored one. The Joe Pye plants have developed small, tight bud clusters, and the wisteria is blooming again on new growth. Continual robin peeping throughout the day, earnest and loud. At John Bryan Park, only avens and hobble bush hydrangea found in bloom. From Madison, Wisconsin, Tat writes: "Ditch lilies out all along the bike path; sweet rocket still hanging on; roses fading; small blue allium still blue."

2018: A second day lily bloomed today, a pink one in the circle garden. The tall, floppy Asiatic lilies are in full flower, forty-two ditch lily blossoms, two day lilies, three Stella d'oros, one yellow rebloomer. Joe Pye with small bud clusters. Monarda starting. Large catbird warbling and warbling high in the spindly black walnut tree on the north border this morning at 8:10.

2019: Fishing in the evening, Hopewell, Virginia: the catfish are ending their spawn but are still not into summer mode. Three fish caught, ten to twenty pounds. We watched the gibbous moon rise over the James River, following Saturn and Jupiter, which were already well up in the southeast.

2020: Dog Day heat settles in. Eight ditch lilies, three Stella d'oro lilies, one pond iris in bloom. Catbird at the suet. From Madison, Tat sends a video of tiny toads, single-file in procession, crossing a sidewalk.

2022: Full song of robins, cardinals and doves when I went outside at 5:30 this morning. Then gradually the clucks of the grackles and the warbling melodies of catbirds. Ditch lilies: 24.

*Our bodies have formed themselves in delicate reciprocity with the manifold textures, sounds, and shapes of an animate earth – our eyes have evolved in subtle interaction with other eyes, as our ears are attuned by their very structure to the howling of wolves and the honking of geese.*

David Abram

## *June 21st*
## *The 172nd Day of the Year*

*The glorious lamp of heaven, the sun,*
*the higher he's a-getting,*
*The sooner will his race be run,*
*And nearer he's to setting.*

Robert Herrick

Sunrise/set: 5:06/8:07
Day's Length: 15 hours 1 minute
Average Hi/Lo: 83/62
Average Temperature: 72
Record High: 98 – 1988
Record Low: 48 – 1897

### *Weather*
Highs in the 60s occur five percent of the time on this date, 70s come on ten percent of the afternoons, 80s on 70 percent, and 90s on 15 percent. The sun appears nine years in ten, but thunderstorms pass through 30 percent of the time. Morning lows in the 40s come only five to ten percent of the time; 50s occur on 25 percent of the nights; 60 percent of the nights are in the 60s, and ten percent are in the 70s

### *Natural Calendar*
Solstice marks the end of Early Summer in Yellow Springs, but time is also space; movement and distance can take the season backwards or forwards, allowing what was and still will be to ride the hinge of the sun's declination. North in Maine, azaleas and columbine are still bright. Lupines hold in Bar Harbor. Foxglove and privet are budding in Bangor, strawberries just ripening. Through the valleys of Vermont, the wheat is deep green wheat (it's golden-brown, almost ready to cut in Indiana). Parsnips are opening in New Hampshire as they go to seed in Tennessee. In upstate New York, catalpas are still flowering, and peonies are still in bloom.

The flora of the upper Midwest reaffirms the Late Spring

and Early Summer of the Northeast. The blossoms of mock orange are still fragrant in Minneapolis. Multiflora roses and the petals of blackberries repeat Cincinnati May. Cottonwood cotton is drifting across the arboretum in Madison, Wisconsin. The thistles are stronger, the hemlock fresher, cattails more delicate and flushed with pollen all across the northern plains.

West in the Rocky Mountains, lupines are in full bloom at 4,000 feet, lilacs and early iris are coming in above 6,000 feet. Southern Ohio April appears in fields of dandelions and spring beauties at 7,000 feet. At 8,000 feet, the heartleaf arnica, like a yellow bloodroot, pushes Middle Atlantic time almost to the end of March.

Then down toward the Pacific, the landscape collapses forward toward a Yellow Springs June. From Tillamook to the ocean, cow parsnips, yarrow, moth mullein, yellow sweet cover, meadow goat's beard, milkweed and great mullein line the roads.

***Daybook***

1983: At Grinnell Swamp: Golden Alexander, henbit, yellow and white sweet clover, privet, angelica, white violets, clustered snakeroot, honewort, forget-me-nots, moneywort, yarrow, fleabane, wild garlic, white waterleaf, black medic all in bloom. Catchweed has burs, foliage yellow. May apples leaves are spotted and old. Decaying garlic mustard leans across the undergrowth.

1984: First monarch butterfly caterpillar found in the carrots. At the Covered Bridge: a third of the parsnips, angelica, and hemlock going to seed. Wingstem and tall coneflowers are five feet high, avens flowering, honewort going to seed, multiflora roses completely gone, damselflies and daddy longlegs everywhere, first spotted touch-me-not and first yellow touch-me-not blooming, white flowered waterleaf and the late henbit still in bloom.

1985: A field cricket heard chirping in the yard last night. Most black raspberries gone.

1986: The sun rose over the house across the street at 60 degrees on the compass; if I'd been able to see it on the horizon, it probably would have been at 45 degrees, all the way northeast. I watched it go down over Fairborn at 310 degrees through the trees, close to perfect northwest.

1987: The inner woods seemed tattered this afternoon, some leaves yellowing, grasses turning. Along the railroad tracks, Deep Summer's wild lettuce was budding. Avens was in full bloom.

1988: Belize City, Central America: Cactus at the Fort George Hotel blossoming at the same time as in our greenhouse in Yellow Springs. Summer solstice in Belize: the sun rises at 5:19 a.m., sets at 6:30 p.m., the day 13 hours 11 minutes long: in Yellow Springs: 15 hours 1 minute. North to the Mexican border: some sugar cane three to four feet high, other fields just emerging. Blue and white dayflowers, *Ipomoea* throughout, just like in Yellow Springs. A waiter at Altun Ha told me that corn is planted here at the middle to the end of May, just before the rains begin. The Central American corn cycle, then, basically follows that of the Midwest.

1989: At South Glen, seeds have formed on half the angelica and maybe a third of the parsnips. First flowers on the wood nettle filling up the undergrowth. Orchard grass brown and old, English rye grass full, bottle grass late bloom, brome grass very late, some timothy still tender, damselflies common, mosquitoes pesky. First touch-me-not, first thimble plant in bloom. Nodding and Canadian thistles still full bloom. Blackberries have set fruit. *Panicum clandestinum* just emerging. Multiflora roses are fading, along with some Japanese honeysuckle. Burning bush, *Euonymus atropurpureus*, found full bloom at South Glen. Four cedar waxwings sighted along the river.

1996: I was doing exercises in the greenhouse before daylight and was surprised by something flying around me. I thought it might be a cecropia moth, but it turned out to be a bat that had somehow gotten inside. I opened the back door, and after a few swoops, it went out. Today the white mulberries were falling heavily to the sidewalk and the street.

1998: Indigo bunting seen by the pond today. Campanula opened in the east garden, the first purple coneflower unraveled completely along the fence, and the first rose of Sharon bloomed along the street. Trumpet vines and Rugosa roses are full now. Wheat is brown. Five Japanese beetles in the roses, the most so far.

1999: Return to Yellow Springs after almost two weeks in Maine: dry here like across the Northeast, but crops holding. Birds still sing in the morning chorus, crows joining in near 5:00 a.m. The wheat is champagne brown. There are fields of thistle down, patches of daylilies. The purple loosestrife is open in the pond, and the heliopsis, achillea and feverfew all started while we were gone. Daisies have been replaced by daisy fleabane. First fireflies seen; there were none before we left, and none in Maine or along the way. A few Japanese beetles in the roses.

### *Notes for the Yellow Springs News After Returning from Maine*

The second week of June, Jeanie and I drove up to Maine, traveling back in time to Yellow Springs May, into lupines everywhere, to poppies, iris, blue flags, peonies and lilacs, to flowering blackberries, and roadsides full of tall buttercups and daisies. Above us, the locust trees were still in bloom, and the catalpas just budding. In the yards and gardens around Bar Harbor, there still were fragrant privets blossoming, and mock orange, bridal wreath spirea, snowball viburnum, rhododendrons and even azaleas.

I always find it magical to jump seasons, to go back or forward from one month to the next. Without the seasonal patterns and a notebook, I would have a hard time knowing when and where I am. My sense of continuity is completely dependent on movement and the picture of how one motion fits with other motions. The markers of my life are fragile. If I didn't anchor events to other events, to colors and odors, buildings, plants, and to artificial paper frames, I would be literally lost in space.

And so I calculate the return to Late Spring by traveling to Maine, evaluating the distance in Yellow Springs degrees, with a Yellow Springs gauge. When I adjust the needle, shifting the measuring device from June to May and back again, I not only break the rules of stasis but apply them too. The familiar becomes a guide to the unfamiliar. I leave home and universalize home in the same step, both dissolving it and applying it to anywhere I choose.

2000: From this noon in time, the hands of the biological clock move down toward winter. And I rationalize about the loss. I create compensation for decay. I philosophize about transcendence and divinity, indestructible souls, heaven beyond the sky, salvation in kindness and love, immortality through children or influence. I try to believe in the resurrection of the dead and life everlasting. I try to understand how matter and energy are one, how nothing is ever truly destroyed, how spirit is forever in motion, transformed from action to atom to action.

But I wonder, really, if life is not only measured in quantity and presence, measured like the longest days. The absence of leaves and flowers and grass and warmth in winter is beautiful only in the context of its covenant with rebirth. An appreciation of snow and empty branches rises primarily from an aesthetic that values cold and dissolution only if their opposites are certain. In that context, I tolerate the receding tide, find meaning in the yellowing foliage, in the autumn flowers, in the departure of the birds. I find consolation in natural history like I find consolation in my own history, in recollection of my finest, longest days.

Summer is measured in quantity, in the experience of bounty. Memory and longing are always second best. Accumulation does not always add up to ecstasy, but it reminds me of what is true. It affirms and proves what I know in this season, that less is not more, and that my imagined God and Paradise are the defiant and fantastic signs of an enduring June's immediate and peerless abundance.

2002: Queen Anne's lace and goosefoot just starting to bloom as water willow fades after a week-long flowering period. New leaves are growing on the white rhododendron. Frances Williams hosta and the great blue hosta are in full bloom.

2003: Green ash tree in front of the house trimmed back: flower clusters turning to seedpods.

2004: Home from southern Wisconsin: The red monarda and two transplanted hollyhocks opened up all the way while we were gone. The yellow primrose and the kousa dogwoods ended their seasons. Lilies are gathering momentum. Lizard's tail still full – but its flowers are moving well up its stalk. Water willow is still blossoming. Japanese beetles have eaten the tea roses.

2006: At Santee in South Carolina, corn tall, tasseling, ears completely formed. Wheat fields cut over. Soybeans and peanuts a few inches high. One field of sunflowers in full bloom. Mimosa trees, first seen flowering in southern Kentucky (along with orange trumpet creepers), were common throughout the region. By the roadside, white swamp mallow full bloom, and a yellow five-petaled water plant. Catfish bit off and on night and day at selected sites, even though few fish were reported taken by others in the area.

2007: No Japanese beetles seen this morning. Birds quiet all day, very little activity at the feeders.

2008: Inventory in Yellow Springs on return from Santee-Cooper: Bright yellow primrose still full, some tall daylilies opening. Asiatic lilies: orange, violet, deep orange, white, yellow. Candy lilies completely gone. Mallow and veronica full. First green-eyed Susan. Full catmint, spiderwort, hobble bush, oakleaf hydrangea, white achillea, red phlox, great blue hosta, Stella d'oros, coral bells, lamb's ear, pink spirea, astilbe, Japanese honeysuckles, very late sweet Williams, monarda blushing, fragments of sweet rockets, heading Queen Anne's lace. Full hollyhocks all over town. Full violet clematis. Rhubarb has recovered. More endless summer hydrangea flowers. Apples in the alley a third of full size, one golf-ball size hairy Osage fruit, first blue campanula, last Japanese iris, last water willow. Lizard's tail is about a fourth to a third open.

2009: Inventory here on return from Santee Cooper: Wheat is golden. Lizard's tail a third in bloom. Monarda flushed, celandine holding, strong spiderwort in the shade, late lamb's ear, full daisy fleabane, pink spirea, oakleaf hydrangea, coral bells, astilbe, ramps, great blue hosta, early heliopsis, full gooseneck, hobblebush, Anna Belle, larkspur, veronica, pink phlox, Stella d'oros clustered bellflower, pink tea rose, campanula, achillea, late catmint, Japanese honeysuckle, sweet Williams, primrose, early yucca in the yard, and purple coneflowers, Russian sage, mallow, and Queen Anne's lace. Japanese iris gone. No bird calls as I walked Bella this evening at 9:00, but Janie reported fecal sacks in her birdbath.

2010: Jeanie saw three Japanese beetles in the ferns this afternoon, the first of the year. I noticed white thrips, "fuzz bugs," on the flower stalk of a hosta.

2011: Ramps up and fully budded.

2012: Mid-season hostas starting to open now, Mateo's rose of Sharon coming in, moth mullein seen full bloom on the way to Dayton, the lily in the dooryard garden has five blossoms, full bloom - and throughout the rest of the yard, thirty-five different lily varieties flowering. Ramps starting to bloom. Just a handful of Stella d'oro lilies and yellow primroses flowering, the last yellow bloom of early June. At the west end of the yard, the oak leaf hydrangea petals are turning soft pale green. Birds much quieter through the day. This afternoon, a monarch in the zinnias and a white "fuzz bug" in the raspberry brambles (and another small picking of berries today). This evening, some cardinal songs as I walked Bella.

2013: Inventory on return from three weeks in Italy: Stella d'oro, pink spirea, penstemon, astilbe, oakleaf hydrangeas (flowers eaten by deer), Anna Belle hydrangea, hobble bush hydrangea, pink hydrangea, heliopsis, spiderwort, lamium, mallow, salvia, roses, celandine, Japanese honeysuckle, great blue hosta, catmint, sweet peas, seven lily plants, and the last of Jeanie's campanulas, grown two feet tall – all in bloom. A few sweet rockets, violet clematis and weigela blossoms and sweet Williams left. Most of the yellow primroses eaten off by deer. Peaches about an inch and a half long. Seedpods found hanging from the wisteria.

Three zinnias have bloomed and a couple of the cosmos in the east garden. The gladiolas that I planted before I left at the end of May are from one to two feet tall. Some of the bee balm is reddening. One of the fish – Daisy, the smallest one – is  sick, hides by the filter. A small dark green frog has moved in to the pond. A great spangled fritillary came by in the afternoon, only the third large butterfly I have seen all year.

2014: White sweet clover along the freeway to Cincinnati. Throughout the countryside, dead ash trees. The autumns will be transformed, will be missing half their color. Arrowhead foliage well developed at Ellis. In the yard, the first monarda flower head is blushing. Stella d'oro lilies along the east fence complement the yellow primroses in the north garden, the first time they have been strong enough to provide real banks of color. Gold finches feed all day at the thistle seed. Five different kinds of dragonflies seen at home and at Ellis. One zebra swallowtail and a glimpse of a monarch or viceroy at the monastery of St Clare.

2015: Twelve different lily varieties open today, although the large number blossoms on Stella d'oros and ditch lilies balances the small amount of standard day lily bloomers. I noticed that the catmint had been spent at the same time as the primrose. Don's cherry tree is still full of cherries, all dark and ready to pick.

2016: Twenty-eight different lily plants in flower this morning, mostly Stella d'oros (in decline) and ditch lilies, but the standard day lilies are now up to four. In the pond, lizard's tail in early full flower, and the first trumpet creeper blossomed by the back porch.

2017: Sixty ditch lily blossoms, five Asiatics, five Stella d'oros, five standard day lilies. Only two flowers left on the primroses, their worst season in years. Jill told about being briefly in a straight-line wind full of cottonwood cotton today.

2018: All day rain. Fifty-nine ditch lily blossoms, three Asiatic plants with several blossoms, five Stella d'oros, two standard day lilies. Primroses holding. An avens plant seen flowering at Jill's, and from Denver she sent me a photograph of a bull thistle plant in full bloom.

2019: Hopewell, Virginia to Yellow Springs: The hills and valleys were rich, deep green, the June rains having produced dense, lush foliage. In Virginia, the large magnolias still kept some of their flowers. Mimosa trees were covered with their pink blossoms. At a rest stop, I found honeysuckles with red berries, budding burdock, fully developed cattails. At home: seven Stella d'oro lilies, one day lily, two Turk's cap lilies, twelve ditch lilies, heliopsis early full, the first bee balm turning, water iris gone, full bloom of the big blue hostas and some bi-colors, first flowers on the milkweed.

2020: The monarda (bee-balm) is starting to blush now at home, but the bright red, larger-flowered variety is open in some yards. Twenty-four ditch lilies are in bloom today, but only one Stella d'oro. No pond iris blossoming today; the first one opened on June 7 this year, a clean two-week season. At Ellis Pond, the elderberry bush is finally in full flower, the parsnips are full and the hemlock is going to seed. In the street, small, hairy Osage fruits the size of a large sweet cherry fallen in the wind. I picked a black walnut the size of a big acorn from Jill's tree and an apple just a little bigger than the Osage from Peggy's tree. The first wild black raspberries are ripe along Davis Street. Tat sent a note saying that she saw the first firefly tonight in Madison.

2021: Seventy-nine ditch lilies are open today, one Stella d'oro, one Asiatic. Around 6:45 this morning, the first *Polygonia* comma came and hid in the ditch lilies, perfectly camouflaged. The monarda is blushing, like last year, and the Endless Summer hydrangea is in full pink and blue bloom for the first time in over a decade. Osage and black walnut fruits are the same size as they were last year. Mid-season hostas are budded near the studio, smartweed in full flower by the ditch lilies.

2022: Two heliopsis flowers open in the night, 35 ditch lilies. Monarda is blushing, and all is like last year except for the Endless Summer hydrangea, which seems disinterested. Burdock buds starting to form at Ellis. The three garden milkweed plants have started to open. Yucca tall and full of flowers throughout town. A large bush of rugosa roses is in bloom along Dayton-Yellow Springs Road.

*We need time's arrow to assure us that sequences of events tell meaningful stories and promise hope for improvement.... If events recur in predictable ways (as days must follow nights, and new birth compensate old deaths), then life includes pattern amidst the flux.*

Stephen Jay Gould

## *June 22nd*
## *The 173rd Day of the Year*

*A warm, gentle day, windless:*
*The seeds we plant are like our hopes.*

Harlan Hubbard

Sunrise/set: 5:07/8:07
Day's Length: 15 hours
Average Hi/Lo: 83/62
Average Temperature: 73
Record High: 98 – 1988
Record Low: 48 – 1897

### *Weather*

Highs are in the 80s six years in ten, and 90s occur 25 percent of the time. Cool 60s or 70s are recorded 15 percent of the afternoons. Sun is the rule for this date, with only two years in a decade producing completely overcast conditions. Chances of precipitation, usually in the form of a thunderstorm: 35 percent. Lows stay above 60 tonight more often than on any other June night.

### *The Weather in the Week Ahead*

Sunny skies are the rule for the last week of June: clouds dominate only about 20 percent of all the days, and that makes this period one of the brighter ones in the whole year. Daily chances of rain throughout this period of the month are 30 percent except on the 25th and 26th; those two days are some of the driest of the entire year, carrying only a 15 percent chance of precipitation. High temperatures rise into the 80s at least 60 percent of all the afternoons and climb above 90 on 20 percent of the days. Cooler conditions in the 70s or even the 60s are most likely to occur on the 23rd and 24th.

### *The Natural Calendar*

When the wheat harvest begins, then bright orange butterfly weed reaches full bloom, and acorns become fully formed. Sycamore bark starts to shed, and thistle flowers change to down. Hemlock season is complete, stalks collapsing into the tall grasses. Clustered snakeroot has gone to seed like the waterleaf. Parsnip heads brown in the sun. Privet is done blooming. Spring lamium has stopped flowering.

### *Daybook*

1982: The red hollyhocks Jeni planted from seed bloomed today.

1983: Fireflies thick now. First wild black raspberry eaten.

1984: Timothy in full bloom.

1986: No geese heard for more than a month in town. When do they start their autumn flights? At the mill, lizard's tail early full bloom, first wood mint flowering, wild leek about to blossom. Small toads, half an inch long, hopping in the mud. Rugosa rose, tall nettle, avens, thimble plant full bloom.

1990: Into western Pennsylvania: Vegetation similar to Yellow Springs, crown vetch magnificent, and all the clovers are in bloom. Coreopsis here and there. Patches of hemlock still flowering. Parsnips still strong at high elevations. Red (small) and large yellow-green staghorns have emerged. Catalpa flowers and thistles are holding in the mountains. Daisies, sweet clover, white and yellow moth mulleins, and sweet peas are everywhere. I don't ever remember the roadsides so lush.

1991: Picking the last black raspberries and cherries after the night-long rain. Misty morning, soft and cool. Robins, flickers, cardinals singing, filtered through the heavy air. Many raspberry leaves yellowed, the smell of August, the humidity and late sweetness, the day so gentle. I hang on to the longest days.

1992: Cherries all ripe, sudden decline.

1996: The first domestic raspberry eaten from the garden tonight. The first black raspberry should be ready in a day. Cherries red on the diseased tree, blackbirds coming to eat them. The lilies have bloomed now. The orange was the first. Then the pink. Then more orange, then pink. Throughout town, the small yellow Stella d'oro lilies are all in flower.

1998: The white and magenta monarda have started now, and the variegated hosta. The great blue hosta is in full bloom, and the Francis Thompson. Late high season for yellow primrose, for spiderwort, midseason for mallow and achillea. Gaura full, helianthus full. Along the roadsides, the orange daylilies (ditch lilies) are all open.

2002: Kelleys Island in Lake Erie, 130 miles north of Yellow Springs: Panicled dogwoods and elderberry bushes common and in full bloom. Early Summer lingering: late peonies, daisy fleabane, bright Canadian thistles. Cottonwood is drifting in the wind. At home, the wheat is mostly gold; in northern Ohio fields are lighter and greener, the season about seven days behind conditions in Yellow Springs and southwestern Ohio. Constant chatter of red-winged blackbirds around the camp.

2003: The birdhouse on the west wall is empty. After weeks of constant activity, flying back and forth with food every few minutes, the sparrows have finally launched their young.

2006: Returned from three days at Santee-Cooper in South Carolina to find the pink hollyhocks open, many more lilies in bloom, the first yucca flowers blooming, a few alley raspberries ripe, Heliopsis full, sweet Williams gone.

2007: More red monarda comes in as lilies gradually increase in number. Lizard's tail has reached full bloom in the pond. Small berries have formed on Mateo's back honeysuckles. Goldenrod in the alley is almost chest high, and avens is in bloom.

2008: No grackles for the past three days. Transplanted one of the east garden endless-summer hydrangeas to the south garden. Young doves, still tame, in the grass this afternoon. Toad found in the triangle park, under the red-leafed redbud.

2009: Doves calling as I walked Bella at 8:00. No grackles. Only peeping robins and sparrows in the yard today. Osage fruits are golf-ball size. Mulberries continue to fall to the street. The first avens seen in the alley. Honeysuckles and panicled dogwoods have green berries. Hackberry leaves are full of galls. Half of the black raspberries are dark.

2010: Sweet gum seed balls, green, sharp protrusions.

2011: Monarda in early bloom throughout, joining common daisies and Shasta daisies, comfrey, blueweed, large bellflowers, blanket flowers, coreopsis, catmint, spiderwort, early hosta, the first purple coneflowers. Peaches are maybe a third of their full size, about as big as the black walnuts fallen to the street. Robins and doves after sunrise. First sparrow fledgling seen begging for food, fluttering its wings, in the back yard. First purple butterfly bush flowers open.

2012: Very faint bird twittering at 4:00 - 4:30 in a soft, warm rain. Then by 4:45, strong robin song, and a cardinal heard at 5:09, sparrows chirping strong then. By 5:30, a very melodious robin singing steadily. The cardinals still sing off and on, but I don't hear the constant calling of earlier in the spring. No birdsong heard on my evening walk, 8:00 p.m. (the evening cooler than it has been, thanks to the cool front arriving exactly on schedule). Thirty varieties of lilies counted today, including the very last of the Stella d'oros. The primroses are down to just a few blossoms also, their season closing with that of the Stella d'oros, dovetailing with the rise of the rose of Sharon, the Russian sage, the purple coneflowers, the Shasta daisies, the midseason hostas.

2013: North to Goshen, Indiana, and then returning to Yellow Springs: In bloom: Queen Anne's lace, purple coneflowers, black-eyed Susans, yellow and white sweet clover, milkweed, chicory, yucca, birdsfoot trefoil, ditch lilies, great mullein and moth mullein, bull thistles and Canadian thistles, daisy fleabane, white yarrow, parsnips, small white bindweed, elderberries, trumpet creepers, crown vetch. The wheat has turned, is almost ready to harvest. Haying throughout. Corn varies from a foot to four feet tall, depending on the area. Cattails have emerged, thin among their foliage. Red-winged blackbirds still guard their territories along the fences. One catalpa seen in bloom. Most hemlock has gone to seed.

At Ellis Pond outside of Yellow Springs, the pawpaw flowers have become two-inch fruits, and the once tiny specks of hickory nuts have grown round and fat. The tulip trees have lost their tulips. The willow has thickened, and the bald Cyprus trees, so bare in May, are bright and fully formed. Mulberries, still ripening when I left for Italy, are black and sweet. The long, feathery fingers of blossoms hang from the sweet hart chestnut tree (a sweet hart seen blooming in Sardinia just a week ago). Ramps budding under the hosta near the shed, avens in flower by the water garden.

2014: Ditch lilies and Stella d'oros provide drifts or points of color in the village gardens this third and fourth week of June. In the yard, the hydrangeas and the spiderwort offer a backdrop and contrast. And more hostas coming in – an early bloom phase. Fireflies seem good so far this summer: normal numbers. Mosquitos biting with more regularity now. Still, no Japanese beetles or squash beetles seen so far, and I've had very few chigger bites. Don's pie cherry tree has lost all but a handful of cherries. Along Dayton Street, the serviceberries are plentiful, dark and sweet.

2016: Thirty-two lilies in bloom this morning, the standard daylilies growing in number to five of the plants. As in 2012, the primroses decline with the Stella d'oros. The first purple coneflower is unraveling. The white waterleaf flowers have become round, green BB–size berries. Monarda bloom spreading quickly across the drift. Green frogs in conversation before sundown in the rushes at Ellis Pond.

2017: Crows heard this morning for the first time this summer. Three Stella d'oro lilies, four Asiatics, five standard day lilies, fifty ditch lilies in bloom. The resident deer has eaten almost a dozen buds. I found the first two Japanese beetles in the northeast garden. Germander in late bloom at Ellis Pond, and a young beaver swam by as we walked along the shore. Late in the afternoon, I heard a great chattering of grackles in the high trees, perhaps an initial gathering after mating and preparing fledglings for adulthood. Or maybe they were making a racket because of a hawk or crows.

2018: Six standard day lily blossoms, forty-eight ditch lilies, five Stella d'oros. The three Asiatic plants remain fully open. Two fully red monarda flowers.

2019: Fourteen ditch lilies, two Turk's caps, eight Stella d'oros. Common plantain finally blooming at the pond.

2020: Twenty-six ditch lilies this morning, two Stella d'oros, and the very first day lily bloomed. Casey called to say he had Baltimore orioles and catbirds feeding and rose-breasted grosbeaks every once in a while (the latest I've heard of them here). Three cabbage whites and one silver-spotted skipper noticed today. At Park Meadows last night, Jill and I saw full blooming orange butterfly weed and early purple coneflowers. Shasta daisies were fully budded but not flowering.

2021: Full moon approaching, barometer rising, cool 50 degrees in the night, cloudless sky. The first few monarda blossoms are fully red. Seventy-seven ditch lilies in bloom. The lone purple coneflower by my daisies is stretching out to flower in a few days. No butterflies at all seen in the garden today, high 68 and a slight wind. No Japanese beetles. Report from Cincinnati: the Brood X cicadas are gone. In the woods here, no more chanting, only soft tree frogs or crickets. In John Bryan Park: wood mint heading up, avens in bloom, many daddy longlegs in the undergrowth, black raspberries turning red.

2022: Ditch lily count: 40. The first monarda blossom is fully red. The primroses are declining quickly, as are the spiderworts.

*A change in the weather is sufficient to re-create the world and ourselves.*

Marcel Proust

### June 23rd
### The 174th Day of the Year

*Horas non numero nisi serenas* (I count only the happy hours)
*Horas non numero nisi aestivas* (I count only the summer hours)

Sundial Inscriptions

Sunrise/set: 5:07/8:08
Day's Length: 15 hours, 1 minute
Average High/Low: 84/62
Average Temperature: 73
Record High: 98 – 1899
Record Low: 43 – 1902

### Weather
This is often a cooler day than the 22nd, due to the passage of the fourth major high-pressure system of the month. The chances of a high in the 60s or 70s jump to 40 percent; 55 percent of the time, however, highs reach into the 80s, and 90s come five percent of the time. The sun appears 85 percent of the days, but thunderstorms occur three times in a decade on this date.

### Natural Calendar
Poison ivy has green berries. The first touch-me-nots and the first thimble plants flower. Rugosa roses are in full flower, accompanied by black-eyed Susans, wild petunias and hobblebush. Staghorns have pushed out on the sumacs. Catmint and the short, bright yellow primrose (*Oenothera*) come to the end of their blooming seasons.

### Daybook
1989: Virginia creeper in full bloom. Garlic headed in the garden. Clustered snakeroot now all gone to seed like the waterleaf. Peaches half size, apples a third size, cherries all ripe, mums cut back. Yucca is open in Xenia. Wild black raspberries are coming in, and mulberries are at their peak.

1990: Virginia creeper seen in full boom, first garden mallow flowers, some sundrops dying back. Grackles in the mulberry tree all afternoon.

1991: Three young grackles were in the back yard this afternoon, fed cherries by their parents. Tonight, a cecropia moth, huge and soft, came to the front porch light.

1992: Grackles are here all day for cherries. Tree of heaven flower clusters noticed high in the branches. Hemlock still strong. Garden carrots getting some orange to their roots. First tomato set. First mallow flowers along the south wall. Zinnias show color in their buds. Bleeding heart foliage is yellowing. Sweet Williams well past their prime, astilbe fading now.

1999: Only a few Japanese beetles so far.

2001: Arboretum at Madison, Wisconsin: Thimble plant, yellow leafy spurge, prairie dock (very first flowering), orange hawkweed, cottonwood cotton, late Rugosa roses, new privets, wood anemone (like at Susi's), basal flowers of the compass plant, budding rattlesnake master, Indian plantain heading, baby toads hopping across the path, and a mourning cloak butterfly.

2002: Kelleys Island: Robins calling by 3:45 a.m. By 4:30, the redwings start cackling, and robins are all over the ground mating, bold and raucous throughout the campground. By 4:50, the robin activity declines, and blackbirds take their place in the grass. All day: mayflies swarming.

2003: Pale blue-bodied dragonflies appear at the pond for the first time. As I talked to Neysa about the morning sounds, I mentioned – and realized at the same time – how the crows have been silent all year. Did the West Nile Virus decimate the flocks?

2005: Inventory before leaving for Florida: Full oak-leaf hydrangea, mallow, heliopsis, coreopsis, primrose, moonbeam coreopsis, Stella d'oros, achillea, larkspur, spiderwort, blue hosta, and yucca. Pink spirea half done. Last Japanese iris in the pond, last daisy. Fist monarda and dahlia opening, first pink and yellow hollyhocks, very late sweet Williams, one clematis. Lizard's tail blooming about a third the way up the tail. Early Queen Anne's lace and purple coneflowers. Thirteen types of lilies open along the north border. Penstemon all done.

2008: The blue jay, sparrows, cowbirds, downy woodpecker and finches continue to appear at the feeder, but the grackles are still absent (until one this evening). The first monarda opens all the way. Don's cherry tree is full of red cherries, and mulberries keep coming in. New elephant ears transplanted near the old ones that have only emerged an inch or two. New England asters transplanted to the far east garden. Young doves in the grass this afternoon; I walked within a few feet of one.

2009: Early morning birdsong strong today at 4:30, even a screech owl in the back trees. In the alley, the black raspberries have reached their best, all the bushes full of berries. Great ragweed has grown waist to chest-high. The great mullein I've been saving at the front sidewalk has opened. The one wild lettuce allowed to grow at the northeast corner of the yard is at least eight feet, maybe ten feet tall. In the vegetable garden, two poke plants are pacing the Jerusalem artichokes at seven to nine feet. Two Shasta daisies have opened today. The new Dutch iris plant has produced one beautiful, dark purple flower, almost like a Japanese pond iris.

2010: Cardinals still strong at 9:00 a.m., doves and robins in the background. Fledgling sparrows still being fed. Fallen Osage fruit larger than golf-ball size.

2011: More transplanting of annuals and perennials in the cool, cloudy afternoon and evening. Another sparrow fledgling begging for attention. I am noticing how our absence during May has made the gaps in the perennial garden more apparent. Without the recent memory of bloom sequencing, I feel an emptiness that is more a disconnection or a failure of connection; I feel only the present, not so much its part in the cycle.

2012: Frog calling off and on through the night. A cardinal woke me at 4:30 this morning. Crows came by around 5:00. At 6:30, a great chorus of sparrows, robins, starlings in the back yard. At 7:30, an even louder confluence, with visits from a cowbird, a jay, several grackles, chickadees, every creature in full voice. The violet monardas are coming in now. One great spangled fritillary in the butterfly bush today, two zebra swallowtails at the lilies, twenty-nine different lily varieties throughout the garden.

2013: Last night, warm and humid: fireflies sparkled in the butterfly bushes and in Jeanie's river birch. This morning at 4:20, full moon setting, the birds were in high chorus, cardinals and robins, sometimes the song sparrows. And down Limestone Street, then up Elm, I heard the soft rattle of the new summer crickets. Before I left for Italy, no crickets, no fireflies; now, finally at home, I am in the middle of them. As I talked to Annie late this morning, blue jays were calling and calling around the yard.

2014: Soft golden dawn, late fourth-quarter crescent moon, so clear and crisp over Lil's house. After I fed the fish, I looked up and noticed that the trumpet creeper had not only crept to the top of the greenhouse wall but had started to bloom, four fresh blossoms. By the crab apple tree, I discovered a lost "Endless Summer" hydrangea (which I thought had been killed by the cold) pushing up through ferns. I cleared it out: it has one bud cluster, maybe the first since Jeanie died. The first Japanese beetle of the year found on one of the yellow primrose blossoms.

2015: Twenty-two different lily plants in bloom this morning. Chigger bite noticed yesterday afternoon. Rhubarb harvested for pie. A great spangled fritillary in the circle garden. Three zinnia flowers, four tithonias: the time of annuals beginning.

2016: Twenty-three lily plants this morning, down nine or ten from yesterday as the Stella d'oros go into quick decline and the ditch lilies thin. One zinnia just starting to open. Last night, a long chain of thunderstorms passed through, seeming to last for hours, Bella very frightened. This morning, flowers and shrubs and bamboo leaning from wind and water. This evening along Polecat Road, I saw most of the Canadian thistles had gone to seed.

2017: Twenty-eight ditch lily blossoms, eight day lilies, two Asiatics, two Stella d'oros. All day rain.

2018: Sixty ditch lily blossoms, ten day lilies, three Stella d'oros, three Asiatic plants with about a dozen flowers in all. I found the first Japanese beetles; they were mating in the ferns. The buds in one lily patch have been eaten off by deer.

2019: Twenty-five ditch lilies, two Turk's caps, six Stella d'oros. Red admirals, hackberry butterflies and the first Japanese beetle seen.

2020: Thirty-two ditch lilies, three Stella d'oros. *Sonchus asper,* a prickly thistle about two feet high with a yellow flower found blooming in the alley this morning. First Shasta daisy seen at Don's house. Tree crickets chirping along the north hedge of the house through the day. Reports of monarch caterpillars in Kentucky. Maggie in Madison says her milkweeds just opened, so Madison has caught up with the Lower Midwest.

2021: Sixty-five ditch lilies open today, and the first day lily, a deep orange one at the east end of the north garden. The Asiatic lily plant continues to produce more flowers, pale violet-pink. Walking through the neighborhood, I saw many clumps of purple coneflowers, one blooming great mullein, patches of full-flowered milkweed, one rich planting of gooseneck loosestrife. As in many past years, I feel that I am losing touch with what is happening around me, am surprised by the progress of the summer!


*Afoot and light-hearted I take to the open road,*
*Healthy, free, the world before me,*
*The long brown path before me leading wherever I choose.*


Walt Whitman

### June 24th
### The 175th Day of the Year

*Inebriate of Air -- am I --*
*And Debauchee of Dew --*
*Reeling -- through endless summer days --*
*From inns of Molten Blue --*

Emily Dickinson

Sunrise/set: 5:07/8:08
Day's Length: 15 hours 1 minute
Average High/Low: 84/62
Average Temperature: 73
Record High: 96 – 1910
Record Low: 46 – 1972

### Weather

Fifteen percent chance of a high in the 90s today, 55 percent of 80s, thirty percent of 70s. Most of the nights are in the 60s, but 40s are recorded ten to 15 percent of the time, and 50s fifteen to 20 percent. The sun almost always shines, and rain almost never falls on June 24th; it is one of the three driest days of the Yellow Springs year.

### Natural Calendar

Leafhoppers and Japanese beetles reach the economic threshold on the farm. Katydids are silent but roving through the undergrowth. The first woolly bear caterpillars, harbingers of winter, cross the road. Snapping turtles and mud turtles hatch.

### Daybook

1982: Pink smartweed found blooming in the lawn, probably started weeks ago. First avens and trumpet creeper seen flowering this afternoon.

1983: First small bowl of both black and red raspberries.

1984: The end of Early Summer: parsnips going to seed at the mill, clustered snakeroot and waterleaf gone. Bamboo grass has fresh growth. Wood mint is budding. Huge black cricket hunters in the garden, ready for July. First large milkweed bug found at Middle Prairie. Bright orange butterfly weed seen in flower on the way to Xenia. Wild lettuce full six feet. First Canadian thistles turning to down (but most full bloom).

1986: Heal-all now open in the yard, woods, fields. First large milkweed bug seen at South Glen. Orange butterfly weed open on the way to Xenia. Nodding and Canadian thistles going to seed quickly along Dayton-Yellow Springs Road. Wood nettle budding. Hemlock gone.

1989: Last of the mulberries.

1991: First white "fuzz bug" seen on the lilies today.

1997: Wheat golden green. Catalpas full bloom. Clear fading of the hemlock. First great blue hosta flower. First red-orange lily. First mallow. Teasel heading. Parsnips three-fourths to seed.

1998: Saw a young toad, maybe an inch long, hopping through the grass this afternoon. Aida talked about seeing one of her toads, raised from a tadpole, on this date; and Lynn told the same story about finding a toad on her land on the 24th. Gooseneck, the very first, blooms in the north garden now.

1999: Purple coneflowers open in the yard.

2001: Returning to Yellow Springs from Madison, Wisconsin: The transition from Wisconsin Early Summer to Lower Midwest Deep Summer was clear by the time we reached central Illinois. Hemlock, parsnips and Canadian thistles all deteriorated quickly the further south we drove. Some fields and roadsides, however, showed a patchwork of mixed seasons, some areas holding on to June, others letting go completely.

2002: Lizard's tail full bloom today, white and soft. Lamb's ear, astilbe, sweet Williams, and daisies are full and late. Three

Japanese iris, pale violet. Monarda and goosefoot just starting. Asiatic lilies and daylilies, heliopsis, daisy fleabane, and mallow early full. Frances Williams and great blue hosta at their peak. No rust on the ferns yet. Oak-leaf hydrangea still blossoming in town. Peaches, two inches across.

2005: To Miami Beach: Mimosa trees and elderberry bushes in bloom from Ohio to Florida.

2008: Another young dove in the lawn this morning. One grackle visited the feeders. At least 18 different lily plants in bloom. No Japanese beetles yet. On the road to Fairborn, Canadian thistles and hemlock half to seed, wheat deep golden.

2009: Lizard's tail has reached full bloom in the pond. Mulberries continue to fall on Limestone and Davis Streets.

2010: End of yuccas along Davis Street. The midseason hostas have begun to flower, and Jeanie said she heard three separate, loud cicada calls this morning.

2012: First robins heard at about 4:15 this morning, a cardinal at 4:40, birdsong steady and loud through the early part of the day, blue jays joining in, too. The lily in the dooryard is lush with six huge blossoms, and a number of daylily plants (29 varieties today) are putting out dozens of flowers, bringing the peak of lily bloom now. This evening when I walked Bella an hour before sunset, I heard no birds singing.

2013: At 5:20 this morning, steady sparrow chirping, crows in the distance, cardinals, titmice and doves calling, wren heard chattering, and maybe a thrush, even a rooster crowing. Cricket trilling steady and strong.

The lilies have been swallowed up by weeds and encroaching foliage this year. They are late, compared to last year, but there are also fewer of them. The zinnias are starting to fill in a lot of spaces, though, and they should tie the surviving perennials together for the rest of the summer. At Peggy's garden, lamb's ear and Russian sage in full flower. Osage fruit fallen to the sidewalk, a little smaller than golf-ball size.

2014: Monarda and purple coneflowers coming in along North High Street. Yesterday, I again found Osage fruits on the sidewalk; some were bigger, some smaller than golf-ball size, similar to what I have found in the same place in the second week of June. Eleven lily plants in bloom here, lilies and roses becoming very prominent in the alley garden that I watch in my walks.

2015: Once again, 22 lily plants in bloom. This morning, I came across Osage fruits , the same sizes as last year, on the same High Street sidewalk. I found the first two Japanese beetles of the summer on castor bean leaves. Two great spangled fritillaries visited the tithonias, the first time I've seen two of them together.

2016: Thirty-two lily plants in bloom this morning, twelve of them now standard lilies (including three blossoms on the dooryard lilies). The Stella d'oros are down to just four plants. The bright primroses have almost disappeared. Monarda and Heliopsis full bloom. Mulberries still falling to the street, Osage fruits, too, as in so many previous years. One zinnia completely open. Motherwort foliage is tattered and diseased in the northwest corner of the garden.

At John Bryan Park, thimble plants were open, their single stalk providing the only light in the undergrowth; even most of the hobblebushes are just starting (but fully developed at home).

2017: Twenty-five day lily blossoms this morning, twenty-eight ditch lilies, two Stella d'oros and two red Asiatics, one tall yellow Asiatic opening. At Clifton Gorge: white sweet clover, a few daisies, hobble bush, thimble plant, avens, common and daisy fleabane, the river, flushed with rain, rushing down the gorge. Along the Xenia bike path, I saw a few purple rose of Sharon flowers open, the earliest so far this year.

2018: Forty-five ditch lilies, five standard day lilies, ten Asiatics today. The Davis Street yucca has completed its blooming time. Midseason hostas are well budded, showing blue. One small metalmark butterfly in the lilies. On a drive to Columbus, the landscape deep green, overflowing, some corn shoulder high, soybeans nicely developed, cattails, teasel and touch-me-nots almost as tall as the corn, many roadside grasses speckled with bright hawkweed and coreopsis.

2019: Leslie reports sighting starling flocks. At home, there is constant robin clucking, steady chirping and chirping of the house sparrows. In bloom: Seventeen ditch lilies, two Turk's caps, seven Stella d'oros.

2020: Fifty-eight ditch lilies this morning, one day lily. A few more Osage fruits on the sidewalk, fruit of yesterday's wind gusts.

2021: A record 101 ditch lilies open today, in spite of deer grazing. Two deep orange day lilies in bloom, two pink-violet Asiatics. Only cabbage butterflies.

2022: Ditch lily count: 52. Primroses down to a handful. Gladiolas so far: 100 planted. Fledglings are whining and scrambling and fluffing, lots of clucking, the back yard full of sound and movement. I surprised a large fritillary in the spiderwort this afternoon, but it sped away up over into Moya's yard before I could get a good look at it. Cottonwood cotton still lining Greene Street.

*Seeing only what is fair,*
*Sipping only what is sweet.*

Ralph Waldo Emerson

### June 25th
### The 176th Day of the Year

*Hey, Old Midsummer! are you here again,*
*With all your harvest-store of olden joys,*
*Vast overhanging meadow-lands of rain,*
*And drowsy dawns, and noons when golden grain*
*Nods in the sun....*

James Whitcomb Riley

Sunrise/set: 5:07/8:08
Day's Length: 15 hours 1 minute
Average High/Low: 84/62
Average Temperature: 73
Record High: 102 – 1988
Record Low: 42 – 1979

## Weather
Chances of highs above 100 degrees today are five percent. Nineties come 15 percent of the afternoons, 80s seventy percent, and 70s just ten percent. Precipitation falls on only 15 percent of all June 25ths, making it one of the drier days of the entire year. The sun appears 95 percent of the time.

## *Natural Calendar*
Cattails are almost fully developed. May apples are ready to harvest in the woods. Blackberries have always set fruit, even in the coldest years. Black walnuts are about half their full size, Osage fruits the size of golf balls. Ditch lilies reach full bloom, Asiatic, Oriental and standard daylilies gather momentum, pacing the monarda.

## *Daybook*
1982: Wheat fields golden brown now, some sweet corn has tassels, field corn is shoulder high.

1984: First milkweed just opening.

1986: Enchanter's nightshade in bloom. First trumpet creeper blossoms seen.

1987: Regressing in time, north to Wisconsin: multiflora roses coming back into bloom as I drove, the fields becoming brighter and greener than in Yellow Springs, shining with more gold, violet, blue.

1993: Returning to Yellow Springs from Houston, Texas, I saw parsnips going to seed through Kentucky, and nodding thistles, which had been so strong a week ago, decaying. When I got home, mallow was open in the south garden.

1996: Great mullein seen blooming along Dayton-Yellow Springs Road.

1997: Great mullein seen open along Brush Row Road. Potentilla in full bloom in town. Snow-on-the-mountain fading at the same rate as the poison hemlock. Privet season is over.

1999: North along the bike path with Walt. We ate mulberries, perfectly dark and ripe, passed a mother groundhog with her half-grown brood. Through town, daylilies everywhere, late full yucca. In the yard, full heliopsis, yellow and pink yarrow, late lamb's ear, mallow, flax. Hollyhocks, gooseneck, Queen Anne's lace heading. First sweet corn from south of Xenia came in on the 24th, planted, the grower said, in early April. As the mid-season hostas bloom, the great blue ends its flower cycle.

2001: First red monarda opened in the southeast garden today. First Japanese beetle found in the roses.

2002: Driving west and north from Yellow Springs: The habitat remained relatively stable between Ohio and Iowa, but by the time we passed Iowa City, the wheat had changed from gold to a dusky blue- green. White false indigo found in late bloom near Iowa City, some pink spirea full, some finished there. Hot and dry throughout.

2003: At 4:05 this morning, the robin chorus was strong. Doves and cardinals had joined in by 4:55. Two robins seen mating across the street at 6:35. When I walked Bella, I found a small Osage fruit about an inch and a half in diameter, still covered with the fibers of its flower stage. First red monarda in the south garden today.

2004: Milkweed is in full bloom at South Glen, but there were no milkweed beetles to be found.

2007: Black walnuts in the alley were at least half size. The birds were very quiet yesterday and this morning. Grackles seem to have left, and all the frantic chatter and the feeding of young have ended. Midseason hosta are fully budded, the Frances Williams bicolor hosta is in full bloom now. In the pond, the lizard's tail has passed its best.

2008: At the back bird feeder, a young dove and a young female grackle scrounge seeds thrown out from above by the sparrows. One large fritillary butterfly came to the garden early this afternoon, seemed to have a wingspan of at least three inches (a great spangled fritillary).

2010: The first monarch of the year seen in the north garden, sipping from the lilies. Its colors were fresh and bright, and it rollicked from flower to flower. A very young black swallowtail came to the butterfly bush after lunch, then a fritillary. Some soybeans are now almost knee high, corn still not tasseling. Jeanie heard cicadas again this morning, loud and close by. I got my first chigger bites when I mowed the lawn.

2011: To Hueston Woods west of Yellow Springs for the weekend: Inventory:  chicory, all the clovers (white, red, yellow sweet clover, white sweet clover), Rugosa roses, elderberry, yellow and orange touch-me-nots, Canadian thistles, cattails tall, enchanter's nightshade, honewort, daisies, daisy fleabane, avens, parsnips, hemlock, Queen Anne's lace, Deptford pinks, one cinquefoil, ditches full of common orange daylilies, and black raspberries just starting to come in. Along the back road, as we returned to Yellow Springs, we saw so many killdeer and doves and blackbirds (whereas most of the other roads were empty).

2012: Cardinals and robins heard when I got up this morning at 4:20. No birdsong this evening. Primrose and pink spirea gone. First hummingbird moth seen, and the first blueberry in the yard was ripe.

2013: Walking Bella at 8:00 p.m.: Robins and doves calling. Black mulberries falling, privets blooming, cottonwood cotton on the street. Full ditch lilies and new Asiatics, yucca throughout the walk. Saw Ed Oxley who talked about how he would sometimes see his cottonwood trees send out a cloud of cotton, then stop for a few hours, and then do it all again, "like snow falling," he said, waving his arms. Ed also said that he'd seen a farmer cutting wheat. So the harvest is beginning in southwestern Ohio..

2014: Again, eleven different lily plants in bloom, and this morning, one deep red one, my favorite, a new Asiatic I must have purchased just before Jeanie died. The bright garden primroses along the north fence are down to just a few blossoms – while the tall sundrops (*oenothera fruticosa*) have opened on the other side of High Street. In the pond, lizard's tail is at mid bloom.

2015: In the yard, many things are similar to last year – except that there are twenty-two lily plants open. This year I have my own *Oenothera fruticosa* and  a few that have survived the phlox beetles have put out one or two flowers apiece. Some of the common green hostas are flowering in the east wall garden. Monarda a mass of red. At the Women's Park, milkweed, heliopsis, violet monarda and purple coneflowers  are all at various stages of early bloom. Two polygonias seen today. Blue jays talking back and forth through the evening, talking to fledglings.

2016: Forty lily plants in bloom today. Great spangled fritillary (and numerous bees) in the bee-balm. Cottonwood continuing to build up beside the street near Jill's house. Avens and daisy fleabane full.

2017: Forty ditch lily blossoms, three Asiatics still, thirty-three day lily blossoms, no Stella d'oros, no primroses. The deer continue to take the buds off the lily plants, another half dozen last night in spite of the repellant spray.

2018: Fifty-five ditch lilies, ten standard day lilies, ten Asiatic blossoms, no Stella d'oros, primroses almost gone. Two small black swallowtails seen, one in the budded winterberry. At the feeder, nuthatches and titmice and red house finches more than grackles and sparrows.

2019: First milkweed bug seen. One great spangled fritillary, one large Eastern black, one red admiral, one hackberry. Two monarchs sped briefly around the milkweed patch. Thirty-six ditch lilies, six Stella d'oros, two Turk's caps in bloom. Now the monarda/bee balm is reaching early full color. The drift of blue spiderwort continues to fill much of the north garden.

2020: Fifty-four ditch lilies counted before Jill and I left for Keuka Lake in New York. The drive through central Ohio showed a palette of elegant Early Summer: deep amber fields of wheat, drifts of golden parsnips, pale blue chicory, yellow sweet clover, orange ditch lilies, pink crown vetch, pale violet Canadian thistles, and freshly cut round bales of hay. In New York: more round hay bales, plus daisies, multiflora roses, sweet peas, green-gold wheat and sweet rockets from Late Spring. Cumulus clouds and dramatic cirrus formations in the big sky throughout.

2021: Ditch lily count: 88. Giant pokeweed in bloom.

2022: Ditch lily count: 85. One bright yellow day lily opened in the night, the garden's first. Great mullein seen in bloom along Fairfield Pike. Rick reports the first monarch in his milkweed patch, first report this year.


*Dignity and beauty and meaning are given to our lives when we see far enough and wide enough, when we see the forces that minister to us, and the natural order of which we form a part.*

John Burroughs

### *June 26th*
### *The 177th Day of the Year*

*Each season brings a parallel change to the human mind and body. Every flower places its subtle signature on us; as the trees fill with leaves, so does our soul fill out for summer; the songs of the birds alter our rhythms; the south winds bring the scent of fulfillment, make us dream new dreams and reshape old ones.*

Leon Quel

Sunrise/set: 5:08/8:08
Day's Length: 15 hours
Average High/Low: 84/63
Average Temperature: 73
Record High: 98 – 1964
Record Low: 48 – 1984

### *Weather*

Like the 25th, today is typically sunny and dry, with little rain (just a 15 percent chance) likely. Highs are in the 90s twenty-five percent of the time, in the 80s sixty-five percent of the time, in the 70s or high 60s just ten percent of the time. Sixty-five percent of the lows are in the 60s, thirty percent are in the 50s, and 40s occur five percent of the years.

### *Natural Calendar*

Deep Summer typically begins near this date and lasts through the first third of August. In those six to seven weeks, approximately an hour is lost from the day's length along the 40th Parallel, and the year turns toward autumn. Even though night lengthens in this middle season, the amount of possible sunshine reaches its zenith, and the percentage of totally sunny days is the highest of the year throughout almost all of North America. And between now and the end of the first week of August, average temperatures vary just one degree.

### *Daybook*

1983: First quarts of pie cherries picked today. Great mullein blooming by the roadside, common sow thistle in the garden. At the Indian Mound, cottonwood cotton drifting through the air. Two May apples picked, size of a small plum, tasted bitter. Low hop clover and Indian hemp identified.

1984: North Glen inventory: catnip, daisies, Deptford pink, fire pink, white sweet clover, trumpet creeper, ditch lilies, wild peppergrass, Japanese honeysuckle, rough-fruited cinquefoil, yarrow, blueweed, daisy fleabane, enchanter's nightshade, forget-me-not, hobblebush, bedstraw, bittersweet nightshade, water horehound all in bloom. Brown berries on the Solomon's plume, green berries on the poison ivy, red berries on the honeysuckles, half of the Canadian thistles to seed, hemlock half gone.

1985: Black raspberries at their peak along the railroad tracks north. Figwort discovered. First soapwort found.

1987: Early acorns well formed by now. Most Canadian thistles going to seed. Sweetheart underwing moth found at school, deep orange inner wings.

1990: American lotus pads have emerged at Caesar Creek, wrinkled at the edges, folded to the center like the claw of a Venus flytrap.

1991: Caesar Creek: Three big catfish and a carp today at far hole in three feet of water. Butterflies came to my hand, early cicadas whined, sporadic. Late blooming privet found in bloom at South Glen.

1996: Into South Glen all the way to Jacoby with Jeanie: First touch-me-nots, a total of three, in bloom. Avens is in early bloom along the river. Galls found on a few goldenrod. St. John's wort and wild petunias seen. White wild yarrow in early bloom. The woods dominated by aging honewort, maybe two-thirds of it going to seed, and old clustered snakeroot. Old wild geranium seeds gathered. First wood nettle flowers have formed. First hobblebush with side flowers. Wood mint heading, maybe a week away from blossoming. First leafcup almost flowering, but most don't even have heads yet. Thin-leafed coneflower is waist high most places, sometimes chest high. One bright green tiger beetle seen. Moneywort found, rich yellow in the dark bushes. Some buckeye leaves rusting in the undergrowth.

1997: Titmouse and flicker calls dominant these days. Grackles clucking in the back trees: mulberries are ready. Into South Glen: large fritillary butterflies. Several red admirals, the old first generation faded, the younger generation bright. Thimble plant in bloom. Aging moneywort. First buds on the wood nettle. Honeysuckles, some with orange, some with red berries. Late tall meadow rue. Late honewort.

One bright green tiger beetle. Timothy is bearded. Cow parsnips have gone to seed. Cabbage moths clustering on the river bank mud, river fast and clear. A few parsnip heads are brown. Great blue heron flies off, low guttural call. Box elders hang with green seeds. Catchweed seed balls yellowing. Birdsong constant. Golden Alexander all to seed. Swarms of damselflies. Peak of wild orange tiger lilies. I surprised a young wood duck, and he scooted off downstream. Very late white violets. Yellowing garlic mustard leaves and buckeye leaves, give an autumnal glow to the woods, making a small but prophetic subseason in the undergrowth.

1998: From Jacoby to High Prairie: Rugosa roses still full. Some of their leaves had blackspot, and the small multiflora roses were losing leaves to the same fungus. Dogbane is complete in some places, some starting pods. Black raspberry still coming in. First blackberry turning red. Rare Turk's turban lily at the middle of its bloom along the river, several hundred yards north of the old bridge bed.

2000: Thinking about fluidity and porousness/porosity of awareness and notes, the way that they interchange, the extent to which events infiltrate the psyche and how they change the perception in a cascade of alterations that leave nothing the way it was at the beginning. Each act of observation transforming the observer and therefore the nature of observations to come, the compounding of minutiae, the construction of new realities….

2001: Cardinal 5:30 a.m. To Caesar Creek: one carp, one drum, one bullhead, two sunfish. Wood thrush heard. Baltimore oriole seen. White beardtongue, in the middle of its season, common along the shore. Rugosas late, but very little else flowering.

2002: Driving across Iowa: The landscape remains stable at the stage of early June for 730 miles north and west of Yellow Springs. Yellow sweet clover, crown vetch, birdsfoot trefoil, and parsnips keep the roadsides bright. The corn is deep green, the elderberry creamy white, the wheat almost blue, the soybeans a middle green. Cottonwood cotton in the wind. At Council Bluffs, banks of poison hemlock in full bloom. One butterfly weed found. Then when we entered Nebraska, there was a quick end to the Midwestern vegetation. To complement the change, all the Nebraska wheat was dark golden and ready to cut.

2003: Japanese iris full bloom. The lily bed is strong now, the bright yellows and oranges complementing the violet of the mallow, the pinks of the hollyhocks, the gold of the heliopsis. More catmint in front would set them off, I think. I got my first chigger bites today; Jeanie was attacked yesterday.

2004: Along the bike path, the leaves are darkening, the summer deepening. Wild black raspberries are ripening. Leather flower and tall tell flowers are in bloom, but few other wildflowers are visible other than honewort, an occasional jewelweed and cutover rockets. At home, the lizard's tail is at the end of its cycle and the very last water willow. Lilies gather momentum, reaching an early bloom stability.

2006: I sort back over all my birthdays to see what has happened on this or that date. The same days of each year fit together easily, wound tightly around my notebooks. There is hardly space at all between one June 26th and all the others.

In linear time, an entire year goes by between one summer and the next, and the distance seems immense. Circular time has none of that separation; like the nonlocality of psychic energy, it turns back upon itself, exists in several places at once, transcends the long, straight road that divides me from the past.

Closely placed like the rings of a tree, all the June 26ths create a radius that cuts through annual intervals. Enhanced by more and more cycles, the June 26ths swell until their cumulative meaning becomes clear: all the days are one day, all the touchstones of memory creating one self.

2007: One yellow rose flower destroyed by several Japanese beetles; no other beetles found. The birds are louder this morning, constant chatter in the woods – after last night's rain. In the afternoon, I went to the Beavercreek wetlands, a brushy cutover swath in the middle of suburbia. The sun was hot, high humidity. Scrub trees and plants, noise of earthmovers all around as more condominiums go up. Habitat of blackberry and black raspberry bramble, wild cherry and honeysuckle. Close to the ground, old sweet clover, aging white yarrow, seeded honewort, red clover, red black raspberries, dry blackberries, late parsnips, faded hemlock all to seed, late Rugosa roses, one delicate Deptford pink, many goldenrod and wingstem stalks, some boneset shoulder tall, not budded. One beautiful clump of full-blooming milkweed, but no milkweed beetles found. Dogbane with white flower buds nearby. A few St. John's wort, and a shrub with 5-petaled flower clusters, palmate leaves. Some webworms had emerged on one of its leaves. A few damselflies by the water, one horsefly, no mosquitoes, two small moths, a cabbage butterfly.

2008: In the alley, black raspberries are ripening, quite a few dark. One summer avens blossoming, panicled dogwood fading, Don's cherry tree still full of cherries. Peggy's cosmos are coming in now. At the women's park, Heliopsis, coreopsis and purple coneflowers are in early bloom Along the bike path south, avens, daisy fleabane and blueweed are open, but the few raspberries there are small and not ripe yet. Canadian thistles, nodding thistles, cow parsnips, standard parsnips, some hemlock are still flowering. Birdsfoot trefoil seen. In the back yard, the lone grackle may have a partner, a brother or a parent nearby – a male appears from time to time as she is feeding. No red-bellied woodpecker calls for a few days.

2009: To Gethsemani, Kentucky: In the woods, the landscape of Deep Summer at first seems so dark. The Late Summer staining of the leaves has not begun yet, and the spring flowers are long gone. The edge of the woods: the plants of August still without buds, ironweed and wingstem. In the hillsides, promise of September, the ubiquitous three-leafed stalks of field clover.

In the heat of the middle of the day, I ruminate on the infra nature of the flowers. The infra natures are, like landscape, figments of the mind, perhaps their angels, working miracles. And landscape, like something out of Genesis, becomes landscape in our own image and likeness.

"Cognition is a delusion," says Zen master Nansen, "and noncogition is senseless. If you want to reach the true path beyond doubt, place yourself in the same freedom as sky."

Rumination, like cognition, I thought after reading Nansen, might be delusion, more projections of false self. And then I read more about the selves in Thomas Merton, the false self being the ego which remakes the world in its own image and likeness and in such arrogance feeds itself, the ego, with its visions. And here I was with names and enumeration, touching the landscape, doing just what Kent Ryden said was the simple state of affairs, what happens to a person just because they are alive.

Walking up from the open fields, I approached an island of trees and shrubs, with a great elderberry bush in swampy ground at its edge, and beneath the elderberry flowers that were breaking up and turning to fruit, a long drift of blackberry bushes, their ripening berries so bright and red. I began musing that, as a mentor of mine had hinted, it was the relationship with the blackberry that mattered, not the blackberry itself, and of course what could either of those ideas mean really, and was not the whole point just to wait until the berry was ripe and then eat it? But what about right now, my emotion when the berry was red and shining in the sun like the underbelly of this great elderberry bush? That too was a relationship, a kind of love.

2010: To South Glen at 9:30 this morning, heat and humidity building: Buckeye leaves rusting at the entry beyond the covered bridge, delicate honewort common and to seed. Rank, imposing wood nettle, chest high, all budded in its habitat close to the river, where the 17-year cicadas will appear again in 2021. Firm berry clusters on the Jack-in-the pulpits. Scattered violet remnants of the sweet rockets. Aging clustered snakeroot full of daddy longlegs. Yellowing garlic mustard and hemlock leaves and stalks, rose hips firm. May apples mottled and tattered, fruit gone. Ripe black raspberries, blackberries tight and green.

Near what was once the butterfly preserve, Canadian thistles half to seed. Nodding thistles still full. Milkweed open but no milkweed beetles seen. Some white yarrow breaking down. Leafcup budded, jewelweed soft and lush. Fruit on the panicled dogwood. Fat Angelica collapsing, old parsnips to seed. Random white clover, red clover, a few white sweet clovers, a few purple vetches, some black medic, then deep in the woods the path is filled with white clover.

I walk under the canopy of exotic honeysuckles and scrub box elder, black walnut, locust, Osage orange, and through a forest of September goldenrod, beside so many young wingstem along the path, through ground covers of clearweed and smartweed and waterleaf. A female mallard with four ducklings the size of my hand feed along the riverbank. Doves calling, red-winged blackbirds chortling and whistling, a grackle clucking, robins peeping, a catbird whining in a high sycamore, crows far off, once in a while a blue jay. Small tan moths rising from the undergrowth.

Near the water, black damselflies with white speckles on their wings, luminescent blue damselflies, some thin darners, one emerald six-spotted tiger beetle. Sleek wood snails nestled on leaves. Shy mosquitoes in the open, hungry in the shade. One black swallowtail, one tiger swallowtail, question mark butterflies, cabbage butterflies. One spitbug hidden in its wet coverlet. One shining Japanese beetle. Houseflies mating in the sun.

2012: To the quarry park: Sunny and warm with a steady breeze. Much of the landscape drying out and past its early June prime. But still a lot of brightness with orange butterfly weed, chicory, blue weed, blue vervain. Fields of white sweet clover and drifts of yellowing hemlock (with violet-gray stems), Queen Anne's lace, scrub dogwoods with green berries, the very first teasel in bloom, a few fading cottonwood leaves, some black-eyed Susans, a few purple coneflowers, small daisies, many lesser daisy fleabanes, common ragweed to twelve inches, cattails sleek and firm, St. John's wort, salsify to seed, silver olive with brown berries, yarrow, galls on goldenrod, violet-flowered wild garlic, red clover drying up, sumac with red seeds, milkweed budded, late Rugosa roses, crown vetch, purple vetch, pokeweed with berries, gray headed coneflower, small flowered bindweed, no berries on the honeysuckles, one thimble plant in bloom, one dogbane ready to flower, many nodding thistles, a few blossoming still, most tattered and to seed, one black swallowtail, one monarch, two sulfurs, flies pesky.

2013: To the Grinnell walkway down to the Swinging Bridge at noon: The woods dark and subdued in this time between seasons. May apples toppled over, foliage dappled with yellow. Leafcup plants had been eaten off by deer, would bloom as they recovered. Near the wetland area, moss on a fallen tree seemed to glow in the twilight beneath the canopy. A few late enchanter's nightshade plants still had tiny blossoms, but Early Summer's honewort was gone. Pollen had disappeared from the clustered snakeroot. Some spicebushes and privets had green berries. Touch-me-nots were tall but not budded yet.

The wood nettle of July was still not ready to flower. Down toward the creek, white hobblebush hydrangeas in bloom brightened the undergrowth, the only landmarks left from Early Summer. Light cobwebs of micrathena spiders, not the stickier ones of the Late Summer, lay across my way. A few inches above last year's layer of leaves, the foliage of spring's ginger, waterleaf, poison ivy, clearweed and bloodroot formed a low, intermittent canopy, replacing the common chickweed that had dominated the forest floor in spring.

A lone daisy fleabane and one wilted ragwort had blossoms near a spring that crossed the path. Other fragments April and May: bare scaffolding of old meadow rue, sweet Cicely, Jacob's ladder, wild geranium, golden alexander. The stalks of August's ironweed, zigzag goldenrod, white snakeroot and the small-flowered asters blended into the honeysuckles, their timing tuned by heat and the amount of sunlight. Algae and spent watercress lay below the Cascades. A few damselflies hovered near the old skunk cabbage. Cardinals called in the distance.

Robins sang to guide their young.

2014: Black walnuts about a third of full size in the alley, avens moving to full bloom there. A zebra swallowtail passed in front of me as I walked along Dayton Street under the serviceberry trees. In the garden, a great spangled fritillary was sipping the milkweed. Now the lilies are picking up, fifteen this morning, the new Asiatics especially beautiful, deep red and violet. The astilbes are in full color now, complementing the hostas beside and around them, well planned by Jeanie. A short walk at the Mill Dam area, river very high from the recent rains: A habitat of harsh wood nettle (just starting to flower) mixed with delicate honewort (gone to seed), four and five foot wingstem stalks lining the path, many avens, patches of touch-me-not and tall coneflower foliage, several wood mint plants with new flowers, a few violet wild petunias *(ruellia)*, and four tall anemones/thimbleweeds *(Rubus parviflorus)*.

2015: Twenty-seven different lily plants open today. Monarda, spiderwort, great blue hosta, heliopsis complementing the lilies. Peggy's gray-headed coneflowers are just starting, and I saw several new rose of Sharon blossoms downtown. (Moya's came in three or four days ago!)

Walking at Clifton Gorge and John Bryan Park: full avens, wood mint, pokeweed, lopseed, hobblebush and great Indian plantain. Clusters of ramps fully budded sticking up through the mulch, all their spring foliage gone. Some white vervain and some leafcup beginning, several tall nettles and thimble plants in bloom. One clump of bright Deptford pinks. Green hickory nuts on the path, a few green acorns. Fat red berries on one honeysuckle by the river. Cow parsnip and honewort to seed. Black cherry trees with black cherries. Only one wild raspberry bush seen: fruit still not ripe. Tight green berry clusters on the Jack-in-the-pulpit.

The woods stained now with yellowing and rusting May apple foliage, sweet Cicely, Solomon's plume (with brown berries) foliage. A few buckeye leaves have turned, the undergrowth showing the summer's age. This evening, John Blakelock called to say that his American toads were singing again, just started today. He'd never heard them try a second round of calls. Perhaps it's the steady rains of the last week or so, the month's precipitation at about six and a half inches, almost three inches above normal.

2016: Down the path to Xenia: Leafcup with early flowers here and there, ditch lilies common, some heal-all in the grass, full clovers and black medic, two touch-me-not blossoms, one patch of wild spiderwort with deep purple blooms, black raspberries mostly red but some sweet for picking, blackberries still small and green, one Rugosa rose bush with many flowers. At the side of the path, sprawling sweet rocket plants with their splayed flower heads gone to seed, garlic mustard stalks browning and green cones on the sumac. At the Women's Park, heliopsis, purple coneflowers and milkweed were the dominant flowers. At home, as the Stella d'oros and ditch lilies decline, the other day lilies ascend: thirty-two lilies in all in the late afternoon.

2017: At home, thirty-seven ditch lily blossoms this morning, fifty-six standard day lilies, three Asiatics, more damage to the day lilies from the deer. Once again, I walked Clifton Gorge and John Bryant Park on my birthday, the varieties of flowers almost the same as when I walked there that date in 2015.

To my description of two years ago, I would add numerous luminescent green damsel flies, two red admirals, two azures, one brown, one pearl, one great spangled fritillary, a small cluster of pale violet spiderworts, a clump of white bee-balm, daisy fleabane common, enchanter's nightshade, Canadian thistles and nodding thistles in flower, parsnips holding, berry clusters on the baneberry, elderberry flowers mostly turned to green berries, timothy and clustered snakeroot all to seed, tattered and disintegrating orchard grass, white vervain and hemlock, some fresh brome and recent bottle grass, yellowing meadow rue and blanched sweet Cicely, horsetail grass budded, leafcup and small-flowered agrimony showing some yellow buds, one orange butterfly weed, wood nettle not quite blooming, fat plumes of lizard's tail, Saint John's wort late full, milkweeds in full flower – but without milkweed beetles, one white yarrow, juniper berries filling the juniper branches, raspberries – some red, some ripe. I heard cardinals, a young crow begging to be fed and a pileated woodpecker. A green frog croaked by the creek.

At the bend of the river before the old mill, a great blue heron flew up from the flooded shoreline. And after I ate lunch at the lower picnic area, a small groundhog approached me and sniffed my boots. When I left he followed me quite a ways, squeaking, running hard to catch up.

2018: To the quarry at 8:30 this morning, cool at first with light wind, then the Sun grew warm and the wind went away. Tree crickets constant. This habitat that I sometimes thought of as barren was so full of flowers today, richer than the Glen fields and woodlands. I walked through long patches of white and yellow sweet clover, daisy fleabane, small white daisies and chicory, one large cluster of black-eyed Susans, past occasional blue vervains and St. John's wort, fat bull thistles (some gone to seeds with puffy dandelion-like heads), crown vetch, great mullein, moth mullein (very late), heal all, Deptford pinks, Queen Anne's lace, avens, black medic, red clover, thimble plant, dogbane budding, one white yarrow plant, one clump of woodland sunflowers, one small cinquefoil, many common milkweeds, many blue weeds, many bright orange butterfly weeds, much reed grass, some brome grass seeded .

The habitat seemed so accessible, a finite number of wildflowers in bloom, a few others yet to bloom: goldenrod, ragweed, teasel, little evidence of spring blooms. Only a few species of trees and shrubs: panicled dogwood and honeysuckle prominent, cottonwood and sycamore the only real large trees, some water willow and silver olive, many juniper and red cedar. And I saw more butterflies than I have all year in town and the Glen: two monarchs, a great spangled fritillary, many many sulphurs. And on the walk downtown this evening: two rose of Sharon blossoms, the first I've seen this summer.

2019: Forty-one ditch lilies in the garden this morning, one standard day lily, two Turk's cap and six Stella d'oros. One hackberry butterfly, one great spangled fritillary noticed as I ate breakfast on the porch. Basswood tree seeds falling near the AME church. Sparrow fledglings begging for food and being fed on the feeders. Mosquitoes were pesky today, really for the first time this year. At the Covered Bridge, wood mint was in full flower, wood nettle starting to bloom, honewort mostly finished, one Rugosa rose bush with blossoms, but no other flowers open. I found a few brome plants, a little English rye grass. The only prominent grass was a species of wild wheat. From Goshen, Indiana, Judy reports that the dove nestlings that hatched a week ago, have still not left the nest.

2020: Keuka Lake, New York: Watching clouds.

2021: Lily count: 28 ditch lilies (down 60 from yesterday), two day lilies. Slow walk at Covered Bridge, 4:30 p.m., 88 degrees: Now the fierce wood nettle guards the undergrowth. Dozens of black damselflies and many green-bodied ones explore that prickly waist-high canopy. The river is low and slow, a few carp visible swimming in the occasional deeper holes. Along the water, lizard's tail is soft and white in early bloom. All the honewort, full flower two weeks ago when the 17-year cicadas were calling, has gone to seed. Garlic mustard and sweet rocket dry and leaning. Skunk cabbage is motley with age, some buckeye trees rusting. Clustered snakeroot getting old. Wild roses gone. Two huge elderberry bushes in full bloom. Avens late. Touch-me-nots waist high, ironweed and wingstem to my shoulders. One *Poligonia* comma butterfly and one moth with black cruciform markings, *Haploa clymene.*

2022: Ditch lilies: 72, day lilies: one creamy colored in the circke garden, The transition to Deep Summer has begun with the end of the primroses and the worn, raggedy nature of the spiderwort. The bee balm is gaining momentum, and the heliopsis is strong, although its plants greatly diminished and no longer anchoring the northwest garden.

*Unlike simple geographical locations, which exist objectively, places do not exist until they are verbalized, first in thought and memory and then through the spoken or written word.*

Kent Ryden

### June 27th
### The 178th Day of the Year

*The earth is all before me. With a heart*
*Joyous, nor scared at its own liberty,*
*I look about; and should the chosen guide*
*Be nothing better than a wandering cloud,*
*I cannot miss my way.*

William Wordsworth

Sunrise/set: 5:08/8:08
Day's Length: 15 hours
Average High/Low: 84/63
Average Temperature: 73
Record High: 98 – 1971
Record Low: 48 – 1927, 50 – 2017

### Weather
The chances of precipitation rise to 30 percent today. Sun, however, is still the rule, with completely overcast conditions occurring just 15 percent of the time. Highs are usually in the 80s (seven days out of ten), climb to 90 fifteen percent of the time, reach only the 70s another 15 percent.

### Natural Calendar
The canola harvest starts near this date in the Lower Midwest. Winter wheat is usually a third ripe, first cutting begun. Cabbage gathering ends in most of Great Lakes area. Summer blueberries are ready to pick. Earliest cornfields start tasseling. Cottony maple scale eggs hatch on the silver maples.

### Daybook
1987: To Kentucky: Orange butterfly weed common by the roadsides below Cincinnati. First corn tassels seen in southern Ohio, angelica all gone to seed. Some sycamore bark has fallen. Teasel blooming near Lexington.

1989: South Glen: Avens in early full bloom, lower buckeye leaves are starting to weather and yellow. First leafcup blooms, some wood nettle full. Last moneywort seen, late tall meadow rue, timothy completely bearded, Virginia roses full like at Caesar Creek. A field of daisy fleabane, more fields of full Queen Anne's lace. Huge prickly sow thistle, six feet high. Lesser stitchwort identified in late bloom, germander heading, last of the blueweed, last of the yellow sweet clover, last of the parsnips. Dozens of cabbage butterflies in a field of Canadian thistles gone to seed.

1993: Home from Houston to a whole new season. The black and red raspberries are coming in now, the Asiatic lilies are in early full bloom, first yellow daylily in the yard. Mid-season hosta budding along the north wall, seen blooming other parts of town. The garden is overgrown, lettuce all gone to seed, tomatoes with fruit an inch in diameter, the second crop of radishes ready to pull, the carrot patch filled in with foliage, the rows indistinguishable. The carnations are done after just seven or eight days, and the sweet Williams have decayed, are tattered and fallen. The cosmos are waist high, some of the first flowers starting. The tall yellow yarrow is open, and the Queen Anne's lace is taller than the rose bushes, the first head blooming. Cherries all red now, branches hanging heavy and low.

1997: First yucca seen open in Kettering.

1998: Jacoby to High Prairie: Some of the wild yarrow fading. Osage fruit maybe a third size. Elderberry bushes half in flower, half berries. Canadian thistles full bloom here. Teasel big, but no flowers. Showers of yellow leaves when I stepped inside a locust grove. Moth mullein late, early Queen Anne's lace, baby robins, field thistles waist high, avens full, first touch-me-nots open, honewort done. Enchanter's nightshade, purple vetch, Deptford pink, hobblebush, wood mint, St. John's wort, thimbleweed, sweet clovers, brome grass, wood nettle, daisy fleabane, milkweed, thin leaf plantain all in bloom. Gray tree frogs heard in another locust grove. Timothy heavily bearded but still sweet to chew. Black butterfly with golden eye on wings. May apples, garlic mustard, rusted buckeye leaves bring faded gold to the woods. One hickory nut fallen, seemed full size. Woods wet and dewy, mosquitoes very bad, river and brooks strong from the rain.

2002: On the road: Catnip, cattails, milkweed provide roadside color across Nebraska. Past the desert in Wyoming, yellow sweet clover reappears. At the Utah border, wild lupine found.

2003: Cardinals, robins, doves loud at 4:35 a.m. A monarch butterfly visited the north garden at mid morning.

2007: First dark green midseason hosta flowers open. First violet monarda blooms – the red are in full bloom. Sticky buds noticed on the burdock in the alley. All morning, robins have been peeping something like their autumn migration call, but this is faster and more intense – still, not a whinny. More rain last night, the drought certainly at an end in Yellow Springs.

2008: The lone female grackle was back this morning, and the red-bellied woodpecker called twice. Mulberries are still coming in, Don's cherries are holding, and more alley raspberries are ripening. White "fuzz bugs" noticed on some struggling astilbe. Heavy rains last night toppled two dahlias. In the vegetable garden, spinach to seed, but lettuce and chard are lush. The first Japanese beetles appeared on the ferns this morning, and inch-long praying mantises were in the ferns and lilies. One rose full of Japanese beetles in the afternoon. In the pond, fingerlings continue to emerge; some are now maybe half an inch, others barely visible. One red-bellied woodpecker call heard this noon, one orange fritillary seen.

2009: Gethsemani, Kentucky: I am used to being here in the fall. Today is so hot, the humidity so high. But I begin to walk and look about in the fields before the sun gets higher and I get too tired.

A reading from Genesis at the service this morning: Abraham's aged wife, Sarah, mocking the angels (disguised as travelers) who had promised her she would bear a son in her old age. Of course, against the odds, the child appeared.

I wander out onto rolling hills, past hay in great round bales, into patches of tall violet monarda and knapweed full of honeybees, bright orange butterfly bushes full of butterflies, white

Queen Anne's lace and yarrow, long drifts of daisy fleabane, the pathway lined with vervain and powder-blue chicory.

I ruminate about Kent Ryden's assertion that place or landscape exists only as a projection of the mind, that the land is not only dependent on our perception but takes its nature, its characteristics from what we formulate its shapes to be. Place is structure that seems so distant but is actually inside us, constructed by us, an outcropping of our vision.

After an hour in the sun, I retreat into the dark and the shade of the forest. I accept the cool with the mosquitoes. The Deep Summer woods offers only fragments of color: a few avens, a lost fleabane, one pale wild petunia, some small yellow sorrel.

I take the foliage for granted, dismiss its dominance that shadows the path in spite of the protection it offers me in sassafras, pawpaw, locust, walnut, yellow poplar, creeper, sycamore, and in spite of the fact that it is so ephemeral and that at any moment it will start turning, become mottled, and then disappear into autumn. I walk past the religious sculptures placed a long the walkway, every few hundred yards a Virgin Mary, a St. Francis, or other storied figure. I think about the written requests placed at their feet, consider miracles. Then at the end, I come across three angels disguised as statues. Landscape as the figment of my mind: What will these three promise me?

2010: I just noticed that Mateo's rose of Sharon is in full bloom – then I came home to find some of ours open, too. On the privet bushes in front of the Champneys': first small berries. When Bella and I walk to the alley at 9:30 this morning, twittering of sparrows, clucking of robins, some scrawing of the starlings. Baby sparrows being fed by parents at the feeders. Red admiral and a black swallowtail at the butterfly bush today. Corn tassels just emerging from the great tall fields on the way to the interstate.

This afternoon, my friend Don Wallis wrote: "As to the South Glen woods, my real-life home: yes, on the First Day of Summer the ticks took over -- they're thirsty for blood, skin oil, scalp juice, etc. Since I have no Bella, the dog, they travel home on my body, and yeah, I got a houseful myself. Spiders, too. Rude guests -- demanding of attention. Always restless and hungry. They never sleep. Plus, I itch. Damn. It's not right. It's not fair.

What the hell is wrong with Nature?" Of course, no one loves it more than Don.

2011: Cardinal loud at 4:24 a.m., then calling for several minutes. Robin chorus continues. At 9:00, grackles clucking, then feeding their fledgling at the feeder. Blue jay restless, red-bellied woodpecker still calling. Then sparrows all around, screaming and feeding their babies. In the alley, more grackle clucking and another baby hopping in TK's yard. Through the afternoon, feeding and calling. Strong robin vespers near sunset, punctuated with cardinal song.

2012: Robins at about 4:20, but their chorus was relatively faint, and lasted only until a little after 5:00. A cardinal first sang at 4:29, and cardinal song lasted maybe half an hour. The last primrose flowers gone today, last of our ditch lilies (but they are still common throughout the area). Still thirty different lily plants in bloom today in the garden. Starling fledgling being fed by the pond early this afternoon, and a spicebush butterfly came by the pond, too. Some cardinal song at my walk this evening. Jeanie heard cicadas, the first so far, at dusk.

2013: Pokeweed flowering, some setting green fruit. One Osage fruit, about a third of its full size, on the sidewalk this morning after last night's rain. Ten different lilies in bloom – but many more are budded. Saw the first Greene County wheat field being cut.

2014: Our few blueberries, blushed magenta just five days ago, are now pale blue. Fifteen different lilies in bloom this morning. At the entry to South Glen: hobblebush lush flowering, leafcup starting to show color, wood nettle fierce, a few full bloom, honewort still full in places, a few enchanter's nightshade, rusting buckeye leaves, several small wood snails on the wood nettle leaves, many tan moths and black damselflies fluttering, gliding in the undergrowth, one bright polygonia butterfly, the first butterfly I've seen all day. At home, the first violet phlox came out in the afternoon, and the tattered chives plant produced one flower.

2015: Thirty-two lily plants in bloom this afternoon, my transplanting of last year producing many more blossoms at this point than in earlier summers. The lush motherwort plant at the northwest corner of the yard has finally reached the end of its flowering, its leaves even drooping. Purple coneflowers and Queen Anne's lace in early bloom at Peggy's and at the Women's Park and downtown.

2016: From last night's storm: a black walnut the size of a golf ball and an Osage twice as big came down. Forty-two lily plants in bloom this morning, 11 alone in the circle garden. The Stella d'oros have completed their season here. And I found the first Japanese beetles in the north garden. Two hackberry butterflies seen in the yard today, one great spangled fritillary yesterday.

2017: Thirty-two ditch lily blossoms, 39 day lilies, three Asiatics. Unusually cool this morning and through the day, low 50, a high of 71.

2018: The first standard hostas have started to open. Twenty-four day lilies, 40 ditch lily, four Asiatic blossoms. Three yellow primrose flowers.

2019: Fifty ditch lilies, one Turk's cap, two Stella d'oros this morning, and one of the tall tree lilies opened this afternoon. The primroses still offer color by the new peach tree, and the spiderwort is lush near the red cannas. Steady blue jay calls heard in the late afternoon. Two sulphur butterflies seen on my jog at Ellis.

2020: Keuka Lake, New York: A mother mallard with four very small ducklings swims back and forth near the dock. Much of yesterday and today, I spent at the lake watching clouds in the big sky. I haven't watched clouds so long since I sat with Jeanie in her hospital room waiting for her to be discharged. That day in middle July, the clouds hardly moved at all, just like the slow time itself as we waited and waited.

2021: Five day lilies are open this morning: one pink, two deep orange, two big gold. Ditch lilies at 55. To Keuka Lake: The southwestern Ohio landscape with deep brown wheat, corn knee high, roads lined with orange ditch lilies, yellow snakeroot, golden trefoil, powder blue chicory, old hemlock to seed, teasel growing tall. Several young groundhogs near the road. Intense heat all the way, but nothing like the rare triple-digit temperatures in Portland, Oregon. Arriving at the Finger Lakes Region in New York: wheat pale beige, gold staghorns prominent on the sumacs. From Portland, Oregon, Jeni reports triple-digit highs.

2022: Sitting on the back porch around eight o'clock this morning, I listened to the steady clucking and cawing of starlings all around.

> *Often I am permitted to return to a meadow*
> *as if it were a given property of the mind*
> *that certain bounds hold against chaos,*
> *that is a place of first permission,*
> *everlasting omen of what is.*

Robert Duncan

### June 28th
### The 179th Day of the Year

*I hear the wild bee wind his horn,*
*The bird swings on the ripened wheat.*
*The long green lances of the corn*
*Are tilting in the winds of morn,*
*The locust shrills his song of heat.*

John Greenleaf Whittier

Sunrise/set: 5:09/8:08
Day's Length: 14 hours 59 minutes
Average High/Low: 84/63
Average Temperature: 74
Record High: 101 – 1934, 102 – 2012
Record Low: 52 – 1926

### Weather

Temperature distribution for today: 20 percent chance of 90s (including a slight chance of 100), seventy percent of 80s, ten percent of 70s. Skies are partly cloudy to sunny 80 percent of the days; precipitation, however, occurs 40 percent of the time as the final high-pressure system of the month approaches and the Corn Tassel Rains get underway. Those rains typically take place in a two-week period between the end of June and the middle of July.

### Natural Calendar

Purple coneflowers, white vervain, horseweed, germander, teasel and wild lettuce blossom in the fields; tall bellflowers and great Indian plantain open in the woods. The first white-flowered thimbleweeds set thimbles.

### Daybook

1984: Nodding thistles going to seed.

1985: Creeping bellflower identified, has probably been open for almost a week.

1987: Rose of Sharon is blooming early.

1990: This has been the greenest June that I remember. And the cardinals have been singing just as loud as in May all month, the decline of spring not so obvious, the roadsides lush.

1991: Mallow still full bloom, lychnis fading.

1992: Astilbe complete for the year. More raccoons killed along Grinnell, foretaste of the Dog Days.

1993: The Corn Tassel Rains are two weeks before the corn tassels this year. The rain batters the perennials. The coreopsis are drooping, lilies and cosmos leaning, hollyhocks broken and fallen forward into the vegetable garden, weeds starting to get the better of us now. Lettuce has gone to seed, and the radishes are hot.

1997: First coreopsis blooms today, planted from seed in March. Riding along the bike path, I found the first dogbane in bloom, first pokeweed. July and August's plants getting tall: leafcup, wild lettuce, ironweed. On the way down Limestone Street, I passed a mulberry tree: black mulberries still all over the road.

1998: First cicadas heard today.

1999: Red monarda opened today. Suddenly coneflowers are everywhere. Birds much quieter now throughout the day.

2000: Portland, Oregon through eastern Washington, June 27 – 29: Cow parsnips, which had been in full bloom a week ago when we arrived in Portland, now mostly gone to seed. Blackberries have set fruit, bushes darkening, many thimbleweed flowers gone, fruit formed. Cattails have emerged and show their pollen. Rhododendrons, late a week ago, are gone. Blue-tint snowball viburnums large, full flowered in Portland, the smaller variety just opening at Quinault Lake in southwestern Washington. Full-blooming sweet peas along the river gorge, and common throughout the trip.

2001: First hollyhock opens.

2002: We left dry Wyoming and came into the green Salt Lake valley. The corn is Yellow Springs height, haying all across the land, and some of the wheat is gold. In Ontario, Oregon (southeastern Oregon): milkweed, pink spirea, hollyhocks, potentilla all full bloom. Salsify, yellow sweet clover, and teasel seen here and there along the roadsides, a little behind southwestern Ohio.

2003: Several lilies done for the year, the pale pink and the tall orange Asiatics. The rest of the lily bed is opening nicely, complemented by pink and cream hollyhocks and violet mallow. The large blue hosta remains at full bloom along the west border. Green thorax noticed on a small thin bee that was visiting the mallow. Small beeflies noticed around the yard the last few days. In the Caribbean, Hurricane "Bill," the second hurricane of the season, is moving north toward Louisiana.

2004: One last Japanese honeysuckle flower dies back, the peak of bloom having passed maybe two weeks ago. The red June phlox that started in early June continues to flower, even as midsummer phlox is starting and the first blackberries are reddening at a few locations around town. The second budding of comfrey is beginning. The final flowers on the pink spirea are rusting, and the spiderwort seems to be declining.

2007: Driving north of Springfield, I saw the roadsides full of the pale green decay of hemlock and the blackening seed clusters of angelica. Coming back from Xenia, I saw a few corn stalks with tassels. Late this afternoon, crows were whining and calling in the back trees – adults and fledglings arguing about something.

2008: A young robin with a speckled breast came to the porch this morning, the first adolescent that I've seen this year. The red-bellied woodpecker called about 9:30. Throughout the morning, clouds, thunder, scattered rain, the weather perfect for transplanting, but wet for walking in the woods. No whining crows so far. Three purple coneflowers open in the yard. One red monarda patch almost full. Midseason hostas are fully budded now, but none have blossomed yet.

2009: At Gethsemani, the chestnut tree's flowers are falling now, browning, soft, unlike their spiny, heavy fruit. Throughout northern Kentucky, the wheat has been cut, and corn is six to eight feet tall. Canadian thistles have all gone to down, and the hemlock is yellowing and bent.

2010: Hard rain and lightning storm last night. This morning, cardinals early, and when I got up about 5:00, doves were calling, and then crows came in. And maybe the crows are starting to flock now, becoming audible as they gather.

2011: Queen Anne's lace and chicory are common, and daylilies increase in variety and number. Now the northwest garden is in full bloom with roses, salvia, heliopsis, gooseneck, spiderwort, monarda, the Annabelle hydrangea, the ditch lilies and new daylilies. A pint of raspberries picked from our few bushes, the best crop of the year! Cardinal vespers this evening around eight o'clock. Field crickets at various points in my walk with Bella. Robin peeping outside our bedroom window just after sunset.

2012: Deep summer now, a high expected past 100 today. A hackberry butterfly seen by the pond late this morning. The Joe Pye weed has been heading up for about a week. Sweet rocket seed stems cut back this morning. Mid-season hostas in full bloom throughout the neighborhood. Ramps in full flower beneath them. First corn tassels seen on the way back from Beavercreek. Everything following suit from the hot spring.

2013: One great spangled fritillary butterfly in the zinnias about noon. John Blakelock has ripening blueberries and a katydid calling. Tree crickets sing through the night and day.

2014: Fifteen lilies again today. Blueberries ripening. Monarda reaching early full. Primroses gone. Two zinnias open. At Ellis Pond, the mulberry bush is done blooming, has very small green berries.

2015: A ragged great spangled fritillary in the lilies this morning. Thirty-three lily plants in bloom this afternoon. Three clymene moths *(Haploa clymene)* seen today in the Glen.

2016: Thirty-eight lilies this morning. Small bee with bright green thorax (*Agapostemon*) noticed on the monarda. Near the shop downtown, I saw the first rose of Sharon open. At the quarry habitat, a predominance of white sweet clover with scattered blueweed and blue vervain, St. John's wort and orange butterfly weed. A few very old daisies are still in bloom. A very simple environment within which to watch the trajectory of the year. Coming back to Yellow Springs, Jill and I noticed the first small flock of starlings, a mini-murmuration above the road and adjacent cornfield.

2017: Seventy-nine day lily flowers, eighteen ditch lilies.

2018: Forty-three day lilies, thirty-six ditch lilies, Asiatics down to three blossoms, the first dahlia opening, the first zinnia slowly unraveling. Many sulphurs in the yard today for the first time, a monarch stayed in the milkweed throughout the morning and a great spangled fritillary and a red admiral came by the hummingbird feeder. Tree frogs strong along Dayton Street as Jill and I walked after sunset.

2019: At 4:30 this morning, robins and cardinals raucous, doves soft in the background. Sixty-eight ditch lilies, one tree lily, three day lilies, one Turk's cap, three Stella d'oros. I noticed that trumpet creeper flowers have appeared on the porch trellis, probably have been out maybe a week. Sparrows chant through the day, abundant at the feeder, fledglings a part of the action, the birds exploding as a flock when startled. Chiggers attacked me as I transplanted canna lilies. One hackberry butterfly came by as I worked. A record-breaking heat wave, temperatures in the 100s, has spread across Europe, and is growing here, as well. Tree frogs calling quietly as I walked Ranger at night.

2020: Scattered inventory: Finger Lake Region, New York:

Dogbane opening, daisies, crown vetch, sweet peas, birdsfoot trefoil, ditch lilies, yellow sweet clover, prickly sow thistle (*Sonchus asper*), roadside buttercup (about ½ inch), plant with umbels of tiny, white, five-petaled flowers, ribbed stem and long-stemmed, opposite palmate leaves in a triangular shape, red clover and white clover, late sweet rockets, elderberries in early flower, white sweet clover.

2021: Intense heat wave covers the Northwest, Portland with record triple-digit temperatures. In the Midwest and western New York State, highs in the 90s. At Keuka Lake, Jill notes how few gulls there are now. She remembers her father in a constant struggle to keep them off of the float out on the lake. No mosquitoes, but one bright yellow tiger swallowtail visited the dock area in the afternoon.

*Once you realize this floating life is the perfect mirage of change,*
*it is breath-taking, this wild joy and wandering boundless and free.*

Han Shan/David Hinton

## *June 29th*
## *The 180th Day of the Year*

*Below Arcturus lies the Virgin,*
*Corn with tassels shining in her hand.*

Aratos

(The verse by Aratos quoted above places the farm year within the context of the heavens. The Boötes star group (including the great star, Arcturus) is directly overhead after dark this week, and below that constellation lies Virgo (the Virgin) in the southwest – both constellations announcing the tasseling of the corn in temperate regions in typical years.)

Sunrise/set: 5:09/8:08
Day's Length: 14 hours 59 minutes
Average High/Low: 84/63
Average Temperature: 74
Record High: 100 – 1934
Record Low: 49 – 1905

### *Weather*
The likelihood of precipitation is 35 percent, and clouds completely obscure the sky 25 percent of the days. The chance of a high in the 90s is 25 percent, of 80s fifty percent, of 70s twenty to 25 percent. This is one of only two Middle-Summer days when a cold afternoon in the 60s is possible (July 13th is the other).

### *Natural Calendar*
Wheat Harvest Season introduces the beginning of Deep Summer, the time when Sycamore Bark Falling Season points to aphelion and the center of the year. Thistle Down Season is another sure sign of Deep Summer. Leafhopper Season and Japanese Beetle Season reach economic levels on the farm and in the garden at this time. Cattail Flowering Season is visible from the roadways, as is Staghorn Season on the staghorn sumacs. The opening of Turtle Hatching Season presages the Dog Days of July, while Woolly Bear Caterpillar Season looks ahead to autumn.

Thimbleweed Setting Thimbles Season, Wood Mint Season, Lopseed Season and Leafcup Season replace Clustered Snakeroot Season and Honewort Season in the shade.

### *Daybook*

1982: First chigger bites from walk in the woods. Common sow thistle blooming in the garden.

1983: South Glen, evening: Early leafcup, wood nettle first blooms, first touch-me-nots. Parsnips are going to seed, wild onions, angelica, too. Tall meadow rue, violet bush clover, water willow, elderberry, panicled dogwood are in full bloom. Osage fruits are an inch in diameter.

1987: First cicadas heard in the yard.

1988: Belize: The abundance of new plants to watch: I think about micro habitats, like archeological squares for excavations, artificial limitations, roping off of climate and landscape, each day or plot or field an extensive case study.

1990: Sundrops almost gone, foxgloves gone. Peak lily time. Milkweed and butterfly weed beginning. Red and violet monardas throughout town, and Shasta daisies. Veronica late, astible late full. First leek seed heads breaking apart. Grackles are still loud in the mulberries, yucca still open.

1991: Teasel early full bloom south toward Kettering. First local sweet corn at the farmer's market. First field corn is tasseling in the fields around Yellow Springs.

1997: One yellow Asiatic lily bloomed today. (The progression has been orange, yellow, pink, and red-orange.) First purple loosestrife today. Almost no yuccas in bloom yet – the latest they've ever been. Tall cressleaf groundsel suddenly gone from the roadsides and fields.

2000: Central Washington State: Milkweed full bloom, wheat pale brown, potatoes lush and two-feet tall. Haying everywhere, field corn knee high, full potentilla. Great mullein open, trefoil, yellow sweet clover. At the gardens in Spokane, a wonderful variety of summer flowers in early full bloom, while the last of the spring poppies, iris and Dutch iris were losing their petals, and a small-flowered mock orange and a privet still blossomed.

2001: Cardinal sings 4:18 a.m.

2002: From southeastern Oregon to Portland: Catalpas and yucca in full bloom, full poison hemlock at Pendleton (about 3,500 feet above sea level), placing the area about ten days behind Yellow Springs. Rugosa roses, white yarrow, tall cinquefoil, salsify, thin-leafed St. John's wort, purple loosestrife open.

2004: At 9:30 this morning, I followed a hummingbird with pale green markings through the red monarda to the first rose of Sharon along the south border. In the stump garden, the violet daylily opened overnight. Mid--season hostas are coming in throughout the yard.

2007: More rain. The lawn is saturated now, squishes when I walk across to the garden. This morning at about ten o'clock – the crows were back, more whining and talking between parent and fledglings. Still very few Japanese beetles around. None at all found yesterday. The ramps are in full flower under the mock orange bush.

2008: Crows call briefly before dawn, the red-bellied woodpecker after dawn. Ramps budded. Philippe, the frog, croaks steadily morning and evening. I watch the fingerlings in the pond, some so small they are like tiny elongated specks of light moving in the morning water. How many hundreds or thousands are there? How many will be eaten even in this seemingly benign, suburban water garden? Philippe swims back and forth - is he hunting the newborns? In the garden tour this afternoon, few new plants seen. Plume poppy identified in bloom at several locations. Buckeye fruits at John Blakelock's garden are prickly and about half size.

2009: Full blooming milkweed seen in Beavercreek. Canadian

thistles still full along Dayton-Yellow Springs Road. Yucca fading in our garden, still quite strong in Mrs. Timberlake's. No Japanese beetles – probably because of the lawn treatment this spring. Black raspberries holding, but aging. Robin peeping (instead of singsong) increasing. When I worked outside near sundown, I walked into a flurry of robins peeping by the shed.

2010: The second monarch butterfly seen while we were driving back home from Xenia.

2011: Cardinals, crows, sparrows, grackles, red-bellied woodpecker calling this morning. Sparrows especially raucous, grackles loud whenever I walked into their fledglings' territory in the alley. One red admiral, one brown seen in the garden. On my walk around 8:30 this evening, field crickets were singing, but there was little birdsong.

2012: Astilbe more than half brown. Forty different day lilies in bloom this morning in the garden. A cowbird fledgling awkward, stumbling toward the bushes as I approached. Heat wave continues. Crows came by at 8:00 a.m.

2013: Grackles, blue jays, doves, robins, cardinals, red-bellied woodpecker, house sparrows all talking at 5:30 this morning. Now ten day lilies are blooming, momentum there just as the Stella d'oros decline quickly. The red bee balm early full bloom. In the neighborhood, Peggy's gray-headed coneflowers started to flower today. I saw green berries on a holly shrub, berries growing quickly on the euonymus, the time for berries deepening near the Catholic church. Heavy rain and storms late in the afternoon.

2014: Serviceberries continue to fall to the sidewalk, about a fourth left.

2016: Forty-one lily plants today, the ditch lilies down to just a handful.

2017: Seventeen ditch lily blossoms, sixty-seven different day lily blossoms today. The butterflies: one azure and a few cabbage whites. Bees were plentiful in the monarda, honeybees, small bumble bees, a few carpenter bees. The mid-season hostas with purple blossoms have started to open now, opening a new phase of the year, full Deep Summer. Fireflies plentiful in the warm night, but no crickets heard around 9:00 p.m.

2018: Twenty-nine ditch lily blossoms, forty-seven day lilies and the first zinnia fully open. A great spangled fritillary flew excitedly throughout the garden, and a red admiral once again visited the hummingbird feeder. First cicada heard. Crows loud the past few days, and blue jay bell calls: the fledglings are out.

2019: Seven standard day lilies blooming this morning, the most ever. Fifty-two ditch lilies are open, two tall tree lilies, no Stella d'oros, one Turk's cap. Blue jays calling. Yucca flowers in the village are still prominent, but declining.

2020: Keuka Lake, New York: Catalpa trees shedding, long seed pods formed.

2021: Keuka Lake: Juniper tree shedding. A second male tiger swallowtail seen. At a country winery, grapes are the size of blueberries.

*One's own landscape comes, in time, to be a sort of outlying part of himself; he has sowed himself broadcast upon it, and it reflects his own moods and feelings.... How has the farmer planted himself in the fields; builded himself into his stone walls, and evoked the sympathy of the hills by his struggle!*

John Burroughs

### *June 30th*
### *The 181st Day of the Year*

*It will not always be summer; build barns.*

Hesiod

*Do not let a flaunting woman coax and cozen and deceive you: She is after your barn.*

Hesiod

Sunrise/set: 5:09/8:08
Day's Length: 14 hours 59 minutes
Average High/Low: 84/63
Average Temperature: 74
Record High: 98 – 1913
Record Low: 46 – 1943

### *Weather*

Statistically, this is the coolest day of Deep Summer, recording a 50 percent chance of a high only in the 70s in my weather history. The last time such odds occurred was June 4th. September 3rd will be the next time the chances return to 50 percent. Highs in the 80s occur 35 percent of the time, 90s fifteen percent. Chances of rain are good: 40 percent of June 30s bring a thunderstorm.

### *Natural Calendar*

June's berries are disappearing: black raspberries and strawberries decline quickly in warmer years; the best mulberries have fallen. July's wild cherries ripen, and elderberries set fruit. Thistledown lies across the pastures in windless afternoons, cottonwood cotton along the streets. The oats matures and the first tier of soybeans blooms in average summers. Maroon seedpods have formed on the locusts. Some green-hulled walnuts are already on the ground. The earliest cicadas chant. This year's ducklings and goslings are nearly full grown. Trumpet vine flowers fall in the midsummer rains.

## *Daybook*

1983: All the strawberries gone now in our patch.

1985: South Glen: Enchanter's nightshade full bloom, some avens fading, scattered daisies, thimbleweed flower a few days old, galls on some goldenrod, wood mint open maybe a week, wild lettuce budding, privet seeding, pale touch-me-nots in bloom, ironweed with small tight heads, white snakeroot – two plants budding, first lopseed flowering, some angelica left.

1987: Katydid seen today, not heard tonight.

1990: To Falling Water, Pennsylvania: More bright, orange butterfly weed flowering, more parsnips gone to seed (maybe half of them now), and most hemlock brown. Clovers and black-eyed Susans still strong, teasel taller but still green, elderberries more than half with fruit set. First tall sundrops (*Oenothera fruticosa*) noticed, cattails fully out in places, some catalpa flowers still holding in the Pennsylvania mountains, weeks later than in Yellow Springs. Back at home, lightning bugs are as thick as they've been for years.

1991: Yucca gone now, catalpa beans long, first red garden phlox.

1992: Cosmos and zinnias are in early full bloom. Gay feather budding, lilies early full, mallow full, yellow yarrow just becoming bright. Full yellow squash harvest, a few peas left, a few tomatoes golf-ball size. Corn still low, no tassels, sweet corn will be late, too. Today is the peak of black raspberries in the yard, the last days for cherries and rhubarb. A large number of raccoons, young and old, were killed on the highways this past week, just prior to the worst heat and humidity of the summer.

1993: First Japanese beetles found in the roses, have probably been out a couple days. Sundrops mostly gone now.

1998: At the orchard, the first peaches have started coming in, and the first of the summer apples. Rugosa roses are gone along Dayton-Yellow Springs Road.

1999: First rose of Sharon blooms.

2000: Home to Yellow Springs after 13 days away: The north garden lush with full orange and yellow daylilies and Asiatics, violet mallow, bright yellow and orange, Shasta daisies, achillea, drooping white cones of goosefoot, tall hollyhocks, ironweed full size and budded. The roses are mostly gone, but only two Japanese beetles found.

Under the apple tree, the mid-season hostas are open, most of the astilbe rusted. In the south garden, last year's snapdragons and bachelor's buttons have finally died back, but the orange perennial gladiolas are open beside the yellow yarrow. Daisies and lamb's ear all gone, and most flax and spiderwort, leaving that far south garden pretty bare. In the pond, purple loosestrife is in bloom, water willow done, the whole pond overgrown with weeds and flowers, needing a full thinning. The fish are doing well, even after two weeks without their waterfall.

2001: Young raccoons continue to be struck along the highway. First yellow coneflower opens at the south wall. Mid-season hosta well underway.

2002: The beach at Tillamook, Oregon: Blackberries and salmon berries in full bloom. Foxglove-like fireweed in mid to late bloom.

2003: First Japanese beetles found in the roses. Lilies coming in strong now. A few peach-leafed bellflowers still in bloom. Yellow primrose declining quickly.

2004: At 4:00 a.m., silence outside; at 4:05 the first distant robin chatter; by 4:30, the cardinals come in, doves by 4:45. In the north garden, the first Shasta daisy opened.

2007: Cardinals and doves strong this morning by 4:30. Sun and cool after days of humidity and storms. The lilies are really coming in now, red monarda full, violet monarda close to full, purple coneflowers filling in the east side of the north wall garden with color, mid-season hostas budded and some are coming in. The first rose of Sharon bloomed a few days ago (one flower only) and has faded now. Zinnias in the east garden have put out six or seven blossoms. One blue bellflower has opened near the geraniums. One rudbeckia has opened at Don's yard. First cicada heard at about noon.

2009: The coolest morning in weeks. Robins were singing at 4:00, and then doves at 4:30, red-bellied woodpecker calling, but no cardinals heard at all. Young grackles in the back bushes, and clucking and cackling in the high trees this afternoon. A monarch butterfly, the first we've seen this year, visited the garden. The Stella d'oro lilies that formed a drift of gold under the peach tree about ten days ago are suddenly completely gone.

2010: More red admirals in the butterfly garden this morning, and a rare southern Polydamas swallowtail (black with a gold band along the bottom edge of its wings - usually found in Florida and the Southwest – or it was an Eastern black swallowtail?) about 1:15 this afternoon. The cats found two baby robins, the youngest I've seen out of the nest this afternoon: both saved in time. In the Gulf, the first hurricane of the season came ashore between Mexico and Texas.

2011: Grackle fledgling insistent. Sparrows loud. Red-bellied woodpecker calling. Daylilies increasing in number, but Stella d'oro rebloomers are exhausted both in the yard and in the landscape plantings throughout the area. Moya's rose of Sharon bush has started to bloom. At Clifton Gorge, avens, honewort, hobblebush and new wood nettle in bloom.

2012: A fierce "land hurricane" swept up out of the northwest, blackened the sky, huge winds and heavy rain, moved east, causing blackouts and damage throughout the Middle Atlantic region and the East. But here the heat wave continued unabated. Indifferent to the storm, 39 different lilies were in bloom through the garden today, maybe just past the peak.

2013: Moya's rose of Sharon opened last night, and sixteen lilies are in bloom this morning, just like in 2011. Pink spirea flowers have suddenly rusted in the back yard. An eastern black swallowtail came to the garden this morning, the first I've seen in Yellow Springs this year.

2014: Peggy's gray-headed coneflowers started to bloom. A few Canadian thistles to seed.

2016: Forty-one lilies in bloom now, the ditch lilies down to four, the blossoms on the standard lilies multiplying quickly, the north and circle gardens filling in with rich color. In the back trees, a catbird has been clucking, first seen yesterday. The mid-season hostas are opening here, have been blooming as much as a week in other yards. Purple coneflowers, monarda, Shasta daisies, heliopsis, spiderwort, hydrangeas, the lone rose, the late, white flowers of the Great Blue hosta, the lone pink spirea, numerous orange trumpet vine trumpets and a handful of zinnias complement the lilies. As Jill and I walked north on the bike path, three red admiral butterflies spun around us in a tight and intense randori. Throughout the county, wheat is a rich caramel brown, still no harvesting seen.

2017: Seventy-nine day lily blossoms counted today, just eleven ditch lilies. A few azure butterflies and cabbage whites, one polygonia in the north garden. Morning bees still relatively common. At dusk, constant peeping and clucking of robins in the honeysuckles. Slowly the fireflies came out, so many!

2018: More cicadas this morning. Cottonwood seeds and cotton still common along Greene Street. Constant sparrow chirping today. Thirty-six day lilies, 25 ditch lilies. And a spicebush swallowtail came to the heliopsis around noon.

2019: Eighty ditch lilies, 12 standard day lilies, five of the golden tree lilies. Tree crickets in the morning. Heat and humidity. At the Covered Bridge, dogbane had white buds, ready to open. Ironweed had tiny tight buds far from bloom time. Tall nettle was in early flower in the field, like wood nettle in the shade. On the way to Fairborn, fields of thistles have gone to seed, gray and spreading in drifts. At the Lutheran church on the west side of Fairborn, I saw the first rose of Sharon blossoms, along with a hummingbird taking advantage of the bloom. The month's average temperature was 69.8 degrees, the coolest and the first average below 70 degrees since 2006. Still, Leslie reported the first cicada call this evening.

2020: Avens blooming in Yellow Springs. Blue-tailed flies (Broad-bodied chasers, *Libellula depressa*) at the pond.

2021: Average temperature for the month was 73.5 degrees (the third highest since 1980), with 4.32 inches of rain. News reports say that this June was the hottest on record for the United States, a 72.6 average, 4.2 degrees above normal.

2022: Nationally, this was the second-warmest June on record. In southwest Ohio, the average was 73.1, with 4.22 inches of rain.

> *The air is full of drifting thistledown,*
> *Grey pointed sprites, that on the breezes ride....*

> Vita Sack-Ville West

## Valediction

*Grounding  in just what lies around me,*
*learning to understand home,*
*feeling the borders of independence,*
*the solitude of landscape,*
*finding enough in plain events,*
*embracing the ordinary,*
*expecting nothing more,*
*accepting this particular passage*
*of time and location in time*
*again and again,*
*seeing salvation in the commonplace,*
*marking the sunlight of solstice on my wall,*
*counting the cracking pussy willows,*
*measuring the height of winter snowdrops,*
*asking nothing more than these pure acts,*
*allowing, opening, watching the finite visions*
*that contain no transcendence,*
*no special compensation,*
*considering the precision of each fragment*
*that names the exact place of Earth's orbit*
*and my exact place within it now.*

\\

Bill Felker has been writing almanacs and nature columns for newspapers and magazines since 1984. The radio version of his commentary is broadcast weekly on WYSO, a National Public Radio station, and it is available on podcast at www.wyso.org. His *Home is the Prime Meridian: Essays in Search of Time and Place and Spirit, Deep Time Is in the Garden: New Essays in Search of Time and Place and Spirit, The Virgin Point: Meditations in Nature,* and the entire twelve volumes of *A Daybook for the Year in Yellow Springs, Ohio,* are available on Amazon. For more information, visit Bill Felker's website at www.poorwillsalmanack.com

9 781986 757423